System/360
Job Control Language

Nils J. Pandens

System/360
Job Control Language

GARY DEWARD BROWN

JOHN WILEY & SONS, INC.
New York • London • Sydney • Toronto

Library of Congress Catalogue Card Number: 79–112589

SBN 471   10870   7

Printed in the United States of America

20   19   18   17   16   15   14   13   12   11

To my wife Lolly — who is patient

PREFACE

This manual is for the person who wants to learn, understand, and use System/360 Job Control Language. It is intended for all System/360 programmers, whether they code in COBOL, FORTRAN, PL/I, assembly language, RPG, or some other language.

The manual presumes that the reader is, or expects to be, an active System/360 programmer having some familiarity with computers and a computer language. The reader is not expected to be familiar with System/360.

Job Control Language is hard to learn and not always easy to use. The manual can be used both as a student text for learning JCL and as a reference for those already familiar with it. It can also serve as an auxiliary text for any computing class using a System/360 computer.

Job Control Language is placed in context by describing the relationship among it, the user's job, and the operating system. Each Job Control Language feature is described in complete detail, examples are given for its use, and possible applications are discussed. Many System/360 facilities are also described in detail, with abundant examples given to show how they can be used through Job Control Language. These facilities include the linkage editor, indexed-sequential data sets, and several IBM-supplied utility programs.

Gary DeWard Brown

Santa Monica, California
January, 1970

JOB CONTROL LANGUAGE PARAMETERS

Parameter	Subparameter of	Positional/ Keyword	Page
ABSTR	SPACE	P	172
ACCT	EXEC	K	59
acct number	JOB	P	40
AFF	DD	K	240
AFF	UNIT	K	98
BLKSIZE	DCB	K	86
BUFNO	DCB	K	86
CLASS	JOB	K	44
CODE	DCB	K	154
COND	JOB, EXEC	K	66
CYLOFL	DCB	K	253
DATA	DD	P	144
DCB	DD	K	85
DD	--	P	82
ddname	DD	P	83
DDNAME	DD	K	146
DEN	DCB	K	188
DISP	DD	K	101
DPRTY	EXEC	K	60
DSN or DSNAME	DD	K	90
DSORG	DCB	K	85
DUMMY	DD	P	156
EXEC	--	P	48
EXPDT	LABEL	K	236
JOB	--	P	38
jobname	JOB	P	39
JOBLIB	DD	P	51
KEYLEN	DCB	K	244
LABEL	DD	K	183
LRECL	DCB	K	86

CONTENTS

System/360
Job Control Language

CHAPTER 1
INTRODUCTION

System/360 was introduced in 1964 as the operating system for IBM's 360 series of computers. Until now, most attention has been directed toward new features of the operating system such as multiprogramming and a new language, PL/I. Little notice has been taken of another new language, Job Control Language (JCL). Yet in many ways JCL is the most important language, for only through it can one use the many features of System/360.

ROLE OF JCL IN SYSTEM/360

JCL is not used to write computer programs. Instead, it consists of a set of control cards used to direct the execution of computer programs and describe the input/output devices used. Traditionally, control cards were just something that had to be placed in front or behind a card deck to get a program running. Now these control cards have become Job Control Language; they must be programmed, perhaps flowcharted and documented, and debugged. The design and coding of the JCL statements can occupy a significant part of the programmer's time.

SCOPE AND PURPOSE OF THIS MANUAL

This manual is written for programmers just learning System/360 who have some familiarity with a higher level language but know little about JCL. It is also written for experienced System/360 programmers who have, nonetheless, never achieved full mastery of JCL. Finally, the manual serves as a reference for the veteran systems programmer already well versed in JCL.

In this manual, individual JCL statements and the system facilities they serve are described in detail. Since JCL is difficult, many examples are given to help the reader learn and apply JCL.

1

This manual corresponds to Release 18 of System/360 dated October 1969. Although IBM releases a new version of System/360 about twice a year, new releases usually do not change existing JCL. However they may add minor new features, and the reader should check each new system release for added features.

Many of the JCL features described in this manual apply only to certain system options and hardware devices. These features are noted in the text, and the reader should feel free to skip over material not appropriate to his needs.

CHAPTER 2

INTRODUCTION TO JCL AND SYSTEM/360

JCL serves as a means of communication between the user's program and the system. JCL statements tell the system how to execute a job, request needed system facilities, and describe required input/output (I/O) devices.

JCL CARDS

The normal JCL statements (or cards)[†] are:

1. The JOB statement. This is the first control card; it marks the beginning of a job.
2. The EXEC (Execute) statement. This card follows the JOB card and names the program or procedure to execute.
3. The DD (Data Definition) statement. This card describes each data set (a file on tape or direct-access device, or a deck of cards), and requests the allocation of I/O devices.
4. The Delimiter (/*) statement. This is the "end-of-file" card for marking the end of a card deck.

Other JCL statements less often used are:

5. The Null (//) Statement. The null may be used to mark the end of a job.
6. The Comment (//*) Statement. Comments may be coded in columns 4 to 80 as an aid in documenting JCL.
7. The PROC Statement. This card assigns default values for symbolic parameters in cataloged procedures.
8. The Command Statement. This card may be used by operators to enter operator commands from the input stream.

[†]Although JCL statements may be contained on magnetic tapes or direct-access devices, they are most often coded on cards.

SYSTEM/360 CONCEPTS AND VOCABULARY

System/360 consists of a new computer (the IBM 360), a new operating system (OS/360), and a new vocabulary. Since the use of JCL statements requires an understanding of System/360 concepts and vocabulary, the remainder of this chapter is devoted to such a discussion.

OPERATING SYSTEM (OS)

The IBM System/360 *Operating System (OS/360)* introduces programs to the computing system, initiates their execution, and provides all the resources and services they require. The operating system, because it must be general enough to accommodate a variety of applications on a wide range of hardware configurations, is made up of a general library of programs that can be tailored to meet many requirements. The user can select the portions that he needs, add his own procedures to them, and update his procedures as his needs change.

The programs and routines that compose the operating system are classified as control programs and processing programs. The three main functions of the *control programs* are to accept and schedule jobs in a continuous flow (*job management*), to supervise each unit of work to be done (*task management*), and to simplify retrieval of all data, regardless of the way it is organized and stored (*data management*). The *processing programs* consist of *language translators* (such as the FORTRAN or PL/I compilers), *service programs* (such as the linkage editor), and *application programs* (such as user programs).

OS/360 Variations

Three variations of OS/360 are supplied by IBM: *PCP* (Primary Control Program), *MFT* (Multiprogramming with a Fixed number of Tasks), and *MVT* (Multiprogramming with a Variable number of Tasks). PCP executes a single job at a time; several jobs can run concurrently under MFT and MVT. PCP is generally for small computers, MFT for medium computers, and MVT for large computers.

Multiprogramming

Both MFT and MVT utilize multiprogramming. Multi-programming, multiprocessing, and time-sharing are often confused. In *multiprocessing*, two or more central processing units share the same core storage. *Time-sharing* allows many people to use a computer at the same time in such a way that each is unaware that the computer is being used by others. The usual case is an on-line system with several consoles using the main computer at the same time. Time-sharing attempts to maximize an individual's use of the computer, not the efficiency of the computer itself.

Multiprogramming is just the opposite in concept. It attempts to maximize the efficiency of the computer by keeping busy all the major components—such as the central processing unit (CPU) I/O devices, and core storage. Most jobs running on a large general-purpose computer do not use all the I/O devices or core storage. Moreover, not all of the CPU is used, since much of the time used to run a job is spent waiting for some I/O action to complete. Rewinding a tape is an extreme case in point.

Since most jobs do not use all of core storage or all I/O devices, multiprogramming can keep more than one job inside the computer at the same time and switch back and forth between jobs. Several jobs are loaded into core, the operating system gives control to one job, and then switches control to another whenever one becomes idle. The system can also *time-slice* by switching to another job after a specified period of time so that one job does not lock up the computer.

Multiprogramming allows I/O-bound jobs, such as sorts, to run economically on a large computer. These jobs generally occupy little core storage and spend most of their time doing I/O.

Many of the facilities of the computer may be shared by several unrelated jobs in core at the same time. Other resources must be dedicated to a single job at a time. The operating system must carefully dole out its resources so that a mixture of jobs in core do not contend for nonsharable resources such as tape units. It is better to hold back a

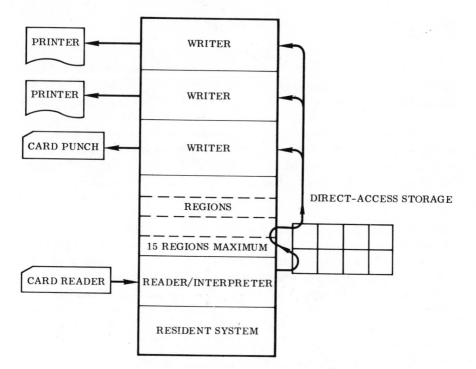

Fig. 1- A MULTIPROGRAMMING SYSTEM

job if it needs an unavailable resource, and schedule another job whose resource requirements can be met.

The system, if it is to schedule jobs based upon their resource requirements, must know what resources each job needs. The jobs make their needs known to the system by the inclusion of JCL statements. For example, if a job needs a tape a JCL statement will describe the type of tape unit needed, and the system will not schedule the job to be run until such a tape unit is available. This prevents the job from sitting idle in core waiting for an available tape unit.

Figure 1 illustrates a multiprogramming system on the 360. Each job occupies a contiguous section of core called a *region* (in MVT) or *partition* (in MFT), and the jobs remain core until they complete. Some regions,† such as the readers

---

†Region is equivalent to partition in the following discussion.

or writers, may never complete and always reside in core. Each region is protected against being destroyed by another region. The system decides which region to run and for how long, and has been made as crashproof as possible, so that although a particular job may fail, the system is not disturbed.

The first region contains the *nucleus* or resident portion of the operating system (those portions of the system not kept on direct-access storage—disk or drum). The *reader/ interpreter* (or *reader*) reads in jobs from the card reader and queues them on direct-access storage. The *writers* write output from direct-access storage, where it has been queued, onto the proper output device. Queuing the input and output on direct-access storage is called *spooling*. The sequence of cards read by the reader is called the *input stream*, and the sequence of output written by the writers is called the *output stream*.

The *unit record* devices (card readers, card punches, printers, etc.) are normally assigned to the readers and writers. All other I/O units except tapes can be concurrently used by any of the regions. A tape unit can be assigned to only one region at a time. This is one reason for using direct-access devices—the job will not be kept waiting for a tape unit to become free.

To capsulate the operation of the system: The reader/ interpreter reads jobs in from the card reader and queues them on direct-access storage. When a job comes to the top of its queue, a system program called the *initiator/terminator* loads it into a region and executes it. If the job reads data cards, the system gets the cards from direct-access storage where they have been stored. (It is much faster to read cards from direct-access storage than directly from the card reader.) If the job prints output or punches cards, this output is again queued on direct-access storage. A job never reads cards, punches cards, or prints directly—it is all done by queuing on direct-access storage. The job will not be aware of this, since it is done automatically by the system. After the output is queued on direct-access storage, the writers write it out to the appropriate output device.

Although the running of a single region was described
here, several regions can be kept running at the same time
in a similar manner.

MFT and MVT systems differ principally in that MFT has
fixed partitions. The size and number of partitions is fixed
when the MFT system is generated, although the computer
operator can change them from the console. The number of
partitions (maximum of 15) limits the number of jobs which
can run concurrently; a single job executes within each
partition.

MVT automatically allocates a region to each job step
based upon the amount of core required by the step. (An
MFT job ties up all core within a partition whether it uses
it or not.) The number of jobs executing concurrently
(maximum of 15) is limited by the number that can be fit
into core. MVT also has *subtasking* which permits the
sophisticated programmer to multiprogram within his job.

COMPUTER JOBS

A computer *job* is the basic independent unit of work. It
begins as a group of computer language statements (often
called *source language* statements) coded on special forms,
which are then keypunched onto cards and submitted to a
computer. A set of source language statements that are
executed together within a job is often referred to as a
program. Programs are usually divided into functional
parts called *modules*, *subroutines*, or *subprograms*, so that
the various parts can be tested and changed without effecting
other parts.

JCL statements direct the operating system on the processing to be done on a job, and describe all I/O units required.
Since these JCL statements are numerous and complex, the
cards for frequently used procedures are kept on direct-
access storage. The user invokes these *cataloged procedures*
by giving the system the name of the cataloged procedure
rather than submitting all the JCL cards.

Each job must begin with a single JOB card.[†]

```
//TEST#7    JOB    6245,JONES
```

The above statement tells the operating system that a job named TEST#7 is charged to account number 6245 and belongs to a programmer named Jones.

Job Steps

Each program execution within a job is called a *job step* or simply a *step*; a job may consist of several steps. A typical job might consist of a compile step to convert the source language statements into machine language, a linkage editor step to combine the compiled program with other programs in subroutine libraries, and an execution step to actually run the program. This entails the execution of three separate programs: the compiler and linkage editor which are system programs, and the user's job. All are executed with JCL statements.

Each job step begins with a single EXEC card that names a program or cataloged procedure.

```
//STEP1    EXEC    PGM=PL1COMP

//STEP2    EXEC    PL1CLG
```

STEP1 executes a program named PL1COMP; STEP2 requests a cataloged procedure named PL1CLG.

Steps within a job are executed sequentially, so that the output from one step can be input to a following step. PCP and MFT systems execute each job step in the same area of core; MVT allocates a new region to each job step based upon how much core the step requires.

[†] The JOB card, along with all other JCL cards, is described in subsequent chapters.

The following example illustrates the difference between jobs and job steps.

```
//RUNA    JOB    7233,LINCOLN

//COMP    EXEC    PGM=FORTCOMP

//LKED    EXEC    PGM=LINKEDIT

//TRY#1    JOB    6221,DOUGLAS

//PL1    EXEC    PGM=PL1COMP

//LKED    EXEC    PGM=LINKEDIT
```

Two distinct jobs, RUNA and TRY#1, are executed. The steps within each job are executed sequentially. However, the jobs may not run sequentially in the multiprogramming environments of MFT and MVT. TRY#1 might execute before RUNA, after RUNA, or both jobs might run concurrently.

Compilation

A card deck that contains source language statements is called a *source deck* or *source module.* A System/360 program called the *compiler* reads in the source deck and translates the language statements into machine instructions. The output from the compiler, which consists of these machine instructions, is called an *object module.* The compiler usually retains the object module on direct-access storage for subsequent execution. The user may also direct the compiler to save the object module by punching it onto cards. Such a deck of cards is called an *object deck.*

Linkage Editor

Before the object module can be executed, it must be processed by the *linkage editor.* The linkage editor accepts object modules passed to it from the compiler, and also previously compiled object decks read in from the card reader. The linkage editor is a system program that determines which subprograms call other subprograms and resolves these *external references* (symbols contained in one subprogram which are referred to in another). The linkage editor also searches various *subroutine libraries* (a group of checked-out subroutines kept on direct-access storage) to gather additional subroutines required to complete the job.

Public libraries, such as the FORTRAN or PL/I library, are usually searched automatically. The user may also create a *private library* containing his own subroutines and instruct the linkage editor to search it.

The linkage editor combines these subroutines into a complete program called a *load module*, ready to be entered (*loaded*) into core from direct-access storage and executed. Many programs too large to fit into core storage must be divided into *segments* that need not all be in core at the same time. The user directs the linkage editor, through special control cards, to divide the program into segments that can *overlay* each other so that core storage can be used and re-used by different segments. Such a *planned overlay structure* can make very effective use of core storage and can be used for programs written in FORTRAN, COBOL, PL/I, and assembly language, but not ALGOL and RPG.

Other programs too large to fit into core cannot be easily segmented because the order in which the various modules of the program are executed cannot be predicted in advance. The *dynamic structure* permits load modules to be brought into core only when needed—during execution. The dynamic structure can be used by all languages except RPG and FORTRAN.

Execution

After the program is link edited, it is loaded into core and executed. This step is usually called the *go step*. When the program is checked out, the user may keep it on direct-access storage in load module form, saving compile and link edit times. Only a fraction of a second is needed to begin executing a load module, whereas several seconds may be required to compile and link edit the same program. Figure 2 illustrates the entire compile, link edit, and execute steps.

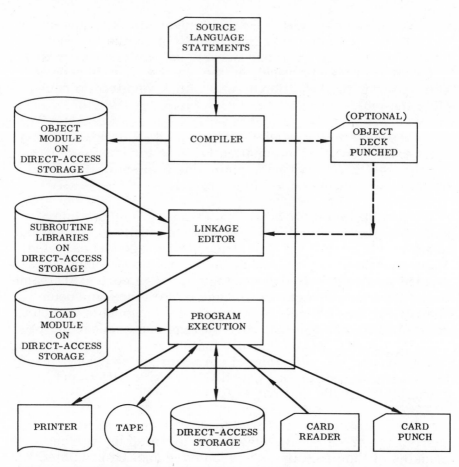

I/O MAY BE PERFORMED ON ANY OF THESE DEVICES.

Fig. 2 – SYSTEM/360 JOB EXECUTION

A job need not consist of a compile, link edit, and execute step. Perhaps only a single step is needed to compile source statements for error checking. Or perhaps several related execution steps are required, with each step performing an operation on some data and passing the results on to a subsequent step. For example, the first step of an automated address labeling system might update the names and addresses in a master file. The second step could select all names and addresses with a given zip code. The final step could then print these names and addresses for mailing labels.

The Loader

A special system program called the *loader* combines linkage editing and execution into one step. Like the linkage editor, the loader accepts object modules passed to it from the compiler, and previously compiled object decks read in from the card reader. It also resolves external references and searches subroutine libraries.

The loader differs from the linkage editor by not producing a load module. Instead it processes all object modules in core. The user must allow enough core storage for both the loader and his program. When processing is complete, the loader passes control to the program for execution. This process is usually called *load and go.*

The advantage of the loader is its speed; it is about twice as fast as the linkage editor. Time is also saved by the reduced overhead of a single job step. The disadvantages are that a load module cannot be saved for later execution, and overlay or dynamic structures are not permitted.

INPUT/OUTPUT

A program, while executing, may read data from the card reader, tapes, or direct-access storage and write output on the printer, card punch, tapes, or direct-access storage. The program may also require *scratch storage* to contain temporary data during execution.

Data Organization

Any named collection of data (source decks, object decks, or data) is called a *data set.* The words data set and *file* are synonymous. Data sets can be organized sequentially, partitioned, direct, or indexed sequential. To understand the difference, visualize several decks of cards. *Sequential* organization consists of stacking the decks one on top of the other and processing the cards one at a time in the order in which they appear in the stack. Magnetic tape, the printer, the card reader, and direct-access devices can contain sequential data sets. Sequential organization is most appropriate when the data set is processed in the order in which it is stored.

If the card decks are left in separate stacks, one can pick up a particular deck and process it by reading it sequentially. This *partitioned* organization, where the individual card decks are called *members*, is used most often for subroutine libraries since one subroutine (member) can be selected or replaced without disturbing the others. A partitioned data set can be processed sequentially by *concatenating* the members, that is, stacking the members end to end. Partitioned data sets can be used only from direct-access devices.

If all the cards are spread out on a table so each individual card could be seen, one can select or replace any card directly, without disturbing the others. *Direct* data set organization can exist only on direct-access devices and is appropriate where records are processed *randomly*; that is, the next record to be processed bears no physical relationship to the record just processed. Some source languages such as COBOL, PL/I, and FORTRAN have direct data set statements which greatly simplify this rather complex data organization.

A better analogy for *indexed-sequential* data sets is the public library where each book is assigned a *key* (a Dewey decimal number) and the books are arranged in *collating sequence* (the sequence in which computer characters are ordered) based on the key. Books are placed on shelves and can be removed or added without disturbing books on other shelves. One can process the "data set" sequentially by strolling through the stacks, or access a book directly by looking it up in the *index*. Indexed-sequential data sets can be created by assembly language, PL/I, COBOL, and RPG.

Forms of Computer Data

Computer data can consist of bits, bytes, words, records, and blocks. A *bit* is a single binary digit, 0 or 1. A *byte* is

the minimal addressable element in the System/360 and consists of 8 bits. All core sizes and storage capacities on the
System/360 are expressed in bytes. A *word* is 32 bits, or
4 bytes, or the amount of core required to store a single-
precision integer or real number. A word was the standard
unit of core on second-generation computers since it was
also the amount of core required to contain a machine instruction. It has been supplanted by the byte on third-
generation machines like the System/360 because more than
one instruction may be contained in a word, and integers or
real numbers may occupy various word sizes.

Since it is very cumbersome to write binary numbers
(a byte containing a binary 1 is written as 00000001),
hexadecimal (base 16) notation is used. A hexadecimal digit
occupies 4 bits and 2 hexadecimal digits equal 1 byte. The
binary equivalence of the hexadecimal digits are:

Binary	Hex	Binary	Hex
0000	0	1000	8
0001	1	1001	9
0010	2	1010	A
0011	3	1011	B
0100	4	1100	C
0101	5	1101	D
0110	6	1110	E
0111	7	1111	F

For example, we would represent the binary number
00110100011101001111000011011011 as 3474F0DB in hexadecimal, which saves space and reduces the chance for
error in copying the number. Hexadecimal notation is
generally used to represent System/360 binary data.

The System/360 representation of a character is 8 bits
so that one character can be contained in a byte. The extended binary-coded-decimal interchange code (*EBCDIC*) is
used to represent the characters internally in the computer.
The characters are subdivided into several character sets
which vary depending upon the context. JCL defines *alphameric* characters as A to Z and 0 to 9; *national* characters
as @, $, and #; and *special* characters as blank , . / ')
(* & + - = .

A *record* is a logical unit of data and may consist of any number of bytes; for example, a payroll record might be all the payroll data relating to an individual such as name, salary, and exemptions. The words record and *logical record* are used interchangeably.

System/360 records have three forms: fixed, variable, and undefined. *Fixed* records are all of the same length; for example, a data set containing card images is fixed length because each card contains 80 characters.

Variable records have varying lengths, with the first 4 bytes of the record specifying the record length. For example, a personnel file containing employee names might have variable-length records because people have different length names.

Undefined records have varying lengths, but the record length is not contained in the record. Records are separated by a physical gap on the storage device called an *interblock* gap (IBG). The computer is able to sense this gap when transmitting a record and thus can distinguish between records. Undefined-length records might be used where the record length is not known until after the entire record is written, for example, a typewriter console.

Data is transferred between core storage and I/O devices in blocks; each block is separated by interblock gaps. Several fixed- or variable-length records may be contained in a single block; an undefined-length record is equivalent to a block. A block then consists of one or more records to be transmitted at a time. Fixed-length records can be processed slightly faster than variable-length records because they are easier to block and unblock. In a block containing variable-length records, the first 4 bytes specify the number of bytes in the block.

Data can be transmitted very quickly (up to 1.2 million bytes per second) between core storage and direct-access devices or magnetic tapes once the transmission of data actually begins. However, it may take quite long (more than 50 milliseconds) to start the transmission because of mechanical inertia, rotation time of the direct-access device, etc. Blocking allows large, efficient groups of data to be transmitted at one time. Blocking also conserves storage space on the device by limiting the number of interblock gaps.

The number of records per block is called the *blocking factor*. A block is sometimes called a *physical record*, but this term is easily confused with logical record. Since blocking is done only for hardware efficiency and is unrelated to the way the user wants to process his data, the system usually does all blocking and unblocking.

A block of data is read into an area of core called a *buffer*. When the last record of a block is processed, the system reads in another block. The reverse occurs when data is written. Several internal buffers can be requested so that while data is being processed in one buffer, the system is reading the next block of data into another buffer. This results in considerable efficiency since I/O is *overlapped*; that is, data can be read or written simultaneously with computations being done in core.

Data sets must be opened before they can be used and closed after processing is completed. The system opens data sets automatically when the first attempt is made to use the data set, and closes them when the job terminates. However, data sets can be opened and closed explicitly in assembler language, COBOL, and PL/I.

When a data set is *opened*, the system creates all the internal core tables needed to keep track of the I/O, positions the data set to the starting point, and generally readies the data set for processing. *Closing* a data set releases all buffers and core tables associated with the data set, frees any tape drive used, releases temporary direct-access storage, and generally cleans up after processing the data set.

Access Techniques

An *access technique* is a method of moving data between core storage and an I/O device. Two ways of reading or writing are provided in System/360, basic and queued. In the *basic* access technique, a READ or WRITE command starts the transfer between core and the I/O device. Since I/O operations are overlapped, the program can continue execution while the I/O action completes. It is the user's responsibility to provide buffers and to *synchronize* the I/O (e.g., ensure that a buffer is completely written before moving more data into it). Basic gives relatively complete control over I/O, but it requires more effort to use.

In the *queued* access technique, the system does all buffering and synchronization. The program gets or puts a record and the system does all the I/O, buffering, blocking, and deblocking. The queued technique is the easiest to use and is provided in most high-level languages.

DATA STORAGE

The three most used means of storing data are on cards, magnetic tapes, and direct-access devices.

Cards

A single card contains 80 characters. Most programs and their data originate on cards. Cards are easy to use, easy to change, and inexpensive. However, large decks are bulky, heavy, and inefficient. Card I/O is sequential; that is, to read the tenth card, the nine preceding cards must be read.

Magnetic Tapes

Magnetic tapes used for storing computer data are similar to those used in home tape recorders, although the recording method and content are quite different. A byte of data is stored across the width of the tape; the position of each bit across the width is called a *track*. The *density* is the distance between successive bits along the length of the tape. Data may be recorded on tape at 200, 556, 800, or 1600 bits per inch (bpi) density; that is, 200, 556, 800, or

1600 bits may be recorded on each track along 1 inch of tape. Older IBM computers had 6-bit bytes, and the data was recorded on 7 tracks (one bit added for parity). Since System/ 360 computers have 8-bit bytes, data is now recorded on 9 tracks.

A single reel of tape can contain up to 26 million bytes; an infinite amount of information can be stored using multiple reels. Tape, like cards, is used to contain sequential data sets. Although several data sets can be stored on a single tape reel by separating them with file marks, this feature is infrequently used because tapes are hard to update—any change requires that the whole tape be regenerated. Because tapes are regenerated by copying the old tape and the changes onto a new tape, an automatic backup is obtained by keeping the old tape.

Tape makes excellent long-term storage because a reel of tape is inexpensive and can contain a great deal of information in a small storage space. Tapes are considerably faster to process than cards and may be faster or slower than direct-access storage depending upon the particular device.

Direct-Access Devices

Direct access, the most versatile storage device, can contain sequential, partitioned, direct, and indexed-sequential data sets. Direct-access storage derives its name from the way data is accessed. Unlike cards or tape, one need not read the first nine records to get to the tenth.

In addition to containing general data, direct-access devices are used for scratch storage, for subroutine libraries, and for storing complete programs in load-module form. Nonresident portions of the system are also stored on direct-access devices.

Direct-access storage consists of drums, disks, and data cell units. *Drums* are the fastest direct-access device but can contain the least amount of data. A drum cannot be dismounted, and another installed in its place. *Disk* is relatively fast and can contain a great amount of data. The 2311 and 2314 disk units have mountable disk packs that can be easily removed and replaced, allowing disk units to contain an infinite amount of data. *Data cell units* are quite slow but can contain an immense amount of data. Data cells can contain only sequential data.

A disk device consists of a stack of rotating recording surfaces similar to a stack of phonograph records. Each disk surface contains many circular *tracks* radiating inward toward the center; tracks are similar to grooves on a phonograph record, except that record grooves are a continuous spiral making it a sequential device.

A set of electronic read/write heads positioned between each disk surface is connected to an *access arm*. When a specific track is read or written, the access arm is moved to position the read/write head over the track. This arm movement is called a *seek*. The read/write head looks for a special marker on the rotating track to tell it where the track begins. Thus there are two physical delays in accessing a specific track; a *seek delay* which depends upon how far the access arm must be moved, and a *rotational delay* which averages out to be one-half revolution.

Since there is a read/write head for each disk surface, several tracks can be read without arm movement. The imaginary cylinder formed by the tracks which lie one on top of the other is called a *cylinder*. All tracks in a cylinder can be accessed without arm movement. Cylinder organization also eliminates rotational delay—after the first track is found—because all tracks begin at the same relative position, and the end of each track is also the start of each track in a cylinder.

A drum device is similar to a disk except it contains a single cylinder of tracks, each with its own read/write head. The seek delay is thus eliminated, and the rotational delay is minimal because of the drum's high rotational speed.

The data cell drive consists of ten data cells, each removable and interchangeable. The data cell is composed of

small strips of magnetic tape; each data cell contains 20 sub-
cells of 10 strips each. The strips of tape are retrieved
similar to the way phonograph records are retrieved in a
jukebox. The data cell drive rotates the appropriate subcell
beneath an access station and the strip of tape is drawn up
and placed on a small drum. As the drum rotates, the tape
passes the read/write heads where it is read or written. The
strip is returned to its original place when processing is
complete.

Volumes

The term *volume* is used to refer to a specific storage
unit. A volume can be a reel of magnetic tape, a drum, a
disk pack, a bin in a data cell, or the part of an IBM 2302
disk storage device served by one access mechanism.

The DD Card

Each data set used within a job step must be described
by a DD (Data Definition) card. The DD card tells the system which I/O device to use, the volume serial number of
any specific volumes needed, the data set name, whether old
data is being read or new data generated, and the disposition
of the data when the job step completes. The following DD
card is typical.

        //DATAIN   DD   DSN=PAYROLL,DISP=(OLD,KEEP),

        //   UNIT=2314,VOL=SER=222222

The DD card is named DATAIN and defines a data set
named PAYROLL. PAYROLL is an OLD data set to KEEP
after it is read. It is contained on a 2314 disk pack with a
volume serial number of 222222. Since the DD statement
does not fit on a single card, it is continued onto another
card.

Data sets may also be *cataloged* by asking the system to
record the data set name, type of I/O unit, and volume serial
number containing the data set. This permits the data set to

be referred to by name without specifying where the data set is stored. If the above data set is cataloged, the DD card can be written as

//DATAIN   DD   DSN=PAYROLL,DISP=(OLD,KEEP)

A cataloged data set should not be confused with a cataloged procedure. A cataloged procedure is a named collection of JCL kept in a special data set; a cataloged data set has its name, type of I/O unit, and volume serial number recorded by the system. Thus, the special data set containing cataloged procedures may be cataloged.

CHAPTER 3
JCL WITHIN A JOB

COMPILE STEP

The JOB, EXEC, and DD cards enable a complete job to be executed. As an example, suppose that some PL/I source language statements are to be compiled. Assume the PL/I compiler is a system program named PL1COMP which requires three data sets: an input data set consisting of source language statements to compile, an output data set to print the compilation listing, and an output data set to contain the object module (that is, machine language instructions produced by the compiler). Such a program might be executed by the following JCL.

```
//TEST    JOB    6245,SMITH

//PL1    EXEC    PGM=PL1COMP

//SYSPRINT    DD    SYSOUT=A

//COMPOUT    DD    UNIT=SYSDA,DISP=(NEW,PASS),

//    SPACE=(80,250)

//SYSIN  DD *

    [source language statements to compile]

    /*
```

Since these JCL statements appear rather forbidding, let us examine each card individually to see what it does. Since a complete description of all parameters is given in the following chapters, the discussion here is brief.

```
//TEST    JOB    6245,SMITH
```

The job is named TEST, the account number is 6245, and the programmer's name is Smith.

```
//PL1    EXEC    PGM=PL1COMP
```

A program named PL1COMP is executed in a step named PL1.

```
//SYSPRINT    DD    SYSOUT=A
```

SYSOUT=A defines a print data set. Print and punch data sets are used so often that a special abbreviation, SYSOUT, is provided. The SYSOUT keyword instructs the system to queue the output on direct-access storage. The general form is SYSOUT=class, where the class is defined by an installation. Traditionally, SYSOUT=A is a printer and SYSOUT=B is a card punch, but other output classes may be established as needed for special forms, high-volume output, etc.

SYSPRINT is the *ddname* (data definition name) of the DD card. The PL1COMP program must internally define a data set with the ddname of SYSPRINT. Those who write their own programs are free to choose any ddname; one must know the ddnames required by existing programs.

```
//COMPOUT    DD  UNIT=SYSDA,DISP=(NEW,PASS),

//    SPACE=(80,250)
```

The COMPOUT DD card defines the data set to contain the object modules produced by the compiler, with the UNIT keyword specifying the I/O unit to be used.

There are three ways of specifying I/O units: by hardware address, by device type, and by device group. Each I/O unit attached to a computer has a unique three-character *hardware address*. For example, if three tapes are attached to the computer, they might have hardware addresses of OC1, OC2, and OC3. UNIT=OC2 would specify a particular tape unit. In multiprogramming systems, it is better to use device type rather than specify hardware addresses; a specific unit might already be busy. The *device type* is the generic type of unit. For example, UNIT=2400-3 permits the use of any available 2400 model 3 tape unit. The *device group* permits the installation to classify groups of I/O units under one name. SYSSQ is often used to include I/O devices which can contain sequential data sets (tapes and direct-access devices). SYSDA is likewise used to refer to direct-access devices.

The DISP (disposition) keyword describes the status of the data set at the start of the job step and its disposition after the step is completed. NEW indicates that the data set will be created in the job step; PASS causes the data set to be passed on to the next job step.

The SPACE keyword allocates direct-access storage space to the data set. SPACE=(80,250) requests space for 250 80-byte blocks. All NEW data sets on direct-access storage must be allocated space.

    //SYSIN   DD   *

The asterisk (*) is a special code telling the system that data cards immediately follow the DD card. The end of the card deck is indicated by the /* card.

LINKAGE EDITOR STEP

Next, the program must be link edited to create a load module that can be executed. Assume that the linkage editor is a system program named LINKEDIT which requires three data sets: an input data set containing the object modules produced by the compiler, an output data set for printing error messages, and an output data set to contain the load module produced.

    //TEST   JOB   6245,SMITH

    //PL1   EXEC   PGM=PL1COMP

    //SYSPRINT   DD   SYSOUT=A

    //COMPOUT   DD   UNIT=SYSDA,DISP=(NEW,PASS),

    //   SPACE=(80,250)

```
//SYSIN    DD    *

    [source language statements to compile]

/*

//LKED    EXEC    PGM=LINKEDIT

//SYSPRINT   DD    SYSOUT=A

//LKEDIN    DD  DSN=*.PL1.COMPOUT,

//  DISP=(OLD,DELETE)

//LKEDOUT    DD     UNIT=SYSDA,DISP=(NEW,PASS),

//  DSN=&&TEMP(GO),SPACE=(1024,(200,20,1))
```

Now examine the added DD cards in detail.

```
//LKED    EXEC    PGM=LINKEDIT
```

Execute the LINKEDIT program.

```
//SYSPRINT    DD    SYSOUT=A
```

The SYSPRINT DD card defines a print data set.

```
//LKEDIN    DD    DSN=*.PL1.COMPOUT,

//  DISP=(OLD,DELETE)
```

The LKEDIN DD card describes the input data set containing object modules for the linkage editor—the data set created in the preceding job step. DSN=*.PL1.COMPOUT tells the system that this is the same data set described in the step named PL1 on a DD card named COMPOUT. (The *.step. ddname parameter is called a *referback* parameter.)

Since the data set already exists, the current status is OLD. The data set is not needed after this job step, and so we can DELETE it, releasing the direct-access storage it occupied.

//LKEDOUT   DD   UNIT=SYSDA,DISP=(NEW,PASS),

//   DSN=&&TEMP(GO),SPACE=(1024,(200,20,1))

This DD card is similar to the COMPOUT DD card in the first step except for the DSN (Data Set Name) keyword parameter. Load module output must be placed on direct-access storage as a member of a partitioned data set. GO is chosen as the member name, and the data set is given a name of TEMP. The ampersands (&&) appended to the data set name mark it as temporary—to be deleted at the end of the job. Space is requested for 200 1024-byte blocks, an additional 20 1024-byte blocks can be allocated if more space is needed, and 1 block is reserved for storing the member names of the partitioned data set.

EXECUTION STEP

The load module is now ready to be executed.

//TEST   JOB   6245,SMITH

//PL1   EXEC   PGM=PL1COMP

//SYSPRINT   DD   SYSOUT=A

//COMPOUT   DD   UNIT=SYSDA,DISP=(NEW,PASS),

//   SPACE=(80,250)

//SYSIN   DD   *

[source language statements to compile]

/*

//LKED   EXEC   PGM=LINKEDIT

//SYSPRINT   DD   SYSOUT=A

//LKEDIN   DD   DSN=*.PL1.COMPOUT,

//   DISP=(OLD,DELETE)

//LKEDOUT   DD   UNIT=SYSDA,DISP=(NEW,PASS),

//   DSN=&&TEMP(GO),SPACE=(1024,(200,20,1))

//GO   EXEC   PGM=*.LKED.LKEDOUT

//SYSPRINT   DD   SYSOUT=A

Again we can examine the added cards in detail.

//GO   EXEC   PGM=*.LKED.LKEDOUT

The referback parameter tells the system that the load module to execute is described in the LKED step on the LKEDOUT DD card.

//SYSPRINT   DD   SYSOUT=A

The SYSPRINT DD card defines a print data set.

CATALOGED PROCEDURE

All JCL cards are now provided to compile, link edit, and execute the program—but there are a great number of them. We should now make them a cataloged procedure so that several programmers can use the JCL. The JCL statements are made a cataloged procedure by storing them on a direct-access device as a member of a special partitioned data set. (The means of doing this is described in Chapter 9.) A name, 1 to 8 characters, is chosen for the cataloged procedure. PL1CLG might be an appropriate name for a PL/I compile, link edit, and execute procedure. The following cards constitute the procedure.

```
//PL1CLG   PROC†

//PL1   EXEC   PGM=PL1COMP

//SYSPRINT   DD   SYSOUT=A

//COMPOUT   DD   UNIT=SYSDA,DISP=(NEW,PASS),
//   SPACE=(80,250)

//LKED   EXEC   PGM=LINKEDIT

//SYSPRINT   DD   SYSOUT=A

//LKEDIN   DD   DSN=*.PL1.COMPOUT,
//   DISP=(OLD,DELETE)

//LKEDOUT   DD   UNIT=SYSDA,DISP=(NEW,PASS),
//   DSN=&&TEMP(GO),SPACE=(1024,(200,20,1))

//GO   EXEC   PGM=*.LKED.LKEDOUT

//SYSPRINT   DD   SYSOUT=A
```

The JOB card, //SYSIN DD   *, the source language statements, and the /* card are omitted; they must be included when the job is submitted. The JCL statements can now be called forth by giving the name of the cataloged procedure on an EXEC card.

---

†The PROC statement, explained in Chapter 9, is the first card in a cataloged procedure.

```
//TEST    JOB    6245,SMITH

//   EXEC    PL1CLG

//PL1.SYSIN    DD    *

    [source language statements]

/*
```

The absence of a PGM keyword on the EXEC card indicates that a cataloged procedure is requested. The PL1.
appended to the SYSIN ddname tells the system that the DD
card is for the step named PL1. Now the JCL has become
manageable.

CHAPTER 4

JCL CARD FORMATS AND RULES

JCL STATEMENT FORMAT

All JCL cards (except the /* card) begin with a // in columns 1 and 2, followed by a name field, an operation field, and an operand field. The name field begins immediately after the second slash, while the name, operation, and operand fields are separated from each other by one or more blank spaces.

//name   operation   operand

The *name field* identifies the control card so that other cards or system control blocks can refer to it. It can range from 1 to 8 characters in length and can contain any alphameric (A to Z, 0 to 9) or national (@ $ #) characters. However, the first character of the name must be in column 3.

Correct	Incorrect
//A	//+TEST (first character not A-Z, 0-9, @ $ #).
//TEST#10	//SPACECRAFT (more than 8 characters)
//PAYROLLS	//TEST-6 (dash is not legal)

The *operation field* specifies the type of control card: JOB, EXEC, DD, PROC, or an operator command.

//TEST20   JOB

//STEP   EXEC

//PRINT   DD

The *operand field* contains parameters separated by commas. Parameters are composites of prescribed words *(keywords)* and variables for which information must be substituted. The operand field has no fixed length or column requirements, but it must be preceded and followed by at least one blank.

```
//TEST20    JOB    2095,CLASS=A

//STEP1    EXEC    PL1CLG

//PRINT    DD    SYSOUT=A
```

PARAMETERS IN THE OPERAND FIELD

The operand field is made up of two types of parameters: a *positional parameter* characterized by its position in the operand field in relation to other parameters, and a *keyword parameter* positionally independent with respect to others of its type and characterized by a keyword followed by an equal sign and variable information. The following example contains both a positional parameter (3645) and a keyword parameter (PRTY=1).

```
//TEST    JOB    3645,PRTY=1
```

A positional parameter or the variable information in a keyword parameter is sometimes a *list of subparameters*. Such a list may comprise both positional and keyword subparameters which follow the same rules and restrictions as positional and keyword parameters. Enclose a subparameter list in parentheses unless the list reduces to a single subparameter. The following JOB card illustrates positional subparameters.

```
//TEST    JOB    (3645,100,40),REGION=(100K,400K)
```

All the subparameters are positional; (3645,100,40) is a positional parameter, REGION=(100K,400K) is a keyword parameter. Subparameters can also consist of keyword parameters. DCB=(LRECL=80,BLKSIZE=1600) represents a keyword parameter consisting of keyword subparameters.

PARAMETER RULES

1. Both positional and keyword parameters must be sepa-
    rated by commas; blanks are not permitted.

    Correct   Incorrect

    6,PRTY=1,REGION=104K   6, PRTY=1,REGION=104K
                                     (blank not permitted)

    (6,106),PRTY=1   (6,106)PRTY=1 (no comma)

    PRTY=1,REGION=104K   PRTY=1,REGION=104K,
                                     (extra comma)

2. Positional parameters must be coded in the order speci-
    fied by IBM, before any keyword parameters in the
    operand field.

    Correct   Incorrect

    (6,106),PRTY=1   PRTY=1,(6,106)

3. The absence of a positional parameter is indicated by
    coding a comma in its place. The second positional
    subparameter in the following JOB card is to be omitted.

    //TEST   JOB   (3645,100,40),MSGLEVEL=1

    //TEST   JOB   (3645,,40),MSGLEVEL=1

4. If the absent positional parameter is the last parameter,
    or if all later positional parameters are also absent,
    subsequent replacing commas need not be coded.

    //TEST   JOB   (3645,,),MSGLEVEL=1

    or

    //TEST   JOB   (3645),MSGLEVEL=1

5. The enclosing parentheses can be omitted if a sub-
    parameter consists of a single value.

//TEST   JOB   (3645),MSGLEVEL=1

or

//TEST   JOB   3645,MSGLEVEL=1

6. Nothing need be coded if all positional parameters are absent.

//TEST   JOB   MSGLEVEL=1

7. Keyword parameters may be coded in any order in the operand field after any positional parameters.

//TEST   JOB   3645,PRTY=1,MSGLEVEL=1,

//   REGION=104K

or

//TEST   JOB   3645,MSGLEVEL=1,REGION=104K,

//   PRTY=1

These rules appear complex, but a little practice makes their application automatic. The following examples should help to establish the rules in your mind.

//A   DD   DCB=(LRECL=80,RECFM=F),

//   SPACE=(TRK,(100,80,30),RLSE,CONTIG,ROUND)

The above DD card does not fit onto one card so it is continued onto another. The rules for continuation are given in the next section. The next DD cards show how the cards are coded as the underlined parameters are omitted.

//A   DD   DCB=(LRECL=80,RECFM=F),

//   SPACE=(TRK,(100, ,30),RLSE, ,ROUND)

//A   DD   DCB=LRECL=80,SPACE=(TRK,100,RLSE),

//A   DD   SPACE=(TRK,100)

GENERAL JCL RULES

1. Start all cards in column 1 with the appropriate // or /*.

2. An entry (sometimes optional) in the name field must begin in column 3 and be followed by at least one blank column.

    //RUN#12   JOB

3. Fields must be separated by at least one blank column.

    //STEP1   EXEC   PL1CLG

    //STEP1   EXEC   PL1CLG

4. There must be no imbedded blanks within fields, and parameters must be separated by commas.

5. Comments may be written on any JCL card by leaving one or more blank columns between the last field and the beginning of the comment.

    //STEPL   EXEC   PL1CLG   THIS IS A COMMENT.

6. Columns 1 to 71 may be used for the JCL information or comments. If more than one card is needed or if you wish to place parameters on separate cards, interrupt the field after a complete parameter[†] (including the comma that follows it) at or before column 71[‡], code // in columns 1 and 2 of the following card, and continue the interrupted card beginning anywhere in columns 4 to 16.

[†] The accounting information on JOB cards, ACCT and PARM parameters on EXEC cards, COND parameters on JOB and EXEC cards, and DCB, VOL=SER, SEP, and UNIT=SEP parameters on DD cards can also be interrupted after a complete subparameter.

[‡] Continuation cards were originally specified by coding a nonblank character in column 72, but this is no longer required.

//TEST   JOB   6245,MSGLEVEL=1,MSGCLASS=A,

//   REGION=104K

or

//TEST   JOB   6245,

//   MSGLEVEL=1,MSGCLASS=A,

//   REGION=104K

7.   Fields containing uppercase or special characters—
PARM (, / . , etc.—are coded exactly as shown. Lower-
case fields must be filled in with values selected by the
user. For example, TIME=minutes could be coded as
TIME=10 to request a time of 10 minutes.

8.   Items in italics are optional. If we recall the rules for
dropping unneeded commas and parentheses,

SPACE=(TRK,(quantity,*increment*),*RLSE*)

could be coded in the following combinations, assuming
a value of 1 for the quantity and 2 for the increment.

SPACE=(TRK,(1,2),RLSE)

SPACE=(TRK,(1,),RLSE)   or   SPACE=(TRK,1,RLSE)

SPACE=(TRK,(1,),)   or   SPACE=(TRK,1)

SPACE=(TRK,(1,2),)   or   SPACE=(TRK,(1,2))

9.   Items stacked vertically above a dashed line indicate
that one of the items must be chosen. If the items are
in italics, they are optional. If one of the stacked items
is underlined, it is the default. For example,

NEW *KEEP*
OLD *DELETE*
DISP=(- - -,- - - - - -)

could be coded as DISP=(NEW,KEEP), DISP=(OLD,KEEP), etc. DISP=(,DELETE) is equivalent to DISP=(NEW,DE-LETE) because NEW is default. Since both positional subparameters are optional, one could code DISP=(,KEEP), DISP=OLD, etc.

10. Some parameters apply only to specific systems or con-figurations. Parameters are ignored if they are inappro-priate for a system or configuration.

CHAPTER 5
JOB CARD SPECIFICATION

The JOB card informs the Operating System (OS) of the start of a job, gives the necessary accounting information, and allows run parameters to be provided. Each job must begin with a single JOB card. Installations usually establish a fixed JOB card format that must be used, and some JOB card parameters described in this chapter may be forbidden.

The JOB card has the following form.

//jobname   JOB   *(acct number,acct information),*

//   *name,keyword parameters*

jobname—name given to job by user.

acct number, acct information—account number to which job is charged and any additional accounting information established by the installation.

name—any name selected by user to identify the run.

keyword parameters—the following keyword parameters may be coded on the JOB card:

MSGLEVEL	Specify whether or not to list all JCL cards.
PRTY	Specify job priority (MFT and MVT only).
MSGCLASS	Specify job scheduler output class (MFT and MVT only).
CLASS	Specify job class (MFT and MVT only).
TYPRUN	Hold job in input queue (MFT and MVT only).

The following optional keyword parameters may be coded on both the JOB and EXEC cards; discussion of them is deferred until Chapter 7.

TIME   Impose a time limit on the job (MVT only).

COND   Specify conditions for executing subsequent job steps if previous steps fail.

ROLL   Specify rollout/rollin options (MVT only).

REGION   Specify region size to allocate to job (MVT only).

RD   Request restart of a job step.

RESTART   Submit a job for restart.

The jobname and the operand JOB are always required, account number and name are usually required, and other parameters may also be made mandatory at an installation.

NAME OF JOB: jobname

The jobname is selected by the user to identify the job to the operating system. It can range from 1 to 8 alphameric (A to Z, 0 to 9) or national (@ $ #) characters; the first must begin in column 3. Jobs in MFT or MVT systems should have unique names because the operator can select or cancel jobs only by the jobname. Unique names can be achieved by assigning job names or by coding some unique characters as a part of the jobname, for example, initials, job number, or man number.

The following should not be used as jobnames since they are operator commands:[†]

[†] If one of these names is used as a jobname, the job will run but the operator must enclose the jobname in quotes if he uses it in a command statement, for example, DISPLAY 'JOBNAMES'.

A	JOBNAMES	R
CONSOLES	N	SPACE
DSNAME	Q	STATUS
		T

Correct	Incorrect
//GDB406	//+J (first character not A to Z, 0 to 9, @ $ #.)
//A8462	//SUPERCOMP (more than 8 characters)
//B8750#12	// RUN#6 (does not begin in column 3)
//X	//Q (invalid name)

ACCOUNTING INFORMATION

Accounting information is coded as (*acct number,additional acct information*). The account number and additional accounting information must be defined by an installation. Subparameters must all be separated by commas.

The account number is optional but can be made mandatory when a PCP system is generated or in MFT or MVT cataloged reader procedures. The total number of characters in the account number and additional accounting information (excluding commas which separate the subparameters) cannot exceed 142 characters. If the account number or additional accounting information contains any special character except a hyphen (that is, blank , . / ') (* & + =), enclose the subparameter in apostrophes ('). The apostrophes are not passed as part of the information. A legitimate apostrophe is coded as two consecutive apostrophes; for example, I'M is coded as 'I''M'.

The usual rules of omitting commas and parentheses in lists of subparameters apply. If the account number is omitted, its absence is indicated by a comma: (,additional acct information). If there is no additional accounting information, the parentheses around the account number may be omitted. Accounting information can be continued onto another card after a complete subparameter, including the comma that follows it.

    //jobname   JOB   2096

    //jobname   JOB   (20746,30,

    //   6,94)

    //jobname   JOB   3042,6

        Wrong!   Parentheses needed if more than one
        positional parameter.

One may alternatively enclose the accounting information in apostrophes rather than parentheses. This obviates having to enclose subparameters containing special characters in apostrophes, but the accounting information must then be coded completely on one card.

    //jobname   JOB   '2256/2240'

PROGRAMMER NAME: name

The name is a 1- to 20-character name selected by the user to identify himself or the job. It must be enclosed in apostrophes if it contains special characters other than a period (that is, blank , / ') (* $ + - =). A legitimate apostrophe is coded as two consecutive apostrophes; for example, O'CLOCK is coded as 'O''CLOCK'.

The name parameter can be made mandatory by an installation when a PCP system is generated or in MFT and MVT cataloged reader procedures.

    //FIRST   JOB   (4562,200,10),SMITH

    //SECOND   JOB   ,A.SMITH

        If the account number is not coded, indicate its
        absence with a comma.

//THIRD   JOB   6542,'O''RIELLY'

//FOURTH   JOB   5642,AL GOLL

Wrong!   Need enclosing apostrophes if name contains special characters other than period.

PRINT JCL CARDS: MSGLEVEL

Code MSGLEVEL=(jcl,allocations) to specify the printing of JCL cards and allocation messages. *Allocation messages,* if requested, appear at the beginning of each job step to show the allocation of data sets to devices, and at the end of the step to show the data set dispositions. Default values set when a PCP system is generated or in MFT and MVT cataloged reader procedures are effective if MSGLEVEL is not coded. The default of the IBM-provided reader procedures is MSGLEVEL=(0,1).

The values for jcl and allocations are as follows:

jcl	Meaning
0	Print only the JOB card.
1	Print all JCL in the input stream and all the JCL in any cataloged procedures invoked, including the internal representation of statements after symbolic parameter substitution.
2	Print only the JCL in the input stream.
allocations	Meaning
0	Do not print allocation messages unless the job abnormally terminates.
1	Print all allocation messages.

//TEST   JOB   6524,'LEWIS N. CLARK',

//   MSGLEVEL=(1,0)

All JCL is printed. No allocation messages are printed.

//RUNFAST   JOB   5540,STOCK,MSGLEVEL=2

Only the JCL in the input stream is printed. Printing of allocation messages depends upon the default.

//AFTERIT   JOB   4422,STACK,MSGLEVEL=(,1)

Printing of JCL cards depends upon the default. Allocation messages are printed.

MSGLEVEL=(0,0) must not default or be coded for jobs using the restart facility in MFT or MVT, or for jobs using the System Management Facility of MVT.

JCL cards submitted in the input stream are listed with // in columns 1 and 2, comment cards (//*) are listed with *** in columns 1 to 3, and cataloged procedure cards are listed with XX in columns 1 and 2. Any DD cards overriding cataloged procedures are listed with X/ in columns 1 and 2. A JCL card considered by the system to contain only comments is listed with XX* in columns 1 to 3.

JOB PRIORITY: PRTY (MFT AND MVT ONLY)

PRTY=priority specifies job *initiation priority*, the priority with which jobs are selected from the queue to be executed, and may range from 0 (lowest) to 13 (highest). A priority established in the cataloged reader procedure is default if PRTY is omitted. Priority 13 is reserved for system use and should not be used.

Priority is within job class. When several jobs of a given class are queued up waiting to be initiated, the job with the highest priority within a class is selected first. The initiator/terminators in MVT and the partitions in MFT determine which job classes have the highest priority for job selection. *Dispatching priority*, the priority with which each job in core gets the CPU, normally depends upon job priority in MVT. In MFT, dispatching priority depends upon the partition; partition 0 has the highest priority, and partition 51, the lowest. (The dispatching priority can be set with the DPRTY parameter on the EXEC card.)

MVT systems with time-slicing are generated so all jobs with given priorities are time-sliced together. The PRTY parameter can thus cause an MVT job to be time-sliced. (The CLASS parameter is used to group time-sliced jobs in MFT.)

        //COMPUTE   JOB   (2252,40,10),'HAP. E. TUPPER',

        //   MSGLEVEL=1,PRTY=6

SYSTEM MESSAGES: MSGCLASS (MFT AND MVT ONLY)

MSGCLASS=class specifies job scheduler message output class. MFT and MVT systems first write print and punch output onto direct-access storage, and output writer procedures later write the output onto printers and card punches. The output class is a single character, A to Z, or 0 to 9. MSGCLASS=A is default if MSGCLASS is omitted and is traditionally the printer.

Job scheduler messages include all messages not printed by the actual job steps being executed, that is, JCL cards and error messages, device allocations, data set dispositions, and accounting information. Since the operator of an MVT or MFT system must start output writers to specific output classes, an active output class must be used; otherwise the output will not be printed.

Special output classes may be used for high-volume output, for special forms, or to separate output (all output of a specific class is printed or punched together). You will seldom have occasion to use a special output writer for job scheduler messages.

        //BIG   JOB   2564,JONES,PRTY=2,MSGCLASS=V

JOB CLASS: CLASS (MFT AND MVT ONLY)

CLASS=class specifies the job class. An installation must specify which of the 15 possible job classes to use. Job classes can range from A to O; CLASS=A is default if the CLASS parameter is omitted. The operator of an MVT system must start an initiator/terminator to each job class, whereas job classes are assigned to partitions when MFT systems are generated but can be redefined by the operator. A class must have a partitioned assigned to it (MFT) or an initiator/terminator started to it (MVT); otherwise the job will remain in the input queue and not be run.

Installations usually attempt to establish job classes that achieve a balance between I/O-bound jobs and CPU-bound jobs, between big jobs and little jobs, etc. In practice, this is difficult to achieve and enforce, partly because a programmer cannot always tell if his job is I/O or CPU bound. Nonetheless, since the performance of multiprogramming systems depends largely upon a balanced mixture of jobs, an attempt at job classification is worth the effort.

Job class also determines the overall priority of a job, along with the PRTY and DPRTY parameters. The operator can start and stop various job classes at his volition, thus controlling when certain job classes are run.

MFT systems with time-slicing are generated so all jobs of specified classes are time-sliced together. The CLASS parameter can thus cause a MFT job to be time-sliced. (The PRTY parameter is used to group time-sliced jobs in MVT.)

//TERMINAL   JOB   6655,JOHNSON,

//   MSGCLASS=W,CLASS=B

HOLD JOB IN INPUT QUEUE: TYPRUN
(MFT AND MVT ONLY)

TYPRUN=HOLD holds a job in the input queue for later execution. The job is held until the operator issues a RELEASE command. Be sure the operator knows the job is to be held; no message is given when the job is read in, and if the operator does not check, he may not know the job is there to execute.

The TYPRUN=HOLD command can be used when one job must not be run until another job completes. However,

MVT and MFT systems are hard to operate, and all operator intervention should be minimized.

```
//XR15    JOB    (2001,10),'J.K.L.',CLASS=M,

//   TYPRUN=HOLD
```

SUMMARY

A single JOB card must begin each job. Various JOB parameters may be mandatory at a particular installation. The simplest form of the JOB card is

```
//jobname    JOB
```

The various JOB card parameters covered so far are:

```
//jobname    JOB   (acct number,acct information),name,

//   (acct number,additional acct information ),name,

//   MSGLEVEL=(jcl,allocations),PRTY=priority,

//   MSGCLASS=class,CLASS=class,TYPRUN=HOLD
```

Since (acct number, acct information) and name are positional parameters, a comma must indicate their absence unless both are omitted.

```
//RUN1    JOB    ,SMITH,MSGLEVEL=1

//RUN2    JOB    (2465,33),,MSGLEVEL=1

//RUN3    JOB    MSGLEVEL=1
```

The following examples show various JOB cards which might be used:

```
//TEST23A    JOB    (6500,100,50),SMITH,CLASS=L,

//   PRTY=8,MSGLEVEL=1
```

A job named TEST23A belonging to Smith is executed and charged to account number 6500. The 100, and 50 represent installation defined accounting parameters; perhaps an estimate of printed and punched output. The job class is L, the priority is 8, and all JCL cards are listed.

```
//DDE    JOB    4524,JONES,MSGCLASS=V,

// TYPRUN=HOLD
```

Job DDE belonging to Jones is charged to account number 4524. System messages are printed as a separate output class V, and the job is held in the input queue until released by an operator command.

CHAPTER 6
EXEC CARD SPECIFICATION

Each job step begins with an EXEC card that either names the program to execute (compiler, linkage editor, applications program, utility, etc.) or invokes a cataloged procedure. A cataloged procedure can contain several job steps, each beginning with an EXEC card naming a program to execute. There may be several (maximum of 255) EXEC cards in a job; each followed by DD cards defining the data sets required by the job step.

The form of the EXEC card is:

```
                              procedure
                              PROC=procedure
                              PGM=program
                              PGM=*.referback
// stepname    EXEC          - - ------------- ,

//   keyword parameters
```

stepname—the name chosen by the user for the job step.

referback—the name of a previous DD card describing the program to execute.

program—the program to execute.

procedure—the cataloged procedure to use.

keyword parameters—the following keyword parameters may be coded on the EXEC card:

PARM	Pass parameters to the job step.
ACCT	Provide accounting information for the job step.
DPRTY	Set the dispatching priority of the Job step (MVT only).

48

The following optional keyword parameters may be coded on both the EXEC and JOB cards; a discussion of them is deferred until Chapter 7.

TIME   Impose a time limit on the job step (MVT only).

COND   Specify conditions for executing subsequent job steps if previous steps fail.

ROLL   Specify rollout/rollin options (MVT only).

REGION   Specify region size to allocate to job step (MVT only).

RD   Request restart of a job step.

NAME OF JOB STEP: stepname

//stepname EXEC names the job step. The stepname is an optional 1 to 8 alphameric (A to Z, 0 to 9) or national (@ $ #) character name selected by the user, and it must begin in column 3. Stepnames within a job or cataloged procedure must be unique. A stepname is required if later JCL statements refer to the job step or if the EXEC card is contained in a cataloged procedure.

//STEP10   EXEC

//COMPUTE   EXEC

//(GO   EXEC

Wrong: First character not A to Z, 0 to 9, @ $ #.

NAME OF PROGRAM: program

//stepname EXEC PGM=program names the program to execute. Programs can reside in a system library named SYS1.LINKLIB, in temporary libraries, and in private libraries. A program is a load module and must be a member of a partitioned data set on direct-access storage.

Programs in System Library

A system library named SYS1.LINKLIB contains all the IBM-supplied system programs, such as compilers, linkage editor, and service programs. One may add his own programs to SYS1.LINKLIB as long as he chooses names that do not conflict with the names of the IBM programs. (If a program is added to SYS1.LINKLIB with the same name as an existing program, the old program is replaced.)

Since SYS1.LINKLIB contains all the IBM-supplied programs, it is perhaps the most important data set in the system. Programs should not be indiscriminately added to it because of the danger of it filling up or of inadvertently destroying an existing program. Only fully checked out, often used programs should be added to SYS1.LINKLIB. A system program in SYS1.LINKLIB is executed by naming the program on the EXEC card:

        //STEP1   EXEC   PGM=IEFBR14

In the absence of other instructions, the system searches SYS1.LINKLIB for the program named. IBM programs have names similar to that shown to decrease the likelihood of someone duplicating the name.

Programs in Private Libraries

Private program libraries are created as output from the linkage editor. Chapter 13 describes how to retain this output as a private library. Programs within a library must have unique names; programs in separate libraries may have the same name. A private program is executed by including a special JOBLIB DD card immediately after the JOB card. (DD card parameters are fully described in later chapters.)

        //TEST   JOB   6245,SMITH

        //JOBLIB   DD   DSN=COMPLIB,DISP=SHR

        //GO   EXEC   PGM=COMP1

JOBLIB DD Card

The above JOBLIB DD card defines COMPLIB as a private library containing the program COMP1. The JOBLIB card is placed immediately after the JOB card and is effective for each job step. It cannot be placed in a cataloged procedure. If the program is not found in the named library, the system searches SYS1.LINKLIB. Libraries must be concatenated if several programs from different libraries are executed.

```
//TEST    JOB    6245,SMITH

//JOBLIB    DD    DSN=COMPLIB,DISP=SHR

//  DD    DSN=PRINTLIB,DISP=SHR
```

PRINTLIB is concatenated to COMPLIB by omitting the ddname on the DD card. The system treats COMPLIB and PRINTLIB as if they were one data set.

```
//STEP1    EXEC    PGM=COMP1
```

COMP1 might be a program contained in COMPLIB.

```
//STEP2    EXEC    PGM=PRINTX
```

PRINTX could be contained in PRINTLIB.

```
//STEP3    EXEC    PGM=IEA001
```

IEA001 could be a system program contained in SYS1.LINKLIB.

One must specify the unit and volume serial number of the direct-access device containing the data set if the library is not cataloged, that is, if its name and location are not recorded by the system.

```
//JOBLIB    DD    DSN=COMPLIB,DISP=SHR,

//  VOL=SER=200,UNIT=2311
```

COMPLIB is not cataloged and is contained on a volume 200 of a 2311 disk.

STEPLIB DD Card

The STEPLIB DD card, similar in form and function to the JOBLIB card, is placed after an EXEC card and is effective only for that job step. STEPLIB provides an alternative means of specifying a private library.

```
//TEST    JOB    6245,SMITH

//STEP1    EXEC    PGM=COMP1

//STEPLIB    DD    DSN=COMPLIB,DISP=SHR

//STEP2    EXEC    PGM=PRINTX

//STEPLIB    DD    DSN=PRINTLIB,DISP=SHR
```

If JOBLIB and STEPLIB DD cards are both included in a job, the STEPLIB card overrides the JOBLIB card for the job step. To negate the effect of the JOBLIB card for a particular step, define SYS1.LINKLIB on the STEPLIB card.

Like the JOBLIB card, the STEPLIB card may be concatenated, and unit and volume parameters must be given if the library is not cataloged. Unlike the JOBLIB card, the STEPLIB card can be placed in a cataloged procedure. The following example shows the use of both JOBLIB and STEPLIB DD cards.

```
//TEST    JOB    6245,SMITH

//JOBLIB    DD    DSN=COMPLIB,DISP=SHR

//    DD    DSN=PRINTLIB,DISP=SHR

//STEP1    EXEC    PGM=ONE

//STEPLIB    DD    DSN=LIB1,DISP=SHR
```

LIB1 and SYS1.LINKLIB are searched in that
order for a program named ONE.

//STEP2   EXEC   PGM=TWO

COMPLIB, PRINTLIB, and SYS1.LINKLIB are
searched in that order for a program named
TWO.

//STEP3   EXEC   PGM=THREE

//STEPLIB   DD   DSN=SYS1.LINKLIB,DISP=SHR

SYS1.LINKLIB is searched for a program named
THREE.

//STEP4   EXEC   PL1CLG

//PL1.STEPLIB   DD   DSN=LIB2,DISP=SHR

//   DD   DSN=LIB3,DISP=SHR,UNIT=DISK,

//   VOL=SER=400

PL1CLG is a cataloged procedure. LIB2, LIB3,
and SYS1.LINKLIB are searched in that order
for the program requested in the PL1 step of
the procedure. COMPLIB, PRINTLIB, and
SYS1.LINKLIB are searched in that order for
programs requested in any remaining job steps
in the procedure.

Programs in Temporary Libraries

Often the output from one job step becomes the program
to execute in a subsequent step. Linkage editor output is
usually executed in a following step. If the load module output from the linkage editor is needed only for the duration of
the job, it is placed in a temporary library. Rather than then
naming the program to execute, it is easier to refer back to
the DD card describing the data set containing the program.
The step executing the program need not immediately follow
the step creating the program.

```
//LK    EXEC    PGM=LINKEDIT

//LKEDOUT    DD    UNIT=SYSDA,DISP=(NEW,PASS),

//    DSN=&&TEMP(GO),SPACE=(1024,(200,20,1))

//STEP2    EXEC    PGM=IEA001

//STEP3    EXEC    PGM=*.LK.LKEDOUT
```

If a cataloged procedure is invoked, the referback must include the cataloged procedure stepname. If the above LK step was part of a cataloged procedure named LKED, the following would be required:

```
//STEP1    EXEC    LKED

//STEP2    EXEC    PGM=IEA001

//STEP3    EXEC    PGM=*.STEP1.LK.LKEDOUT
```

The referback parameter is not limited to temporary data sets. A program may be executed from any library using the referback.

```
//STEP1    EXEC    PGM=IEFBR14

//PROGRAM    DD    DSN=COMPLIB(RUN6),

//    DISP=SHR

//STEP2    EXEC    PGM=*.STEP1.PROGRAM
```

STEP2 executes a program named RUN6 contained in the COMPLIB cataloged data set. The PGM=IEFBR14 is not arbitrary; it is a null program contained in SYS1.LINKLIB. The program executes a single end-of-program statement and is useful in providing a place for DD cards. As is seen in subsequent chapters, one may want to allocate space to a direct-access data set or delete data sets without executing a program. Or, as the above example shows, one may define data sets for subsequent referbacks. (The above program could also be executed using a JOBLIB or STEPLIB card.)

NAME OF CATALOGED PROCEDURE: procedure

//stepname EXEC procedure names a cataloged procedure to use. Chapter 9 explains how to create cataloged procedures.

//STEP1   EXEC   PL1CLG

//STEPA   EXEC   FORTCL

// EXEC   COBOLC

The stepname is often omitted on the EXEC card invoking a cataloged procedure. One may code just the procedure name or the keyword PROC=procedure: // EXEC PL1CLG and // EXEC PROC=PL1CLG are equivalent.

KEYWORD PARAMETERS

The keyword parameters (PARM, TIME, etc.) are coded on the EXEC card after the program or procedure name and apply only to the step being executed.

//STEP1   EXEC   PGM=STUDY,TIME=4,

// PARM=LIST

> The TIME and PARM parameters apply to STEP1 only. The keyword parameters may be coded in any order after the PGM parameter or procedure name.

Parameters can be added to any step of a cataloged procedure by appending the stepname to the keyword.

// EXEC   PL1CLG,TIME.GO=4

> The TIME parameter is added to the GO step of the PL1CLG procedure. Any TIME parameter already coded on the GO step in the procedure is overridden. Other parameters on that or other steps in the procedure are not affected.

Each parameter may be coded as many times as there are steps in the procedure. However, the parameters for each step must appear on the EXEC card in the order the steps appear in the procedure. If the PL1CLG procedure has a PL1 step, a LKED step, and a GO step, the following might be coded.

    //   EXEC   PL1CLG,PARM.PL1=DECK,

    //   TIME.PL1=6,TIME.LKED=7,TIME.GO=4

One could not code the following because the LKED step precedes the GO step.

    //   EXEC   PL1CLG,TIME.GO=24,TIME.LKED=7

A parameter applies to all steps of a procedure if the stepname is omitted.[†] It may appear before or after parameters coded with appended stepnames. To nullify an existing parameter within a step in a cataloged procedure, code just the keyword and appended stepname, and an equal sign.

    //   EXEC   PL1CLG,TIME.PL1=,PARM.PL1=MAP,

    //   PARM.LKED=DECK,ACCT=6

> The TIME parameter in the PL1 step is nullified, the ACCT parameter applies to all steps, and the PARM parameters apply to the PL1 and LKED steps.

PASS PARAMETERS TO JOB STEPS: PARM

PARM=value passes control information to the job step when the step is initiated. The value may be 1 to 100 characters of data.

    //STEP1   EXEC   PGM=ONE,PARM=XREF

[†] The PARM parameter applies only to the first step in the procedure, and any PARM parameters in subsequent steps within the procedure are nullified.

If the value consists of several subvalues separated by commas or if it contains special characters (blank , . / ') (* & + - =), enclose the value in apostrophes. Code a legitimate apostrophe as two consecutive apostrophes: PARM='O''CLOCK,XREF,SIZE=100'.

Parentheses may also be used to enclose several subvalues; any subvalues containing special characters must then be enclosed in apostrophes: PARM=('O''CLOCK', XREF,'SIZE=100'). An ampersand must also be coded as two consecutive ampersands, unless it designates a symbolic parameter. The value may be interrupted for continuation only by enclosing it in parentheses and interrupting it after a complete subvalue, including the comma following it.

        //STEP1   EXEC   PGM=ONE,PARM=('K=6',

        //   FIVE,'I=3','J=4',SEVEN)

            K=6, FIVE, I=3, J=4, and SEVEN are passed to
            the step.

        //   EXEC   PL1CLG,PARM=STOP

            STOP is passed to the first step of the cataloged
            procedure; any PARM values in subsequent steps
            within the procedure are nullified.

        //   EXEC   PL1CLG,PARM.LKED=MAP,

        //   PARM.GO=LIST

            MAP is passed to the LKED step, and LIST is
            passed to the GO step of the procedure.

One must know what values the processing program expects to be passed to it. If PARM is omitted, no values are passed. Programs supplied by IBM, such as the compilers and linkage editor, expect the value to represent various run options. Programs written in assembly language may also accept PARM values. When the system gives control to a program, general register 1 points to a full word containing the address of an area of core. The first halfword of this area contains the number of characters in the value, the remainder of the area contains the value itself.

IBM processing programs may have three levels of values: default values generated into the system, PARM values in cataloged procedures which override the defaults, and PARM values coded on EXEC cards invoking the procedures. If a single PARM value is overridden in a cataloged procedure step, all PARM subparameters in the procedure step are nullified and the default values are re-established. For example, a FORTRAN compile procedure might contain

```
//FORTC   PROC

//FORT   EXEC   PGM=IEYFORT,

//   PARM='LIST,MAP'
```

If the PARM is overridden when the procedure is invoked, all PARM subparameters are overridden.

```
//   EXEC   FORTC,PARM.FORT=DECK
```

> The LIST and MAP subparameters are replaced by DECK, and the FORT step appears in the run as

```
//FORT   EXEC   PGM=IEYFORT,PARM=DECK
```

The loader program may be used to combine link edit and program execution into one job step. Parameters must be coded for both the loader and the program being loaded, in a single PARM field. Values for the loader must be coded first, and any program values must be separated by a slash (/).

```
//LKEDGO   EXEC   PGM=LOADER,

//   PARM='MAP,PRINT/RUN'
```

> MAP and PRINT are passed to the loader. RUN is passed to the program being loaded.

//LKEDGO   EXEC   PGM=LOADER,PARM=MAP

MAP is passed to the loader.

//LKEDGO   EXEC   PGM=LOADER,PARM='/RUN'

RUN is passed to the program being loaded.

JOB STEP ACCOUNTING INFORMATION: ACCT

Any accounting information for job steps must be defined by an installation. To supply step accounting information, code ACCT=(acct information) where the accounting information may be one or more subparameters separated by commas but cannot exceed 142 characters including the commas: ACCT=(2645,30,17). The outer parentheses may be omitted if there is but one subparameter: ACCT=6225.

If subparameters contain any special characters except hyphens (blank , . / ') (* & + =), enclose the subparameter in apostrophes. Code a legitimate apostrophe as two consecutive apostrophes: ACCT=(2645,'O''CLOCK','T=7').

//STEP1   EXEC   PGM=ONE,ACCT=(24,53,

//   45,'A=17')

Accounting information may be continued onto another card by interrupting it after a complete subparameter, including the comma that follows it.

//   EXEC   ALGOLCLG,ACCT=2647

The accounting information applies to each step of the ALGOLCLG procedure.

//   EXEC   PL1CLG,ACCT.PL1=('T=7','K=9'),

//   ACCT.GO=('T=9')

T=7 and K=9 are supplied to the PL1 step; T=9 is supplied to the GO step of the PL1CLG procedure.

DISPATCHING PRIORITY: DPRTY (MVT ONLY)

Code DPRTY=(v1,v2) to set the dispatching priority. *Dispatching priority* is the priority with which the several steps in core from different jobs are given control of the CPU. In the multiprogramming system of MVT, the step with the highest priority is given the CPU until it must wait for an I/O action to complete, until its time slice expires, or until a step with a higher dispatching priority needs the CPU. Control of the CPU is then passed to the awaiting step with the highest dispatching priority.

The dispatching priority assigned to the step is computed as 16(v1)+v2 where v1 and v2 may have values from 0 to 15. The value of 15 for v1 should be reserved for system use. If v1 is not coded, a value of 0 is assumed, but if v2 is not coded, a value of 11 is assumed. Thus DPRTY=(10,2) yields a dispatching priority of 162, DPRTY=10 a priority of 171, and DPRTY=(,2) a priority of 2.

If DPRTY is not coded, the system assumes a default dispatching priority equal to 16(job selection priority)+11. The job selection priority is the value set by the PRTY parameter.

    //STEP1   EXEC   PGM=ONE,DPRTY=(5,2)

The dispatching priority is set to 82.

    //   EXEC   PL1CLG,DPRTY.LKED=(,2),

    //   DPRTY.GO=3

The dispatching priority of the LKED step is set to 2 and the GO step to 59 in the PL1CLG cataloged procedure. The outer parenthesis may be omitted if v2 is not coded.

    //   EXEC   PL1CLG,DPRTY=13

The dispatching priority of each step in the PL1CLG cataloged procedure is set to 219.

In systems with the time-slicing option, jobs are selected to be time-sliced together based upon their dispatching priorities. To make a step part of a group of jobs to be time-sliced together, code v1 equal to the group priority and either omit v2 or give it a value of 11.

ABNORMAL TERMINATION DUMPS: SYSUDUMP, SYSABEND

It is often difficult to find the source of an error when a program abnormally terminates. The SYSUDUMP DD card provides a dump of the user's program area in hexadecimal, including the contents of registers, a traceback of subroutines called, and data sets used. The SYSABEND DD card additionally dumps the system nucleus. Use SYSUDUMP unless you have a particular reason for examining the nucleus. A core dump can be extremely valuable when you need it, but can waste paper and printer time if you do not need it.

Place either the SYSUDUMP or SYSABEND card after each step in which a dump is wanted. A dump results only if the step abnormally terminates.

```
//STEP1    DD   EXEC   PGM=ONE

//SYSUDUMP   DD   SYSOUT=A

//STEP2   EXEC   PGM=TWO

//SYSABEND   DD   SYSOUT=A
```

For cataloged procedures, append the name of the step for which a dump is wanted. See Chapter 9 for a complete description of adding DD cards to cataloged procedures.

```
//   EXEC   PL1CLG

     .

     .

     .

//GO.SYSUDUMP   DD   SYSOUT=A
```

The SYSUDUMP card is effective for the GO step of the PL1CLG procedure.

SYSUDUMP and SYSABEND are both DD cards; their parameters are described in later chapters. Although many special parameters may be coded on the DD card if the dump is to be saved on disk, placed on magnetic tape, etc., SYSOUT=A usually suffices if the dump is to be simply printed.

SUMMARY

An EXEC card either names a program to execute or invokes a cataloged procedure. The various EXEC card parameters covered so far are

                            procedure
                            PROC=procedure
                            PGM=program
                            PGM=*.referback
//*stepname*   EXEC   --------------,*PARM=value,*

//   *ACCT=(acct information),DPRTY=(v1, v2)*

JOBLIB and STEPLIB DD cards are required to execute programs contained in private libraries. PGM=IEFBR14 executes a null program. A SYSUDUMP or SYSABEND DD card must be included to obtain a core dump if a step abnormally terminates. The following job illustrates EXEC cards.

//TEST#1   JOB   5545,'PHYLLIS ELLWUN'

//JOBLIB   DD   DSN=SYS1.PROGRAM,DISP=SHR

Private programs can now be executed which are contained in a data set named SYS1.PROGRAM.

//ONE   EXEC   PGM=PRIMARY,PARM='SIZE=200'

A program named PRIMARY is executed. It must be contained in either SYS1.LINKLIB or

SYS1.PROGRAM. SIZE=200 is passed to the program as a parameter.

//TWO   EXEC   PGM=SECOND,DPRTY=(6,4)

//STEPLIB   DD   DSN=OWNLIB,DISP=SHR

A program named SECOND is executed. It must be contained in either SYS1.LINKLIB or OWNLIB. The dispatching priority is 100.

//THREE   EXEC   PGM=IEFBR14

Step THREE executes a null program.

//FOUR   EXEC   ASMCLG,DPRTY=(,12),

//   PARM.ASM=LIST,ACCT.LKED=(3345,12),

//   PARM.GO='VAR1=22,VAR2=24'

The ASMCLG cataloged procedure is invoked. Each step within the procedure has a dispatching priority of 12. A PARM value of LIST is passed to the ASM step, the LKED step is passed accounting information of (3345,12), and the GO step is passed PARM values of VAR1=22,VAR2=24.

//LKED.SYSABEND   DD   SYSOUT=A

If the LKED abnormally terminates, a dump of the program area and the system nucleus will result.

//GO.SYSUDUMP   DD   SYSOUT=A

If the GO step abnormally terminates, a dump of the program area will result. Cataloged procedures must be overridden in the order of the steps within the procedure. It is assumed here that the GO step follows the LKED step in the procedure.

CHAPTER 7
PARAMETERS COMMON TO JOB AND EXEC CARDS

Several parameters may be coded on either the JOB or EXEC cards: time limits, conditions for bypassing job steps, region size, rollout/rollin conditions, and restart conditions. If a particular parameter is coded on the JOB card, it applies to each step within the job and any corresponding parameters on EXEC cards are ignored. This is convenient if there are many steps in the job; the parameter need be coded only once on the JOB card.

TIME LIMIT: TIME (MVT ONLY)

The TIME parameter sets a CPU time limit for an entire job when it is coded on the JOB card. TIME may also be coded on the EXEC card to set a CPU time limit for a specific step. Code TIME=minutes or TIME=(minutes, seconds) on either the JOB or EXEC cards. Minutes may range from 0-1439 (24 hours); seconds must be less than 60. If the total CPU time for the job exceeds the limit set on the JOB card, or if the elapsed CPU time within a step exceeds the time limit for that step, the entire job is abnormally terminated.

Use of the TIME parameter is good practice; it prevents wasting machine time if the program goes into a continuous loop. The TIME parameter sets a limit for CPU time, not real time. CPU time, the time a job is executing instructions, does not include wait time (when the job is waiting for I/O actions to complete), system time, and time that other jobs in the multiprogramming environment are using the CPU.

A job is abnormally terminated if it is in the wait state for 30 consecutive minutes. Code TIME=1440 to eliminate this limit, and any CPU time limit. A default time limit set by the cataloged reader procedure is effective if the TIME parameter is omitted.

The System Management Facility, if installed, provides the installation with a means of adjusting the normal 30 minute wait time limit. The installation may also build in a feature to extend the CPU time limit for a job or step. Thus if a job exceeds its time limit, it can be given additional time as a safety margin, perhaps to terminate itself in a graceful manner.

TIME on EXEC Cards

        //STEP1   EXEC   PGM=ONE,TIME=(10,30)

> The time limit for the step is set to 10 minutes, 30 seconds. The step may be terminated sooner if a time limit set on the JOB card is exceeded.

        //STEP2   EXEC   PGM=ONE,TIME=7

> The limit is set to 7 minutes. The outer parenthesis may be omitted if seconds is not coded.

        //   EXEC   PL1CLG,TIME.LKED=(,15),TIME.GO=1

> The limit is set to 15 seconds in the LKED step and 1 minute in the GO step of the PL1CLG cataloged procedure.

        //   EXEC   PL1CLG,TIME=3

> The limit is set to 3 minutes for each step of the PL1CLG cataloged procedure.

TIME on JOB Cards

        //TEST   JOB   (54621,5,2),'LIMIT JOB',TIME=9

> The job is abnormally terminated after 9 minutes of CPU time. It will be terminated sooner if a time limit set on an EXEC card within the job is exceeded.

CONDITIONS FOR BYPASSING JOB STEPS: COND

Each job step may pass a return code to the system when it reaches normal completion. The COND parameter permits the execution of steps to depend upon the return code from previous steps. For example, if a compilation fails, there is no need to attempt subsequent linkage editor or execution steps in the job. If the COND parameter is omitted, no tests are made and steps are executed normally.

Programs written in PL/I (by calling the IHESARC library routine), in FORTRAN (by the STOP statement), and in assembly language (by placing the condition code in general register 15) can issue return codes. RPG programs issue condition codes automatically, but COBOL and ALGOL cannot issue return codes.

Return codes can range from 0 to 4095. The return codes issued by the compilers and linkage editor are:

0	No errors or warnings detected.
4	Possible errors (warnings) detected but execution should be successful.
8	Serious errors detected; execution likely to fail.
12	Severe error; execution impossible.
16	Terminal error; execution cannot continue.

The COND parameter on an EXEC card can test any or all return codes from previous steps. If any test is satisfied, the step making the test is bypassed. The COND parameter on the EXEC card can also make step execution depend upon the abnormal termination of previous steps. When the COND parameter is coded on the JOB card, any successful test causes all subsequent steps to be bypassed.

COND on EXEC Cards

The parameter is coded on the EXEC card as
COND=((number,comparison,*stepname*), . . . ,(number,

comparison,*stepname*)) where each number is compared against a return code. As many as eight tests may be coded. If a stepname is included, the test is made against the return code from that step only; otherwise the test is made against the return codes from all previous steps. If any test is satisfied, the step is bypassed. The comparisons are:

GT   Greater Than   LT   Less Than

GE   Greater than or Equal   LE   Less than or Equal

EQ   EQual   NE   Not Equal

For example, COND=(8,LT) is read "if 8 is less than the return code from any previous step, bypass this step."

    //STEPA   EXEC   PGM=ONE

    //STEPB   EXEC   PGM=TWO,COND=(4,EQ,STEPA)

        STEPB is bypassed if 4 is equal to the return
        code issued by STEPA. The outer parentheses
        may be omitted if only one test is made.

    //STEPC   EXEC   PL1CLG,COND.GO=((12,GE),

    //   (8,EQ,STEPB),(4,EQ,STEPA))

        The GO step of the PL1CLG procedure is by-
        passed if 12 is greater than or equal to the
        return code of any previous step, if 8 is equal
        to the return code of STEPB, or if 4 is equal
        to the return code of STEPA. The COND param-
        eter can be continued onto another card after a
        complete test, including the comma that follows
        it.

    //STEPD   EXEC   PL1CLG,COND=(4,NE,STEPC.GO)

        Any step in the PL1CLG procedure is bypassed
        if 4 is not equal to the return code of the GO
        step in the PL1CLG cataloged procedure invoked
        by STEPC.

If the job has a JCL error, MVT and MFT systems will not attempt to execute it. The PCP system will execute the job until it comes to the job step containing the JCL error; it then terminates the job. If a job step abnormally terminates, no return code can be issued and all subsequent steps are bypassed—unless the EVEN or ONLY subparameters are used.

COND=EVEN permits the job step to execute EVEN if previous steps abnormally terminate. COND=ONLY causes the step to execute ONLY if previous steps abnormally terminate, and it is often used to skip job steps. EVEN and ONLY can be coded with up to seven return code tests. The step making the test COND=((EVEN,(8,EQ),(7,LT,STEPA)) is bypassed if 8 equals the return code from any previous step or if 7 is less than the return code from STEPA; if not, it is executed EVEN if previous steps abnormally terminate.

The relative position in which the individual tests are coded does not matter. COND=((2,EQ),EVEN) and COND= (EVEN,(2,EQ)) are equivalent.

EVEN and ONLY cannot be coded in the same step because they are mutually exclusive. The tests for EVEN and ONLY are made only if the job goes into execution; JCL errors or the inability to allocate space on I/O devices cause the remainder of the job steps to be bypassed regardless of the COND parameters.

```
//STEPA    EXEC    PGM=ONE

//STEPB    EXEC    PL1CLG,COND.LKED=EVEN,

//    COND.GO=( (ONLY,(4,EQ,STEPB.LKED) )
```

The LKED step of the PL1CLG procedure is executed EVEN if a previous step abnormally terminates. The GO step is bypassed if 4 is equal to the return code of the LKED step; it is then executed ONLY if a previous step has abnormally terminated.

COND on JOB Cards

A COND parameter on the JOB card nullifies any COND parameters on EXEC cards within the job. The parameter is coded on the JOB card as COND=((number, comparison),..., (number, comparison)). A stepname cannot be used, and EVEN and ONLY are also prohibited. The tests are made at the end of each step against the return code of the step. If any test is satisfied, all remaining steps are bypassed. The comparisons are the same as for the EXEC card, and up to eight tests may be coded.

//TEST   JOB   6245,SMITH,COND=((4,LT),(6,GT))

Terminate the job if 4 is less than a return code or if 6 is greater than a return code (that is, terminate the job unless the return code equals 4, 5, or 6).

//RUN#10   JOB   (6452,200),JONES,COND=((4,EQ),

//   (5,EQ),(6,EQ))

Terminate the job if a return code equals 4, 5, or 6. This is just the opposite of the above JOB card.

ROLLOUT/ROLLIN SPECIFICATIONS: ROLL (MVT ONLY)

Rollout/rollin, if generated into the system, permits additional storage to be allocated to a job step that has exceeded its region size. An attempt is first made to obtain core from unassigned main storage. If none is available space is obtained by *rolling out* another job (i.e., temporarily moving it onto secondary storage). The job being rolled out must consent through a ROLL parameter of its own and is rolled back in as soon as the job step causing it to be rolled out completes. If no job consents to being rolled out, the job requesting rollout is placed in a rollout queue to await a consenting job or unassigned main storage.

Rollout/rollin, to be effective, must be carefully controlled since everyone usually wants to rollout other jobs, but not be rolled out themselves. Teleprocessing jobs with the autopoll option must not be rolled out.

The rollout/rollin conditions are coded as ROLL=(be rolled out,cause rollout). Code YES or NO in the appropriate place in the ROLL parameter if the job can be rolled out or cause rollout. For example, ROLL=(YES,NO) specifies that the step can be rolled out, but cannot cause rollout.

The cataloged reader procedure specifies a default ROLL parameter, effective if the ROLL parameter is omitted. The IBM-supplied reader procedure specifies ROLL=(YES,NO).

ROLL on EXEC Cards

        //STEP12   EXEC   PGM=WIDGIT,ROLL=(YES,YES)

        STEP12 may both cause rollout and be rolled out.

        //   EXEC   PL1CLG,ROLL.LKED=(NO,NO),

        //   ROLL.GO=(YES,NO)

        The LKED step in the PL1CLG procedure may neither cause rollout nor be rolled out. The GO step may be rolled out but cannot cause rollout.

        //   EXEC   PL1CLG,ROLL=(NO,YES)

        No steps in the PL1CLG procedure may be rolled out, but all can cause rollout.

ROLL on JOB Cards

A ROLL parameter on the job card applies to each step within the job. Any ROLL parameters on EXEC cards are ignored.

        //BIG   JOB   5426,'O''HENRY',ROLL=(NO,NO)

        No steps within the job may cause rollout or be rolled out.

REGION SIZE: REGION (MVT ONLY)

MVT operating systems allocate contiguous core to programs as requested. The REGION parameter on the EXEC card requests core for a specific step; REGION coded on the JOB card allocates the same region size to all steps. A default main core region size specified in the cataloged reader procedure is used if the REGION parameter is omitted.

The REGION parameter may also request hierarchy storage. The IBM 2361 core storage unit permits up to 8 million bytes of bulk core to be added to the computer. Bulk core is relatively slow (two to four times as slow as model 50 main core), but inexpensive. When the IBM 2361 core storage unit is installed, it is referred to as hierarchy 1; main core is then referred to as hierarchy 0.

Code REGION=mainK for main core, or REGION=(mainK, bulkK) for hierarchy storage. Main and bulk specify the number of 1024-byte (K) areas of core to allocate; main requests hierarchy 0 (main core), and bulk hierarchy 1 (bulk core). Linkage editor control cards described in Chapter 13, direct portions of programs to hierarchy 0 or 1.

REGION=104K	104K bytes of main core are allocated.
REGION=(,104K)	104K bytes of bulk core are allocated.
REGION=(104K,228K)	104K bytes of main core and 228K bytes of bulk core are allocated.

Main and bulk can range from one to five digits, but neither main nor the total of main and bulk may exceed 16,383 (or the maximum core available on the computer). Bulk cannot exceed 1024 if a single Model 1 2361 is attached, or 2048 for a single Model 2. Main and bulk should be even numbers; the system rounds them up if they are odd. If hierarchy 1 storage is requested but is not attached to the computer, hierarchy 0 storage is allocated—if available. (The second hierarchy 0 area may not be contiguous to the first area.)

The default region set by the reader procedure when REGION is omitted can only be in hierarchy 0. The system always obtains a hierarchy 0 region large enough to contain the initiator (minimum of 12K if the terminator is made resident in the Link Pack Area) even if REGION does not request any hierarchy 0. Since programs are directed into hierarchy 1 storage only by the linkage editor, two copies of a program are needed if it is to execute in either hierarchy.

If bulk core is attached to the computer but hierarchy support is not generated into the system, the bulk core is treated as an extension of main core. One cannot easily control where a particular program may execute; caveat emptor.

Estimating region sizes is difficult. If too little is requested, the step is abnormally terminated. If too much is requested, the wasted core may hamper performance of the multiprogramming system. A linkage editor load map gives the size of the program, but the user must add an estimate for the amount of dynamic storage required. The job will fail during execution if it cannot obtain dynamic storage.

For example, a FORTRAN job might fit nicely into its region, do some calculations, and then print the results. Since FORTRAN obtains dynamic core for buffers when the first read or write is issued, the program could abnormally terminate before the results are printed. There are numerous ways of alleviating this problem (checkpoint/restart, rollout/rollin, opening all data sets first), but the simplest solution is to allow a safety margin in estimating region size.

REGION on EXEC Cards

The REGION parameter on the EXEC card requests core for individual steps.

        //STEPA   EXEC   PGM=ONE,REGION=64K

        STEPA is allocated 64K bytes of main core.

    //   EXEC   PL1CLG,REGION.LKED=88K,

    //   REGION.GO=(20K,512K)

The LKED step of the PL1CLG procedure is allocated 88K of main core. The GO step is allocated 20K of main core and 512K of bulk core.

    //   EXEC   COBOLCLG,REGION=104K

Each step in the COBOLCLG procedure is allocated 104K bytes of main core.

REGION on JOB Cards

The REGION parameter on the JOB card must allow enough core for the maximum region required by any step, wasting core for smaller steps. For example, a FORTRAN H job may require 228K to compile, 104K to link edit, and 52K to execute. A REGION parameter on the JOB card must allow enough core for the largest step (228K), wasting 124K during link edit, and 176K during execution. Since core storage is a scarce resource in MVT systems, specify region sizes on the EXEC card wherever possible.

    //JOB27   JOB   4625,MIDICI,REGION=300K

All steps within the job are allocated 300K bytes. Any REGION parameters on EXEC cards within the job are ignored.

RESTART CONDITIONS: RD, RESTART

System/360 allows programs that abnormally terminate to be restarted so the entire job need not be rerun. Restart may be automatic (the system restarts the job immediately) or deferred, permitting one to examine his output and make appropriate changes before resubmitting the job.

All programs with long run times should probably use the restart feature. A hardware failure, program error, system error, or operator error may all cause the job to fail, and a considerable amount of time may be saved if the job can restart from the point of failure rather than from the beginning. The RD (Restart Definition) parameter controls automatic restart, whereas the RESTART parameter allows the user to resubmit the job for a deferred restart.

Restart can be made from the start of a job step with no extra programming. To restart from within a step, one must *checkpoint* his program during execution of the step, and restart from the checkpoint. Several checkpoints may be taken during a job, each accomplished by executing the assembly language CHKPT macro instruction. The RERUN clause issues a CHKPT macro in COBOL. If the program is not written in COBOL or assembly language, an assembly language subprogram must be written to execute the CHKPT macro. A unique name called the *checkid*, assigned by the user or the system, is printed on the operator's console to identify each checkpoint as it occurs.

The restart may be initiated automatically from the last checkpoint or job step, or it may be initiated later in a separate run from any job step or checkpoint. Automatic restart can occur only if the completion code accompanying the step agrees with a set of eligible completion codes specified by the installation when the system was generated, and if the computer operator gives his consent.

Restart Definition: RD

The RD parameter controls automatic restart and may also suppress the CHKPT macro so checkpoints are not taken. The parameter is coded as RD=restart conditions. The following table describes the restart conditions.

Restart Conditions	Automatic Restart?	Suppress CHKPT?
R—Restart	Yes	No
NC—No Checkpoint	No	Yes
NR—No Automatic Restart	No	No
RNC—Restart and No Checkpoint	Yes	Yes

For example, RD=RNC permits automatic restart and suppresses the CHKPT macro. If automatic restart is requested, the restart is made from the last checkpoint in the step (*checkpoint restart*). If no checkpoint occurred because the CHKPT macro was suppressed or omitted, or the step terminated before the macro was executed, restart is made at the start of the step (*step restart*). If the RD parameter is omitted, automatic restart occurs only if a CHKPT macro was executed.

Automatic restart requires that the system make special dispositions of data sets. When a step is automatically restarted, any data sets created in the step are deleted, and data sets existing when the step was first initiated are kept. If restart is made from a checkpoint, all data sets currently used by the job are kept. Any CPU time limit for a step is reset to its original value when restart occurs.

MSGLEVEL=(0,0) must not default or be coded on the JOB card in MFT and MVT systems for restart to occur. Each step within the job must have a stepname, and each stepname must be unique to the job because the system uses the stepname to decide which step to restart.

RD on EXEC Cards

        //SLOW   JOB   5426,SMAUG,MSGLEVEL=1, . . .

    MSGLEVEL=1 is required on the JOB card for MFT and MVT systems.

        //STEP1   EXEC   PGM=CSMP,RD=R

    STEP1 may be automatically restarted.

        //   EXEC   FORTCLG,RD.LKED=NR,RD.GO=NC

    The LKED step of the FORTCLG procedure may not be automatically restarted. The GO step may not be automatically restarted and any CHKPT macros are suppressed. Each step in the FORTCLG procedure must have a stepname, and the stepname must be unique to the job.

// EXEC   FORTCLG,RD=RNC

Automatic restart is permitted and the CHKPT macro is suppressed in each step of the FORTCLG procedure.

RD on JOB Cards

RD coded on the JOB card applies to each step within the job, and any RD parameters on EXEC cards withn the job are ignored.

//FAST   JOB   4562,SMAUG,RD=R,MSGLEVEL=1

All steps within the job may be automatically restarted.

Resubmitting a Job for Restart: RESTART

One may examine the output from his job and elect to restart it later from a checkpoint or the start of a job step. A deferred restart can be used regardless of the way the job terminates—abnormally or normally—and irrespective of whether automatic restart occurred. Deferred restart also allows the user to correct or change data and to fix program errors before resubmitting the job. The RESTART parameter coded on the JOB card requests deferred restart.

Step Restart

A deferred restart from a job step simply causes the system to begin execution at a specific step within the job, bypassing all preceding steps. Data sets are not passed from previous steps because the previous steps are not executed. Referbacks cannot be used except in the DCB parameter and in VOL parameters that refer back to a DD card giving the volume serial number. Remember that new data sets created in the previous run may still be in existence—attempts to re-create them may cause the job to fail because of duplicate data sets on the same volume. The JCL may have to be modified to circumvent the above restrictions.

Always examine the output from the previous run to reconstruct conditions so that the step may be restarted. Perhaps the step cannot be restarted. If a temporary data set passed from a previous job step has been deleted, restart from the step that created the data set. If a passed data set was kept, identify the data set with name, unit, volume, and label information. Only the name and volume are needed if the data set was cataloged. For direct-access data sets created and kept previously within the step, either change the disposition on the DD card from NEW to OLD or MOD, or delete the data set before resubmitting the job, or define a new data set.

Restart can be simplified by cataloging data sets when they are created so they can be referred to by name without having to specify the unit and volume. Conditional data set dispositions may be used to delete new data sets or catalog passed data sets. Additional changes can be made to the JCL if required. Different devices or volumes may be used, data can be modified, or different data sets used.

Step restart is requested by coding RESTART=stepname on the JOB card, where the stepname gives the name of the step from which to restart.

```
//TEST    JOB    2256,ROI,RESTART=STEP6

//STEP1    EXEC   ...
          .
          .
          .
//STEP6    EXEC   ...
```

Execution resumes at STEP6.

Restart may also be made from a step within a cataloged procedure.

```
//TEST    JOB    2249,DAUPHIN,RESTART=RUN.LKED

//STEP1    EXEC   ...

//RUN    EXEC    PL1CLG
```

Execution resumes at the LKED step in the PL1CLG cataloged procedure.

If RESTART=* is coded on the JOB card, execution begins at the first step. (The same of course happens if the RESTART parameter is omitted.)

    //TEST   JOB   2564,CONSORT,RESTART=*

    //GO   EXEC   . . .

Execution begins with the GO step.

Restart from a Checkpoint

Many of the modifications required for step restart can be eliminated by restarting from a checkpoint. The system retains the job's JCL and changes the status of any new data created to OLD. It also retains unit and volume information for all but passed data sets. One need change only the JCL to supply unit, volume, and label information for passed data sets—unless the passed data set was cataloged. Other changes may be made to the JCL before the job is resubmitted: existing DD statements may be modified, new DD statements added, and data may be altered, unneeded DD cards may be made DUMMY, etc.

To restart a job from a checkpoint, code RESTART= (stepname,checkid) on the JOB card. The stepname is the name of the step from which to start, and the checkid is the name assigned by the user or system to the checkpoint. RESTART=(*,checkid) restarts the job from the first job step. (The checkid must be enclosed in apostrophes if it contains special characters (blank , . / ') (* & + - =); code a legitimate apostrophe as two consecutive apostrophes.)

A SYSCHK DD card describing the checkpoint data set must also be included to restart from a checkpoint. One must have previously coded a DD card for the CHKPT macro to write the checkpoint onto, and the SYSCHK DD card must then define this data set. The SYSCHK DD card is placed immediately after the JOB card and any JOBLIB card, preceding the first EXEC card.

```
//TEST    JOB    2566,JONES,

//    RESTART=(STEP1.GO,CK10)
```

Restart is made from the GO step of the PL1CLG cataloged procedure invoked by STEP1. The restart is made from the CK10 checkpoint.

```
//JOBLIB    DD    DISP=SHR,DSN=PROGLIB

//SYSCHK    DD    DISP=OLD,DSN=CHKPTLIB
```

The SYSCHK DD card follows the JOB and any JOBLIB card.

```
//STEP1    EXEC    PL1CLG
```

The SYSCHK DD card may include other DD parameters as needed. If the checkpoint data set is not cataloged, unit and volume information must be included. Do not include a member name if the checkpoint data set is partitioned. SYSCHK must imply or specify a disposition of OLD and KEEP.

SUMMARY

The TIME, COND, ROLL, REGION, and RD parameters may be coded on either the JOB or EXEC cards. Parameters coded on the JOB card nullify any corresponding parameters on the EXEC cards within the job. The RESTART parameter is coded on the JOB card for deferred restart.

The complete JOB card parameters are

```
//jobname    JOB   (acct number,acct information),

//    name,MSGLEVEL=(jcl,allocations),

//    PRTY=priority,MSGCLASS=class,
```

```
//   CLASS=class,TYPRUN=HOLD,

//   REGION=(mainK,bulkK),TIME=(minutes,seconds),

//   COND=((number,comparison), . . .),

//   RD=restart conditions,

//   ROLL=(be rolled out,cause rollout),

                     *
                 stepname
//   RESTART=(--------,checkid)
```

The complete EXEC card parameters are

```
                     procedure
                     PROC=procedure
                     PGM=program
                     PGM=*.referback
//stepname    EXEC  ---------------- ,PARM=value,

//   ACCT=(acct information),TIME=(minutes,seconds),

//   DPRTY=(v1,v2),

                     EVEN
                     ONLY
                     (number,comparison,stepname)
//   COND=( ---------------------------, . . . ),

//   ROLL=(be rolled out,cause rollout),

//   REGION=(mainK,bulkK),RD=restart conditions
```

CHAPTER 8
DD CARD SPECIFICATION

A DD (Data Definition) card must be included after the EXEC card for each data set used in the step. The DD card gives the data set name, I/O unit, perhaps a specific volume to use, and the data set disposition. The system ensures that requested I/O devices can be allocated to the job before execution is allowed to begin. A maximum of 255 DD cards are permitted per step.

The DD card may also give the system various information about the data set: its organization, record length, blocking, etc. If a new data set is created on direct-access storage, the DD card must specify the amount of storage to allocate. A specific file on a multiple-file magnetic tape is also indicated with the DD card. I/O can be optimized by requesting that data sets be grouped together on the same device or separated from each other on different devices or I/O channels.

A great deal of information must be supplied to read or write a data set: the data set organization, record type, record length, block length, buffering, type of I/O device, etc. System/360 permits this information to come from three sources: a data control block (DCB), DD cards, and data set labels.

DATA CONTROL BLOCK

The data control block is a table of data in core that describes each data set used by the program. It is usually supplied by the language compiler, but may be coded directly in assembly language. The language compiler fills in various parameters for the programmer; the assembly language programmer must supply his own and has greater control over the data set.

When a data set is opened, information is taken from the DD card and merged into blank fields of the data control block. The data set label is then read (if it is an existing data set with a label), and any data from it is merged into any remaining blank fields of the data control block. The hierarchy is data control block first, DD cards second, and data set labels third.

For example, device type need not be coded in the data control block; it can be supplied on a DD card to make the program relatively device independent. Record length and blocking are often omitted in the data control block, and the information is supplied later by either the DD card or the data set label.

The user must know which data control block fields are blank so that he can supply them on the DD card. The assembly language programmer will of course know because he codes his own data control block. The users of other languages must refer to the appropriate IBM programmer's guide for this information.

Since there may be several data control blocks, one for each data set used, a data definition name (*ddname*) is assigned to each. A DD card with a corresponding ddname must be included for each data set used. The system may then read the data set label for further information.

DD CARD FORMAT

The format of the DD card is

//ddname   DD   *optional parameters*

The ddname is the name given to the DD card. The optional parameters consist of three positional parameters (DUMMY, DATA, and *), and several keyword parameters.

DUMMY	Gives the data set a dummy status.
DATA	Indicates that card data with // in columns 1 and 2 immediately follows the DD card.
*	Indicates that card data immediately follows the DD card.

DCB	Specifies data control block parameters.
DSN	Names the data set.
UNIT	Specifies the I/O unit.
DISP	Specifies data set disposition.
VOL	Provides volume information.
LABEL	Provides label information and data set protection.
SPACE	Requests the amount of direct-access space to allocate.
SPLIT	Splits direct-access cylinders between data sets.
SUBALLOC	Suballocates direct-access space from another data set.
UCS	Specifies a character set for printing.
SYSOUT	Routes a data set through the system output stream.
DDNAME	Postpones definition of a data set.
SEP	Separates data sets on channels.
AFF	Places data sets on the same channels.

DUMMY, DATA, and * are positional parameters and must be coded first in the operand field if they are required. (DUMMY, DATA, and * are all mutually exclusive.) The keyword parameters may be coded in any order in the operand field, after any positional parameter.

The ddname, DCB, DSN, UNIT, DISP, and VOL parameters required on many DD cards for a variety of devices are described in the remainder of this chapter. The remaining parameters generally depend upon specific devices or are less often used; they are described in the following chapters.

DATA DEFINITION NAME: ddname

The ddname must be 1 to 8 alphameric (A to Z, 0 to 9) or national (@ $ #) characters. Each ddname within a step should be unique; if duplicate ddnames exist within a step, device and space allocations are made for each card, but all references are directed to the first card. The required ddnames vary with each language processor as shown.

Language	Data set requested by	Required ddnames
ALGOL	ALGOL unit 0	//SYSIN DD . . .
	ALGOL unit 1	//ALGLDD01 DD . . .
	.	.
	.	.
	.	.
	ALGOL unit 15	//ALGLDD15 DD . . .
Assembler	DCB=ddname	//ddname DD . . .
COBOL	SELECT file ASSIGN TO ddname	//ddname DD . . .
FORTRAN	FORTRAN unit 1	//FT01F001 DD . . .
	.	.
	.	.
	.	.
	FORTRAN unit 99	//FT99F001 DD . . .
PL/I	DECLARE ddname FILE or OPEN FILE (ddname)	//ddname DD . . .
RPG	filename	//filename DD . . .

REFERBACK PARAMETER: referback

The referback parameter, similar to the // EXEC PGM=*.referback in Chapter 6, is also used on DD cards to copy information from a previous DD card. The following example in which data control block information is copied from a previous DD card illustrates the referback.

```
//COMP    PROC

//STEP1   EXEC   PGM=ONE

//DD1   DD   DCB=BLKSIZE=80, . . .
```

//DD2   DD   DCB=*.DD1, . . .

> To refer back to a DD card in the same step, code *.ddname.

//STEP2   EXEC   PGM=TWO

//DD3   DD   DCB=*.STEP1.DD1, . . .

> To refer back to a DD card in a previous step, code *.stepname.ddname.

To refer back to a DD card within a cataloged procedure, refer first to the stepname invoking the procedure, next to the stepname within the procedure, and then to the ddname. If the COMP cataloged procedure above is invoked, the following could be coded.

//STEP3   EXEC   COMP

//STEP4   EXEC   PGM=FOUR

//DD4   DD   DCB=*.STEP3.STEP1.DD1

DATA CONTROL BLOCK INFORMATION: DCB

The DCB parameter is coded as DCB=subparameter or DCB=(subparameter, . . . ,subparameter). Appendix A lists all possible DCB subparameters; several of the most frequently used subparameters are described here.

Data Set Organization: DSORG

Code DSORG=organization to specify the type of organization. The organization can be one of the following: (Data sets are unmovable if the data contains absolute track addresses.)

PS	Physical Sequential
PSU	Physical Sequential Unmovable
PO	Partitioned Organization

POU   Partitioned Organization Unmovable

IS   Indexed Sequential

ISU   Indexed Sequential Unmovable

DA   Direct Access

DAU   Direct Access Unmovable

```
//OUTPUT   DD   DCB=DSORG=PS
```

Logical Record Length: LRECL

Code LRECL=length to specify the length of the logical record in bytes for fixed- or variable-length records. LRECL is equal to the record length for fixed-length records and is equal to the size of the largest record, including the 4 bytes describing the record's size, for variable-length records.

```
//OUTPUT   DD   DCB=(DSORG=PS,LRECL=80)
```

Block Size: BLKSIZE

Code BLKSIZE=blocksize to specify the block size in bytes. The block size must be a multiple of LRECL for fixed-length records; for variable-length records it must be equal to or greater than LRECL (the longest record length) plus 4. For undefined-length records, the block size must be as large as the longest block.

```
//OUTPUT   DD   DCB=(DSORG=PS,LRECL=80,
//   BLKSIZE=1600)
```

DCB subparameters can be continued after a complete subparameter, including the comma following it.

Number of Buffers: BUFNO

Code BUFNO=number to specify the number of buffers.

```
//OUTPUT   DD   DCB=(DSORG=PS,LRECL=80,
//   BLKSIZE=1600,BUFNO=2)
```

Record Format: RECFM

Code RECFM=format to specify the record format. (See Figure 3.) The format can be one or more of the following characters.

U   Undefined-length records. LRECL should not be coded, and BLKSIZE must be greater than or equal to the largest record.

V   Variable-length records. BLKSIZE must be the length of the longest record plus 4 bytes if the records are blocked.

F   Fixed-length records. BLKSIZE must be a multiple of LRECL for blocked records. (U, V, and F are mutually exclusive.)

B   Blocked records. (FB and VB are permitted; UB is not.)

T   Track overflow used. (See Chapter 14.)

S   Standard blocks. (See Chapter 14.) For F format records, there are no truncated blocks or unfilled tracks within the data set. For V format records, logical records are spanned over more than one block.

A   ASA control character is the first byte of data. (Control characters are described in Appendix B.)

M   Machine code control character is the first byte of data. (A and M are mutually exclusive.)

//OUTPUT   DD   DCB=(DSORG=PS,LRECL=80,

//   BLKSIZE=1600,BUFNO=2,RECFM=FB)

//OUTPUT   DD   DCB=RECFM=FBSA

RECFM=F   Fixed-Length Records

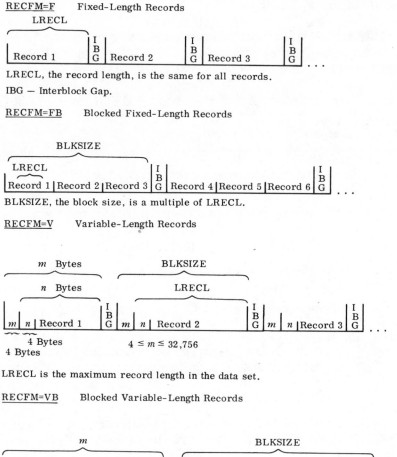

LRECL, the record length, is the same for all records.

IBG — Interblock Gap.

RECFM=FB   Blocked Fixed-Length Records

BLKSIZE, the block size, is a multiple of LRECL.

RECFM=V   Variable-Length Records

$4 \leq m \leq 32,756$

LRECL is the maximum record length in the data set.

RECFM=VB   Blocked Variable-Length Records

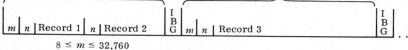

$8 \leq m \leq 32,760$

BLKSIZE must be equal to or greater than the maximum record length in the data set.

RECFM=U   Undefined-Length Records

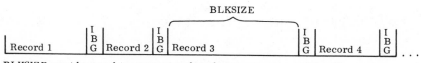

BLKSIZE must be equal to or greater than the maximum record length in the data set.

Fig. 3 – RECORD FORMATS

DCB Information from Labels

A data set label is created as part of nontemporary data sets having standard labels. The DCB subparameters DSORG, RECFM, BLKSIZE, and LRECL are recorded in the label and become part of the data set. These parameters need not be specified when referring to an old data set; the system retrieves them from the data set label. If all required DCB information is contained in the data control block or in the data set label, the DCB parameter may be omitted.

Copying DCB Values from a Previous DD Card or Data Set: referback, name

Often one would like to create a data set with the same DCB subparameters as an existing data set. This is done by either naming the other data set or referring back to a DD card containing the desired DCB.

DCB=(name,*subparameter*, . . . ,*subparameter*)

DCB=(*.referback,*subparameter*, . . . ,*subparameter*)

If a name is coded, the DCB information is copied from the named data set. It must be a cataloged data set on direct-access storage, and the volume containing the data set must be mounted before the step begins execution. (The volume sequence number and retention date are copied along with the DCB subparameters unless they are coded on the DD card.) If a referback is coded, the DCB subparameters are copied from those coded on the previous DD card. (It does not copy DCB information from the label of the data set described by the previous DD card.) Any subparameters can be coded after the name or referback to override or augment the copied DCB subparameters.

//INPUT   DD   DCB=SYS1.LINKLIB, . . .

DCB subparameters are copied from SYS1.LINKLIB.

//INPUT   DD   DCB=*.DDONE, . . .

DCB subparameters are copied from the DDONE DD card. DDONE must be a previous card in the same step.

//INPUT   DD   DCB=(*.STEP1.DDTWO,

//   BLKSIZE=800, BUFNO=3), . . .

DCB subparameters are copied from the DDTWO DD card in STEP1. STEP1 must be a previous step. Any BLKSIZE or BUFNO subparameter in the copied DCB is overridden.

DATA SET NAME: DSN

The DSN[†] parameter names the data set. Data sets can be temporary or nontemporary. A temporary data set is created and deleted within the job, whereas a nontemporary data set can be retained after the job completes. All non-temporary data sets must be given names; the name is optional for temporary data sets. If the data set is new, DSN assigns a name to it; if old, DSN gives its existing name.

Temporary Data Sets

Temporary data sets are used for scratch storage. If the DISP parameter does not delete the data set, the system deletes it. Deleting a tape data set dismounts the tape, whereas deleting a direct-access data set releases the direct-access storage.

A data set is marked temporary by omitting the DSN parameter or by coding DSN=&&name. The system assigns a unique name to the data set when the DSN parameter is omitted, and any subsequent steps using the data set must

---

[†]The DSN parameter can also be coded as DSNAME; for
  example, DSN=MYLIB and DSNAME=MYLIB are equivalent.

refer back to the DD card. (The DSN=*.referback parameter
can be used to refer back to any data set, temporary or
nontemporary.)

```
//STEP1    EXEC    PGM=ONE

//DATA1    DD    UNIT=SYSSQ,DISP=(NEW,PASS), . . .

//STEP2    EXEC    PGM=TWO

//DATA2    DD    DSN=*.STEP1.DATA1,

//    DISP=(OLD,PASS), . . .
```

A temporary data set is assigned a name by coding
DSN=&&name; the ampersands mark it as temporary. A
single ampersand can be coded (DSN=&name) as long as the
name does not conflict with symbolic parameters (see Chapter 9). The name is a 1- to 8-character name beginning
with either an alphameric (A to Z, 0 to 9) or national (@ $ #)
character. The remaining characters may be alphameric,
national, the hyphen (-), or +0 (12-0 multipunch). The temporary data set can be referred to later by coding either
DSN=&&name or DSN=*.referback.

```
//STEP1    EXEC    PGM=ONE

//DATA1    DD    DSN=&&STUFF, . . .

//STEP2    EXEC    PGM=TWO

//DATA2    DD    DSN=&&STUFF, . . .
          or
//DATA2    DD    DSN=*.STEP1.DATA1, . . .
```

Nontemporary Data Sets

Nontemporary data sets can be retained after the completion of the job. A data set label created along with the
data set is filled with the name and DCB subparameters.
The data set may also be cataloged so that the system
records the unit and volume on which the data set resides,

along with the file number if the data set is on magnetic tape. Although a nontemporary data set may be created and deleted in the same step, it is wasteful; a temporary data set should be created instead.

A nontemporary data set is denoted by coding DSN=name, where the name is a 1- to 8-character name. NULLFILE should not be used because it gives the data set a dummy status (see Chapter 10). The first character can be either alphameric (A to Z, 0 to 9) or national (@ $ #), and the remaining characters can be either alphameric, national, the hyphen (-), or +0 (12-0 multipunch). The referback is often used to refer back to DD cards so that if the data set name is changed, only one DD card is affected.

```
//STEP1    EXEC    PGM=CREATE

//A    DD    DSN=OMNIBUS, . . .

//STEP2    EXEC    PGM=READ

//B    DD    DSN=OMNIBUS, . . .
       or
//B    DD    DSN=*.STEP1.A, . . .
```

The name can contain special characters (blank , . / ') (* & + =) under the following circumstances.

1. The name is enclosed in apostrophes. A legitimate apostrophe is coded as two consecutive apostrophes: 'O''CLOCK'. A data set name enclosed in apostrophes may contain 44 characters.
2. The data set name does not refer to a partitioned, indexed-sequential, or generation data set.
3. The data set is not cataloged.
4. The name is not used in a referback.
5. The data set is nontemporary; that is, DSN=&&name is not coded.
6. The data set name is not qualified.

Names can be extended or *qualified* by concatenating names. Each level of name, called an *index*, must conform to the above naming conventions and must be separated from

other names by a period, for example, A.B.Z. Qualified
names can contain up to 44 characters including periods (35
characters if it is a generation data group name), and so 22
levels of qualification are possible. Qualified names are
used to group data sets or to ensure unique names. For
example, DATA.A27.B74276 is likely to be a unique name,
and data sets named SMITH.SOURCE, SMITH.DATA, and
SMITH.REPORT could all belong to Smith.

    //INPUT   DD   DSN=JONES.2267.TEST6, . . .

    //OUTPUT   DD   DSN=LAX.UNITED.707.SEAT32, . . .

A new data set with qualified names must have an index
built for each level of index. The IBM-supplied utility program IEHPROGM, described in Chapter 14, creates indexes.
For example, the data set named A.B.C must have indexes
built for A and A.B before the data set is created.

Other Data Sets

The DSN parameter has a slight variation for partitioned,
generation, and indexed-sequential data sets. (These data
sets are covered in detail in later chapters.) The general
form is DSN=name(value) or DSN=&&name(value), depending
upon whether the data set is nontemporary or temporary.
The name is the data set name, and the value depends on the
type of data set.

To refer to a member of a partitioned data set, code
DSN=name(member), giving the member name within the
data set; for example, DSN=HOLD(IT) requests member IT
in data set HOLD. To refer to a particular generation of a
generation data group, code DSN=name(number), giving the
relative generation number, zero or a signed integer; for
example, DSN=TAX(-1) refers to relative generation -1 of
data group TAX. An indexed-sequential data set can consist
of an index, prime, and overflow area, and one must code
DSN=name(INDEX), DSN=name(PRIME), and DSN=name
(OVFLOW), respectively.

I/O UNIT: UNIT

An I/O unit is a particular type of I/O device: a 2311 disk, 2400 tape, 1403 printer, etc. The I/O unit requested by the UNIT parameter should not be confused with the volume. A volume is a specific storage container: a tape reel, a drum, a disk pack, a bin in a data cell, or the part of an IBM 2302 disk storage device served by one access mechanism. Thus a volume is mounted on an I/O unit. Specific volumes are requested by the VOL parameter described later in this chapter.

UNIT requests an I/O unit by hardware address, device type, or group name or by requesting the unit used by another data set in the same step. Other UNIT subparameters request that multiple volumes be mounted in parallel, that volume mounting be deferred until the data set is opened, and that a unit be chosen separate or identical to that used by other data sets. UNIT is generally required unless the data set is passed or cataloged. The following list gives other circumstances in which the UNIT is not needed:

1. SYSOUT is coded on the DD card. UNIT is optional; if omitted, a default unit specified in the cataloged reader procedure is used.
2. DUMMY is coded on the DD card. UNIT is again optional; if coded, it is ignored.
3. The data set already exists, either as a cataloged data set or as a data set passed from a previous job step, and the VOL=SER parameter is not coded.
4. The data set is assigned volumes used by an earlier data set in the same job with the VOL=REF parameter.
5. The data set shares space or cylinders with an earlier data set by the SUBALLOC or SPLIT space parameters.

To request an I/O unit, code UNIT=address, UNIT=type, or UNIT=group. The address is the hardware address, the type is the numeric model type, and the group is a name assigned by the installation to a group of units. To request a unit or units used by another data set, code UNIT=AFF= ddname, where the ddname is the name of an earlier DD card in the same step. The system will select a unit with affinity for the unit specified in the named DD card.

Hardware Address

Code UNIT=address to request a specific I/O unit by giving the three-digit hardware address of the device, set when the computer is installed. For example, if a specific tape unit is on 0C4, code UNIT=0C4. Do not use hardware addresses unless you want a specific hardware unit; multiprogramming systems may already have allocated the device to another job. It is better to ask for one of a group of devices and let the system select one that is available.

To request a specific bin on a 2321 data cell, code UNIT=address/bin, where the bin is a numeric digit (0 to 9). For example, UNIT=30D/2 requests bin 2 of the 2321 data cell whose hardware address is 30D, whereas UNIT=30D requests any available bin of the 2321.

Type

Code UNIT=type to request a type of I/O device by the IBM model number. Each IBM device has a predefined model number automatically provided. For example, UNIT=2311 requests an available 2311 disk. Table 1 lists the available unit types.

Table 1. Device Types

Tape Units

Unit Type	Unit
2400	2400 series 9-track magnetic tape drive, 800 bpi density.
2400-1	2400 series magnetic tape drive with 7-track compatibility and without data conversion.
2400-2	2400 series magnetic tape drive with 7-track compatibility and data conversion.

Table 1. Device Types (Continued)

Tape Units (Continued)

Unit Type	Unit
2400-3	2400 series 9-track magnetic tape drive, 1600 bpi density.
2400-4	2400 series 9-track magnetic tape drive, 800 and 1600 bpi density.
2420-5	2420 model 5 tape unit, 1600 bpi density.

Direct Access Units

2301	2301 drum storage unit.
2302	2302 disk storage drive.
2303	2303 drum storage unit.
2311	Any 2311 disk storage drive.
2314	2314 storage facility.
2321	Any bin mounted on a 2321 data cell drive.

Unit Record Equipment

1052	1052 printer-keyboard.
1403	1403 printer or 1404 printer (continuous form only).
1442	1442 card read punch.
1443	Any 1443 printer.
2501	2501 card reader.
2520	2520 card read punch.
2540	2540 card read punch (read feed).
2540-2	2540 card read punch (punch feed).
2671	2671 paper tape reader.
2741	2741 communication terminal.

Table 1. Device Types (Continued)

Graphic Units

Unit Type	Unit
1053	1053 model 4 printer.
2250-1	2250 display unit, model 1.
2250-3	2250 display unit, model 3.
2260-1	2260 model 1 display station (local attachment).
2260-2	2260 model 2 display station (local attachment).
2280	2280 film recorder.
2282	2282 film recorder/scanner.
2760	2760 optical image unit.
1130	1130 computer.

Group

Code UNIT=group to request one of several I/O devices grouped by the installation. UNIT=SYSDA is traditionally defined to be direct-access storage devices, and UNIT=SYSSQ is traditionally units which can contain sequential data sets. An installation can define one group name for temporary and another name for nontemporary direct-access storage. Both groups might include different devices. The following examples show the distinction between hardware address, type, and group.

	Available Devices			
	2311#1	2311#2	2314#1	2314#2
Address	130	131	230	231
Type	2311	2311	2314	2314
Group	SYSDA	SYSDA	SYSDA	SYSDA
	SCRATCH	SCRATCH	SCRATCH	

UNIT=130 selects 2311#1 only, UNIT=2311 requests either 2311#1 or 2311#2, and UNIT=SYSDA allows any of the four devices to be selected. Either 2311#1, 2311#2, or 2314#1 is selected if UNIT=SCRATCH is coded. If the volume is mounted in systems with the automatic volume recognition feature (AVR), UNIT=group requests the operator to mount the volume on a specific device, whereas UNIT=type requests the operator to mount the volume on any available device of that type.

Unit Affinity: AFF

Code UNIT=AFF=ddname to assign data sets on mountable volumes to the same unit used by another data set. The ddname must be the name of a previous DD card in the same step. Unit affinity conserves I/O units by forcing data sets onto the same physical device. The unit is used sequentially; that is, each data set must be closed before the next data set is opened. Unit affinity implies deferred mounting (the volume is not requested to be mounted until the data set is opened), and so it can be requested only for units with removable volumes: 2311 and 2314 disks, 2400 tapes, and 2321 data cells.

If affinity is requested for a 2321 data cell drive, the data sets are assigned the same unit but may be assigned different cells. If the ddname refers to a dummy DD card (DUMMY or DSN=NULLFILE), the requesting DD card is also assigned a dummy status.

```
//STEP1    EXEC    PGM=ONE

//A    DD    UNIT=2314, . . .

//B    DD    UNIT=AFF=A, . . .

//C    DD    UNIT=AFF=D, . . .
```

   Wrong!   Must refer to a previous DD card.

```
//D    DD    UNIT=DISK, . . .
```

Special Options

Multiple volumes, deferred mounting, and unit separation from other data sets can be specified with the UNIT parameter.

type *P*
group *volumes*
UNIT=(-----,-------,*DEFER*,*SEP=(ddname, . . . ,ddname)*)

Parallel volume mounting: volumes, P

If a data set resides on more than one volume, all volumes can be mounted at the same time by coding UNIT=(device,volumes, . . .). The device can be either a type or group, and volumes is the number of volumes (2 to 59) to mount in parallel. The volumes must not exceed the number of drives available.

Mounting volumes in parallel can save time by eliminating the need for the operator to dismount and mount volumes on a single unit as they are needed. However, parallel mounting denies the use of these units to other jobs in multiprogramming systems. Parallel mounting allows data sets to be processed that are contained on more than one direct-access volume. One unit is assumed if volumes is omitted or if zero is coded.

If the data set is cataloged or if the VOL parameter indicates the number of volumes, code P rather than volumes. The number of volumes is then obtained from the catalog or the VOL parameter. The device type or group should be omitted for cataloged data sets since this information is contained in the catalog.

    //A   DD   UNIT=(2311,2), . . .

Two 2311 disks are mounted in parallel.

    //B   DD   UNIT=(,P), . . .

All volumes containing the cataloged data set are mounted in parallel.

//C   DD   UNIT=(TAPE,P)VOL=SER=(200,300), . . .

Two volumes (200 and 300) are mounted in
parallel.

Deferred volume mounting: DEFER

To defer volume mounting until the data set is opened,
code UNIT=(device,,DEFER, . . .). The system will not
request the volume to be mounted until the data set is opened.
DEFER can be used to prevent a volume being needlessly
mounted because a particular run does not require it. DEFER
is ignored if the volume is already mounted; in addition, it
cannot be used for new direct-access data sets because space
must be allocated before the step is initiated. Nor can DEFER
be used for indexed-sequential data sets.

//A   DD   UNIT=(TAPE, ,DEFER), . . .

//B   DD   UNIT=(DISK,2,DEFER), . . .

//C   DD   UNIT=(,P,DEFER), . . .

Separating data sets: SEP

To separate a direct-access data set from access mech-
anisms used by other data sets, code UNIT=(device, . . . ,
SEP=(ddname, . . . ,ddname)). Since SEP is a keyword subparameter, it is coded after the last positional subparameter.
The ddname names 1 to 8 previous DD cards in the same step
from which to separate the data set.

SEP limits arm contention by forcing concurrently used
data sets onto units with separate access arms; thus it may
significantly reduce processing time. For example, if the
same disk volume contains an input and output data set, the
disk arm must be moved whenever reading and writing alternate. When the data sets are separated, the arm contention
is eliminated. (There may still be arm contention with data
sets used by other jobs in multiprogramming systems, but
this is beyond the user's control unless he requests a
private volume.)

//STEP1   EXEC   PGM=ONE

//A   DD   UNIT=SYSDA, . . .

//B   DD   UNIT=(SYSDA,SEP=A), . . .

//C   DD   UNIT=(SYSDA,SEP=D), . . .

Wrong!   Must refer to a previous DD card.

//D   DD   UNIT=(SYSDA,3,DEFER,SEP=(A,

//   B))

The SEP subparameters can be continued after a complete ddname, including the comma following it.

If the SEP request cannot be satisfied, PCP systems ignore it; MFT and MVT systems request the computer operator to either cancel the job or ignore the SEP request. If one of the ddnames defines a dummy data set (DUMMY or DSN=NULLFILE), the unit separation for that ddname is ignored. If the system has the automatic volume recognition feature and the volume is premounted, SEP is again ignored. (The system will not force the operator to dismount a volume to satisfy a SEP request.) SEP can be used to request that 2321 data cell volumes be mounted on separate devices because the system normally mounts them on as few devices as possible.

DATA SET DISPOSITION: DISP

The DISP parameter describes the current status of the data set (old, new, or to be modified) and directs the system on the disposition of the data set (pass, keep, catalog, uncatalog, or delete) either at the end of the step or if the step abnormally terminates. DISP is always required unless the data set is created and deleted in the same step. The general form of the DISP parameter is

DISP=(*current status,normal disposition,abnormal disposition*)

The various options are

$$
\text{DISP}=(\underbrace{\begin{array}{l} \\ NEW \\ MOD \\ OLD \\ SHR \end{array}}_{-\,-\,-},\underbrace{\begin{array}{l} KEEP \\ DELETE \\ PASS \\ CATLG \\ UNCATLG \end{array}}_{-\,-\,-\,-\,-\,-\,-},\underbrace{\begin{array}{l} \\ KEEP \\ DELETE \\ CATLG \\ UNCATLG \end{array}}_{-\,-\,-\,-\,-\,-})
$$

Current Status

The current status, NEW, MOD, OLD, or SHR, is the status of the data set at the beginning of the step. If the data set is new, the system creates a data set label; if it is old, the system locates it and reads its label.

New data sets: NEW

DISP=(NEW, . . .) creates a new data set. The UNIT parameter is required, the VOL parameter can be used to place the data set on a specific volume, and the SPACE parameter is required for direct-access devices. The step abnormally terminates if a data set with the same name already exists on the same volume.

NEW is default if nothing is coded; for example, DISP= (,KEEP) is the same as DISP=(NEW,KEEP). If DISP is omitted entirely, NEW is also assumed.

Modifying data sets: MOD

DISP=(MOD, . . .) modifies a sequential data set. When the data set is opened, MOD positions the read/write mechanism after the last record in the data set, providing a convenient means of adding data to sequential data sets.

If the data set does not exist, the system changes MOD to NEW—unless the VOL parameter requests a specific volume. When VOL is coded, the system expects to find the data set on the specified volume and terminates the step if it cannot find it. If VOL is not coded, the system looks to see whether the data set was passed or is in the catalog; if neither is the case, it assumes the data set does not exist and creates it as if NEW had been coded.

A new data set does not contain an end-of-data-set marker until it is opened and closed for output. Often one allocates space for a direct-access data set with the expectation that subsequent jobs will add data to it with a disposition of MOD. An attempt to read the data set yields unpredictable results unless the data set has been opened and closed for output to write an end-of-data-set marker.

MOD can be used to add to a data set that extends onto several volumes; it is the usual way of extending data sets onto several direct-access volumes. Always specify a disposition of CATLG with MOD for cataloged data sets, even if they are already cataloged, to record additional volume serial numbers in the catalog. If the volumes onto which the data set extends are not already mounted, specify either a volume count with the VOL parameter or deferred mounting with the UNIT parameter so that the system will request dismounting and mounting of volumes.

DCB parameters contained in the data set label of a data set being extended with MOD should not be coded on the DD card extending the data set because a data set must not be written with conflicting sets of DCB parameters. If DCB parameters are coded on the DD card, be sure that they do not conflict with the data set.

Old data sets: OLD

DISP=(OLD, . . .) designates an existing data set; it can be an input data set or a partially complete output data set. The step is given sole access to the data set. (In multiprogramming environments, several jobs have the potential of concurrently reading the same data set on direct-access storage.)

If the old data set is cataloged or passed from a previous step, the DSN parameter is usually the only other DD parameter needed. (The LABEL parameter may also be

needed for magnetic tapes.) If the old data set is not cataloged or passed from a previous step, UNIT and VOL parameters are required.

Sharing data sets: SHR

DISP=(SHR, . . .) permits old data sets to be shared.
SHR is identical to OLD except that several jobs may use
the data set concurrently in multiprogramming environments.
SHR must be used only for input data sets; use OLD or MOD
if the data set is modified. Sharing data sets is necessary in
MFT and MVT because public libraries like SYS1.LINKLIB
or the subroutine libraries should be available to every job
in the system. If SHR is coded in PCP systems, it is treated
as OLD. Generally SHR should be used for all input data
sets. (If the data set is being modified by another job, that
job will have a disposition of OLD to prevent the data set
being shared.)

```
//STEP1    EXEC    PGM=FIRST

//A    DD    DISP=(,PASS),UNIT=2311,DSN=RECORDS,

//    SPACE=(80,100)
```

The data set named RECORDS is created. Since
it now exists, any later usage of it must be with
the dispositions MOD,SHR, or OLD.

```
//STEP2    EXEC    PGM=SECOND

//B    DD    DISP=(MOD,CATLG),DSN=BOOKS,

//    SPACE=(80,100),UNIT=2314
```

If data set BOOKS is not found in the catalog, the
system assumes it does not exist and creates it.
If it does exist, any new data written into it is
placed after the last record in the data set.

```
//C    DD    DISP=(MOD,CATLG),DSN=LIBRARY,

//    UNIT=2314,VOL=SER=200
```

LIBRARY must be an existing data set, and any new data written into it is placed after the last record in the data set.

//STEP3   EXEC   PGM=THIRD

//D   DD   DISP=OLD,DSN=SYS1.FORTLIB

SYS1.FORTLIB must be an existing data set, and the step is given sole use of it. If the system cannot locate it in the catalog, the step is terminated.

//E   DD   DISP=SHR,DSN=SYS1.FORTLIB

The only difference between D and E is that E permits other jobs to read SYS1.FORTLIB concurrently.

Normal Disposition

Normal disposition, the second term in the DISP parameter, indicates the disposition of the data set if the job terminates normally. The normal disposition can be omitted if the data set's status is not to change—existing data sets (MOD, OLD, or SHR) continue to exist; NEW data sets are deleted.

Dispositions for direct-access and magnetic tape data sets differ. Direct-access space must remain intact if the data set is to be kept, and space is released for other use if the data set is deleted. Keeping and deleting a magnetic tape data set are similar; the tape is rewound and unloaded. The computer operator is then told whether the tape is to be kept or deleted. Presumably the operator will reserve a kept tape and put a deleted tape back into circulation, but nothing actually happens to the data on the tape. (The CLOSE macro, coded in assembly language, can override the normal tape disposition.)

A direct-access data set passed between job steps is retained on direct-access storage. Passing tape data sets rewinds the tape between steps but does not dismount it.

Disposition is not performed under the following special circumstances:

1. The step is not initiated because of JCL errors.
2. The step is bypassed because of the COND parameter on JOB or EXEC cards. Disposition is performed only for passed data sets.
3. The data set is not opened, and either a nonspecific request was made for a tape (VOL=SER not coded), or deferred mounting is specified for direct-access volumes (UNIT=(. . . ,DEFER) is coded)).
4. The step abnormally terminates after devices have been allocated but before the step begins execution because direct-access space cannot be obtained. Existing data sets (OLD, MOD, and SHR) continue to exist; NEW data sets are deleted.

Pass data sets: PASS

DISP=(. . ,PASS, . .) passes the data set on to subsequent job steps, and each step can use the data set once. PASS saves time because the system retains the data set location and volume information, and a mountable volume containing the data set remains mounted. Both temporary and nontemporary data sets can be passed.

Final disposition is left to a subsequent step. If the data set is not referred to by an intervening step, the data set continues to be passed. If PASS is coded in the last step or no disposition is given, temporary data sets are deleted and nontemporary data sets assume their original status—existing data sets (MOD, OLD, or SHR) continue to exist; NEW data sets are deleted.

PASS does not pass the file number of a tape data set. If the data set resides on other than the first tape file, the LABEL parameter must specify the file. If several data sets in the job have the same name, only one can be passed at a time. Subsequent steps can refer to a passed data set by name or by referback. UNIT and VOL parameters need not be coded since this information is passed with the data set.

//STEP1   EXEC   PGM=ONE

//A   DD   DISP=(,PASS),DSN=&&IT,UNIT=2311,

//   VOL=SER=400,SPACE=(80,100)

//STEP2   EXEC   PGM=TWO

//B   DD   DISP=(OLD,PASS),DSN=&&IT
   or
//B   DD   DISP=(OLD,PASS),DSN=*.STEP1.A

Keep data sets: KEEP

DISP=(. . ,KEEP, . .) keeps nontemporary data sets; a data set residing on direct-access storage is retained, and a data set residing on magnetic tape is rewound and dismounted. A keep message is issued to the operator if the data set resides on a mountable volume. If KEEP is attempted for a temporary data set, the disposition is changed to PASS. (The data set is deleted if no DSN parameter is coded and DEFER is specified in the UNIT parameter.) If KEEP is used for a NEW data set, a data set label is retained with the data set.

//READ   DD   DISP=(,KEEP),DSN=LEDGER,

//   UNIT=2314,VOL=SER=300,SPACE=(80,100)

LEDGER is created and is kept after the step terminates. Since LEDGER is not passed or cataloged, any later use of the data set, either in a subsequent step or in a later job, must give the volume and unit.

//LATER   DD   DISP=(OLD,KEEP),DSN=LEDGER,

//   UNIT=2314,VOL=SER=300

The system locates LEDGER on the volume and unit specified. OLD, MOD, or SHR must be

used to refer to an existing data set. If NEW
had been used instead of OLD, the system would
terminate the step because a data set with the
same name already exists on the volume.

Delete data sets: DELETE

DISP=(. . ,DELETE, . .) deletes data sets; storage
occupied by a direct-access data set is released; a magnetic
tape is rewound and unloaded and the operator is told that
the tape data set is deleted (nothing actually happens to the
data on tape). If the data set is located through the catalog
(UNIT and VOL not coded), the data set is also uncataloged.
If DISP=(SHR,DELETE) is coded, DISP=(OLD,DELETE) is
assumed.

Catalog data sets: CATLG

DISP=(. . ,CATLG, . .) catalogs a nontemporary data set.
CATLG is similar to KEEP except that the unit and volume
of the data set are recorded in the catalog along with the
data set name. The file number of a tape data set is also recorded in the catalog, but the type of tape label and the tape
density is not. (The system assumes standard labels, and
so the user need code the LABEL parameter only for nonstandard labels.)

UNIT and VOL parameters are always required for
CATLG, unless the data set is already cataloged. If the data
set is already cataloged, the disposition is the same as PASS.
If CATLG is attempted for temporary data sets, the disposition is changed to PASS. (The data set is deleted if no DSN
parameter is coded and DEFER is specified in the UNIT
parameter.) All volumes of a multivolume data set are recorded in the catalog. If a multivolume data set is being
expanded onto more volumes, DISP=(MOD,CATLG) records
the additional volumes in the catalog.

If the data set name is qualified (for example, A.B.C)
the IBM-supplied utility program IEHPROGM described in
Chapter 14 must be used to create an entry for each higher-
level index.

```
//CARDS    DD    DISP=(,CATLG),UNIT=2400,

//    DSN=BALANCE,VOL=SER=500
```

BALANCE is created and cataloged. A later DD card can refer to the data set by its name, omitting the unit and volume.

```
//LATER    DD    DISP=(OLD,CATLG),DSN=BALANCE
```

   or

```
//LATER    DD    DISP=(OLD,KEEP),DSN=BALANCE
```

CATLG and KEEP are equivalent if the data set is already cataloged. However, if a multivolume data set is expanded onto more volumes, use CATLG to record the additional volumes in the catalog.

```
//SAVE    DD    DISP=(OLD,CATLG),UNIT=2400,

//    DSN=BUDGET,VOL=SER=300
```

An existing data set can also be cataloged.

Uncatalog data sets: UNCATLG

DISP=(. . ,UNCATLG, . .) uncatalogs a data set. UN-CATLG is the same as KEEP except that the data set name is removed from the catalog. If the data set is not cataloged, UNCATLG is equivalent to KEEP.

```
//RID    DD    DISP=(OLD,UNCATLG),DSN=BALANCE
```

BALANCE is removed from the catalog. SHR should not be used in uncataloging data sets because shared data sets should not be changed. If BALANCE were not cataloged, the system could not locate the data set and would terminate the step.

//A   DD   DISP=(OLD,UNCATLG),DSN=IT,

//   UNIT=2311,VOL=SER=600

IT is removed from the catalog. If IT is not cataloged, UNCATLG is treated as KEEP.

Abnormal Disposition

The abnormal dispositions, effective only if the step abnormally terminates, are the same as normal dispositions except that PASS is not allowed. KEEP, CATLG, UNCATLG, and DELETE are all permitted: DISP=(NEW,PASS,DELETE), DISP=(OLD,DELETE,CATLG), etc.

If an abnormal disposition is not specified and the step terminates abnormally, the normal disposition is assumed; for example, DISP=(OLD,KEEP) is equivalent to DISP=(OLD, KEEP,KEEP). The abnormal termination disposition for temporary data sets is always DELETE, regardless of what one codes.

A passed data set assumes the conditional disposition specified the last time it was passed if a step abnormally terminates. If no conditional disposition was specified, the data set is deleted if it was new when first passed; otherwise it is kept. The following example illustrates the use of the abnormal disposition.

//STEP1   EXEC   PGM=CREATE

//A   DD   DISP=(,KEEP),DSN=JUNK,UNIT=2314,

//   VOL=SER=200,SPACE=(800,20)

If STEP1 abnormally terminates, the data set named JUNK is kept. If the program is corrected and the job re-submitted with the same JCL, it will abnormally terminate again; this time because the data set JUNK already exists on the volume. One must change the disposition on the A DD card to DISP=(OLD,KEEP). This inconvenience is avoided by deleting the data set if the step abnormally terminates.

```
//STEP1   EXEC   PGM=CREATE

//A   DD   DISP=(,KEEP,DELETE),DSN=JUNK,

//   UNIT=2314,VOL=SER=200,SPACE=(800,20)
```

Now if STEP1 abnormally terminates, JUNK is deleted and the disposition need not be changed to OLD when the job is resubmitted. The abnormal disposition is very useful for direct-access data sets because, as the above example shows, subsequent runs may depend upon the disposition of data sets in previous runs. The abnormal disposition, in addition to deleting unwanted data sets, can also retain information about the data set.

```
//STEP1   EXEC   PGM=ONCE

//A   DD   DISP=(,PASS),UNIT=2314,

//   SPACE=(80,200),DSN=SAVIT
```

If STEP1 abnormally terminates, SAVIT is deleted because PASS is assumed, and passed nontemporary data sets assume their original disposition if the step abnormally terminates.

```
//STEP2   EXEC   PGM=TWICE

//B   DD   DISP=(OLD,DELETE,CATLG),DSN=SAVIT
```

If STEP2 abnormally terminates, SAVIT is cataloged and the unit and volume information are retained in the catalog. If the restart feature is used to restart the job from STEP2, the B DD card need not be changed.

The current status, normal, and abnormal disposition are all optional. The following examples show the actual dispositions in effect if parameters are omitted. The reader should reread the description of the dispositions if the assumed dispositions are not clear.

//A   DD   UNIT=2314,SPACE=(80,100)

DISP=(NEW,DELETE,DELETE) is assumed.

//B   DD   DISP=NEW,UNIT=2314,SPACE=(80,100)

DISP=(NEW,DELETE,DELETE) is assumed.

//C   DD   DISP=SHR,DSN=LIB

DISP=(SHR,KEEP,KEEP) is assumed.

//D   DD   DISP=MOD,DSN=TURNON,

//   SPACE=(80,100),UNIT=2311

DISP=(OLD,KEEP,KEEP) is assumed if TURNON
is cataloged or passed from a previous step.
DISP=(NEW,DELETE,DELETE) is assumed if
TURNON does not exist.

//E   DD   DISP=(,KEEP,DELETE),UNIT=2314,

//   SPACE=(80,20),DSN=IT

DISP=(NEW,KEEP,DELETE) is assumed.

//F   DD   DISP=(OLD,PASS,KEEP),DSN=&&IT

DISP=(OLD,PASS,DELETE) is assumed.

//G   DD   DISP=(OLD,,CATLG),DSN=IT,UNIT=2311,

//   VOL=SER=400

DISP=(OLD,KEEP,CATLG) is assumed.

//H   DD   DISP=(,KEEP),DSN=&&IT,UNIT=2314,

//   SPACE=(80,100)

DISP=(NEW,PASS,DELETE) is assumed.

VOLUME PARAMETER: VOL

The VOL parameter[†] requests a specific volume, multiple volumes, specific volumes of a multivolume cataloged data set, and private volumes. A volume can be a tape reel, a disk pack, a bin in a 2321 data cell, a drum, or the part of an IBM 2302 disk storage device served by one access mechanism.

Each volume can have a label. There are two types of labels (actually three if one includes the external label pasted on a tape reel or disk pack): a volume label and a data set label. Both the volume and data set labels are contained in the volume itself as data. The volume label contains the volume serial number and is read by the system to ensure that an expected volume is actually mounted.

The volume label is also used by the automatic volume recognition feature which allows the operator to mount a volume before it is requested. The system reads the volume label and retains the serial number. When the volume is needed, the system knows the volume is already mounted and allows processing to begin immediately.

Volumes can be permanently mounted, mounted by the operator, or mounted because they are required by the user's job. Volumes become permanently mounted if critical portions of the system reside on them, if the volume cannot be physically dismounted, or if they are so designated at the installation by an entry in a special member (PRESRES) of the SYS1.PARMLIB data set. Direct-access volumes are often permanently mounted, although 2311 and 2314 disk packs can be mounted by operator or user requests. Tapes are usually mounted when they are required by user jobs.

VOL must always give the volume serial number for an existing data set unless it is cataloged or passed. A new data set can be created on specific or nonspecific volumes.

[†] The VOL parameter can also be coded as VOLUME; for example, VOL=SER=200 and VOLUME=SER=200 are equivalent.

The VOL parameter requests specific volumes, but if it is omitted, the system selects an appropriate volume for the type of unit specified. The installation can designate appropriate volumes to select for such nonspecific volume requests by a PRESRES entry. Such an entry may designate volumes to be public (temporary data sets only), storage (temporary and nontemporary data sets), private (user requested), or scratch (scratch tapes).

Request a Specific Volume: SER, REF

To request specific volumes, code VOL=SER=volume for one volume, or VOL=SER=(volume, . . . ,volume) if several volumes are needed. The volume serial numbers are 1 to 6 alphameric (A to Z, 0 to 9) or national (@ $ #) characters, or the hyphen (-). Special characters (blank , . / ') (* & + =) can also be used by enclosing the volume in apostrophes; code a legitimate apostrophe as two consecutive apostrophes.

        //A   DD   VOL=SER=PACK12,UNIT=2311,

        //   DISP=(,CATLG),DSN=SAVE,SPACE=(80,200)

            A 2311 disk pack labeled PACK12 is requested.
            If the pack is not mounted, the system will request the operator to mount it.

        //B   DD   UNIT=(TAPE,3),VOL=SER=(TP1,TP2,

        //   TP3),DSN=MANY,DISP=(OLD,KEEP)

            Three tape volumes are requested to be mounted
            in parallel: volumes TP1, TP2, and TP3. A DD
            card specifying several volumes can be continued
            after a complete serial number, including the
            comma following it.

Rather than specifying volume serial numbers, one can request the same volumes used by another data set. If the other data set is cataloged or passed from a previous step, code VOL=REF=name to name the data set. The name cannot contain special characters. If the data set is not cataloged or passed, or assigned a temporary name, code

VOL=REF=*.referback to refer back to a previous DD card describing the data set. If the earlier data set resides on multiple volumes, only the last volume is assigned for tapes; all volumes are assigned for direct-access volumes. If a referback is made to a DD card defining a dummy data set, the DD card making the referback is also assigned a dummy status.

```
//STEP1   EXEC   PGM=START

//A   DD   DSN=HOLDUP,DISP=(,PASS),UNIT=2314,

//   VOL=SER=200,SPACE=(800,100)

//B   DD   VOL=REF=*.A,DSN=REPORT,

//   DISP=(,PASS),SPACE=(200,50)
```

Disk volume 200 is also assigned to REPORT. No unit parameter is needed since the system already knows to which unit the pack is assigned.

```
//STEP2   EXEC   PGM=FINISH

//C   DD   VOL=REF=*.STEP1.A,DISP=(,CATLG),

//   DSN=MORE,SPACE=(400,30)
      or
//C   DD   VOL=REF=HOLDUP,DISP=(,CATLG),

//   DSN=MORE,SPACE=(400,30)
```

The data set named MORE is also assigned to pack 200.

Special Options

Options are provided to request private volumes, to ensure that the private volumes remain mounted between steps, to request multiple volumes, and to request a specific volume of a multivolume data set. All subparameters are

optional and can be coded in any combination. Code commas
to omit any positional subparameters.

SER= . .

REF= . .

VOL=(*PRIVATE,RETAIN,sequence,volumes,- - - - - -*)

Private volumes: PRIVATE

To give exclusive use of a mountable volume to a particular data set during a step, code VOL=(PRIVATE, . . .). No
other data sets are assigned to the volume, and the volume is
dismounted after its last use in the step. Either a specific or
nonspecific request can be made; the system asks the operator to select a private volume if the volume serial number is
not specified. If a permanently mounted volume is requested,
the volume is assigned, but PRIVATE is ignored.

Tape data sets are assumed to be PRIVATE if the data
sets are nontemporary or if a specific volume is requested.
Otherwise they are assigned as scratch and can be dismounted and used by another job at the end of the step. PRI-
VATE should be coded in the receiving step if a scratch tape
is passed, to prevent another job from using it.

//STEP1   EXEC   PGM=PRIMARY

//A   DD   VOL=(PRIVATE,SER=200),UNIT=2311,

//   DSN=ALL,SPACE=(80,100),DISP=(,CATLG)

The system will request the operator to mount
pack 200. No other data sets are assigned to the
pack, and it is dismounted after its last use in
the step.

//B   DD   UNIT=TAPE,DISP=(,PASS)

A scratch tape is requested.

//STEP2   EXEC   PGM=SECONDRY

```
//C   DD    VOL=PRIVATE,DSN=*.STEP1.B,

//    DISP=(OLD,DELETE)
```

The scratch tape passed from the previous step is retrieved.

Retain private volumes: *RETAIN*

To keep a volume mounted between steps, code VOL=(PRIVATE,RETAIN, . . .). The volume remains mounted until it is used in a subsequent step or until the end of the job. Only the last volume of a multivolume data set is retained. RETAIN is often used when a tape is used in several job steps, to minimize mounting. (The PASS disposition also keeps the volume mounted between steps.)

If RETAIN is not coded and the data set is not passed, a mountable volume is dismounted at the end of the step. Then if a subsequent step requests the volume, the operator may have to mount it on another I/O unit. (The CLOSE macro coded in assembly language has precedence over DD card parameters and may specify a different disposition.)

```
//A   DD    VOL=(PRIVATE,RETAIN,SER=300),

//    UNIT=DISK,DISP=(,CATLG),DSN=DISKFILE,

//    SPACE=(1600,20)
```

Pack 300 is not dismounted at the end of the step.

Sequence

When a multivolume data set is cataloged, all volume serial numbers are recorded in the catalog. To begin processing at other than the first volume, code VOL=(. . , . . . , sequence, . . .), giving a 1- to 4-digit sequence number. If the sequence number is omitted or zero is coded, processing begins with the first volume.

//A   DD   VOL=(PRIVATE,RETAIN,2),DSN=MULT,

//   DISP=OLD

Processing begins with volume 2 of the MULT
data set. The volume serial numbers and I/O
unit are omitted since they are contained in the
catalog.

//B   DD   VOL=(,,3),DSN=IRS,DISP=OLD

Processing begins with volume 3 of the cataloged
IRS data set.

Volumes

If a data set extends onto more than one volume, one
can either list the volume serial numbers with SER for
specific volumes or give the number of volumes for a nonspecific request. To request nonspecific volumes, code
VOL=(. ., . . , . . ,volumes, . . .), giving the number (2 to
255) of volumes needed. The number of volumes can also be
given for a cataloged or passed data set to indicate that additional volumes may be required. If volumes is omitted or
zero is coded, one volume is assumed.

//A   DD   VOL=(PRIVATE, , ,2)DISP=(,CATLG),

//   DSN=IRS,UNIT=TAPE

The operator will be requested to assign and
mount a maximum of 2 tapes.

If a multivolume data set is created or extended and the
number of volumes the data set requires is unknown, a
maximum number can be specified.

//A   DD   VOL=(, , ,6,SER=(100,200)),UNIT=TAPE,

//   DSN=FILE,DISP=(,CATLG)

Tape volumes 100 and 200 are assigned to the
data set. The operator may be requested to

assign and mount up to 4 additional volumes if they are needed. The volume serial numbers of all volumes used are recorded in the catalog.

Alternatively, deferred mounting can be used.

//A   DD   VOL=SER=(100,200),

//   UNIT=(TAPE, ,DEFER),DSN=FILE,

//   DISP=(,CATLG)

The effect of this statement is the same as that above except that the data set is not limited in the number of volumes onto which it can extend.

If the number of volumes exceeds the number of direct-access units requested with the UNIT parameter, PRIVATE must also be coded, e.g., UNIT=(2314,2),VOL=(PRIVATE, , ,3). If PRIVATE is not coded and the job requires more than the specified number of units, the job is abnormally terminated. Coding PRIVATE is not required for tape units.

A single DD card is limited to a maximum of 255 volumes; a job step is limited to 4095 volumes. SYSIN should not be used as a serial number because PCP systems preempt this name for their own use. Each volume at an installation should have a unique serial number, regardless of the type of volume.

Now consider two special problems. Suppose we wish to write a data set on a volume, but we do not know the volume serial number. The following must be coded on the DD card.

VOL=PRIVATE,DISP=(NEW, . . .),UNIT=(address, ,DEFER)

For example, suppose the external label pasted on a tape reel is lost and we do not know the volume serial number. The following job opens the data set for output and catalogs the tape. The volume serial number is then listed in the system data disposition messages and is recorded in the catalog.

// EXEC   PGM=OPEN

The program must open the data set.

//A   DD   VOL=PRIVATE,DISP=(NEW,CATLG),

//   UNIT=(0D0, ,DEFER),DSN=WHAT

Next, suppose that a data set is used twice in the same step; perhaps it is first opened for output, closed, and then opened for input. Normally one DD card would suffice, but the program might be coded to require two DD cards. The second DD card must contain

DSN=*.ddname,VOL=REF=*.ddname,DISP=(OLD, . . .)

The following example illustrates a program that uses a data set twice in the same step.

// EXEC   PGM=INOUT

//A   DD   UNIT=2314,SPACE=(80,200)

DD card A creates a scratch data set.

//B   DD   DSN=*.A,VOL=REF=*.A,DISP=OLD

DD card B refers to the scratch data set.

SUMMARY

A DD card must be included after the EXEC card for each data set used in the step. The general form of the DD card is

$$*$$
$$DATA$$
$$DUMMY$$
//ddname   DD   ————,*keyword parameters*

The parameters discussed in this chapter are as follows.

DCB Parameter:

    DCB=(*subparameter*, . . . ,*subparameter*)

    DCB=(name,*subparameter*, . . . ,*subparameter*)

    DCB=(*.referback,*subparameter*, . . . ,*subparameter*)

DSN Parameter:

    DSN=name   DSN=&&name

    DSN=*.referback

    DSN=name(member)   DSN=&&name(member)

    DSN=name(generation)

    DSN=name(INDEX)   DSN=&&name(INDEX)

    DSN=name(PRIME)   DSN=&&name(PRIME)

    DSN=name(OVFLOW)   DSN=&&name(OVFLOW)

UNIT Parameter:

```
         type
         group    P
         address  volumes
UNIT=( ------- , ------- ,DEFER,
  SEP=(ddname, . . . ,ddname) )
```

    UNIT=AFF=ddname

DISP Parameter:

DISP=(current status,normal disposition,abnormal
disposition)

```
            KEEP
   NEW  DELETE   KEEP
   MOD  PASS     DELETE
   OLD  CATLG    CATLG
   SHR  UNCATLG  UNCATLG
DISP=( - - - , - - - - - - - , - - - - - - - )
```

VOL Parameter:

VOL=(*PRIVATE,RETAIN,sequence,volumes,*

REF=name
REF=*.referback
SER=(volume, . . . ,volume)
-)

CHAPTER 9
CATALOGED PROCEDURES

In this chapter begins the discussion of DD card parameters in all their myriad detail to describe concatenated data sets, placement of DD cards, and cataloged procedures.

CONCATENATING DATA SETS

Several input data sets can be read as if they were a single data set by concatenating them together. The data sets may reside on different output devices, but they must have similar characteristics(record format, length, device type). Data sets are concatenated by coding a DD card for each data set in the order they are to be read. A ddname is coded on the first DD card only, and a maximum of 255 sequential data sets may be concatenated. NAMES, ADDRESS, PHONES, and the card data in the input stream are read sequentially in the following example.

```
//DATAIN   DD    DSN=NAMES,DISP=SHR

//   DD    DSN=ADDRESS,DISP=SHR,UNIT=2311,

//   VOL=SER=222

//   DD    DSN=PHONES,DISP=OLD,UNIT=TAPE,

//   VOL=SER=002

//   DD    *

[card data]

/*
```

A maximum of 16 partitioned data sets may also be concatenated together, but they cannot be concatenated with sequential data sets. However, individual members of partitioned data sets are treated as sequential data sets and

may be concatenated with other members or other sequential
data sets. In the following example, a partitioned data set
containing three members is read sequentially by concatenating the members.

```
//DATAIN   DD   DSN=LIB(ONE),DISP=SHR

//  DD    DSN=LIB(TWO),DISP=SHR

//  DD    DSN=LIB(THREE),DISP=SHR
```

Members ONE, TWO, and THREE in LIB are read in
that order. The next example concatenates sequential data
sets with a member of a partitioned data set.

```
//DATAIN   DD   DSN=LIB(ONE),DISP=SHR

//  DD    *

[card data]

/*

//  DD    DSN=NAMES,DISP=SHR
```

Member ONE in LIB is read first, then the card data,
and finally the sequential data set NAMES. A member name
must be given for any partitioned data set concatenated with
a sequential data set. In the following example, an I/O error
occurs when DATAIN is read because LIB is a partitioned
data set. To read LIB in its entirety, concatenate each
member.

```
//DATAIN   DD   DSN=NAMES,DISP=SHR

//  DD   DSN=LIB,DISP=SHR
```

PLACEMENT OF DD CARDS

All DD cards for a particular step must immediately
follow the EXEC card.

```
//RUN    PROC

//FIRST    EXEC    PGM=ONE

//INPUT    DD    DSN=PIANO,DISP=OLD

//SCRATCH    DD    DSN=&&TEMP,UNIT=2311,

//    SPACE=(TRK,200),VOL=(PRIVATE,SER=200),

//    DCB=(RECFM=FB,LRECL=80,BLKSIZE=160)
```

INPUT and SCRATCH apply to step FIRST.

```
//SECOND    EXEC    PGM=TWO

//OUTPUT    DD    DUMMY,SYSOUT=A
```

OUTPUT applies to step SECOND.

Parameters on DD cards in cataloged procedures can be overridden, nullified, or added, or an entire DD card can be added. The stepname is appended to the ddname to override or add DD cards to procedures. If the ddname of the submitted card matches a ddname within the procedure, parameters on the DD card are overridden; if the names do not match, the submitted card is added. DD cards must be overridden in the order they appear in the procedure, and added DD cards must follow any overriding cards.

DD cards are added in their entirety, whereas an overridden DD card is modified parameter by parameter. Parameters are overridden if parameters on the overriding card match parameters on the procedure card; parameters are added if they do not match. The order of parameters on overriding DD cards does not matter. The changes made to a cataloged procedure by overriding DD cards are effective only for the run and do not change the cataloged procedure permanently. The following example illustrates DD cards overridden in the RUN procedure above.

```
//    EXEC    RUN
```

```
//FIRST.INPUT    DD    DSN=GUITAR,UNIT=2311,

//   VOL=SER=222
```

INPUT matches a ddname in step FIRST so that
parameters are overridden or added: DSN is
overridden, DISP is unchanged, and UNIT and
VOL are added.

```
//FIRST.SCRATCH    DD    UNIT=2314
```

The UNIT parameter is overridden. The card
overriding SCRATCH must follow the card overriding INPUT because SCRATCH follows INPUT
in the procedure.

```
//SECOND.OUTPUT    DD    SYSOUT=B
```

The SYSOUT parameter is overridden.

```
//SECOND.MORE    DD    DSN=DRUM,DISP=SHR
```

Since the DD card is added, it must follow the
card overriding OUTPUT.

The cataloged procedure is interpreted as follows for
the run.

```
//FIRST    EXEC    PGM=ONE

//INPUT    DD    DSN=GUITAR,DISP=OLD,UNIT=2311,

//   VOL=SER=222

//SCRATCH    DD    DSN=&&TEMP,UNIT=2314,

//   SPACE=(TRK,200),VOL=(PRIVATE,SER=200),

//   DCB=(RECFM=FB,LRECL=80,BLKSIZE=160)

//SECOND    EXEC    PGM=TWO

//OUTPUT    DD    DUMMY,SYSOUT=B

//MORE    DD    DSN=DRUM,DISP=SHR
```

The system listing produced by the MSGLEVEL=1 option on the JOB card lists the cards as they are coded, not as the system interprets them. Each overriding DD card is listed immediately preceding the card it overrides; added DD cards are listed at the end of the step. DD cards submitted in the input stream are listed with // in columns 1 and 2, cataloged procedure cards with XX, and overridden cards in the procedure with X/. The system listing of the above produced by MSGLEVEL=1 would appear as

    // EXEC   RUN

    XXFIRST   EXEC   PGM=ONE

    //FIRST.INPUT   DD   DSN=GUITAR,UNIT=2311,

    // VOL=SER=222

    X/INPUT   DD   DSN=PIANO,DISP=OLD
               :
               :

Unfortunately the manner in which the system interprets the DD cards is not shown, and one should check carefully to see that the overriding and added DD cards are in the proper order. The following example shows a common error caused by misplaced DD cards.

    // EXEC   RUN

    //SECOND.MORE   DD   DSN=DRUM,DISP=SHR

    //SECOND.OUTPUT   DD   DSN=VIOLIN,DISP=OLD

MORE should follow OUTPUT since it is an added DD card. However, the system does not detect this error and assumes that OUTPUT is also to be added. Since two DD cards in the step now have the same ddname, the second OUTPUT DD card is ignored. Thus a card which was meant to override a DD card is ignored with no error message printed. The error is difficult to detect if MSGLEVEL=1 is not coded on the JOB card to list the JCL. The SECOND step appears in the run as

XXSECOND   EXEC   PGM=TWO

XXOUTPUT   DD   DUMMY,SYSOUT=A

//SECOND.MORE   DD   DSN=DRUM,DISP=SHR

//SECOND.OUTPUT   DD   DSN=VIOLIN,DISP=OLD

Parameters can be coded on overriding DD cards in any order; those appearing in the procedure are overridden; those not appearing are added. All except the DCB parameter are overridden in their entirety. DCB subparameters rather than the entire DCB parameter must be overriden or added.

// EXEC   RUN

//FIRST.SCRATCH   DD   DCB=BLKSIZE=800,

// VOL=SER=666

The SCRATCH DD card is interpreted as

//SCRATCH   DD   DSN=&&TEMP,UNIT=2311,

// SPACE=(TRK,200),VOL=SER=666,

// DCB=(RECFM=FB,LRECL=80,BLKSIZE=800)

Nullify parameters by coding the keyword followed by an equal sign but omitting the value. To nullify the entire DCB parameter, nullify each subparameter. (DCB= cannot be coded to nullify the entire DCB parameter.) To nullify a dummy data set (DUMMY or DSN=NULLFILE), code a DSN parameter on the overriding DD card. If the DD card does not require a data set name, code just DSN=.

// EXEC   RUN

//FIRST.SCRATCH   DD   DSN=,

// DCB=(RECFM=F,BLKSIZE=)

//SECOND.OUTPUT   DD   DSN=

SCRATCH and OUTPUT are interpreted as

//SCRATCH   DD   UNIT=2311,SPACE=(TRK,200),

//   VOL=(PRIVATE,SER=200),DCB=(RECFM=F,

//   LRECL=80)

//OUTPUT   DD   SYSOUT=A

If a DD card is overridden with parameters mutually exclusive from ones on the overridden DD card (e.g., SYSOUT and DISP), the mutually exclusive parameters on the over-ridden DD card are automatically nullified. Do not attempt to nullify them on the overriding DD card.

Concatenated DD cards within a cataloged procedure must be overridden individually in the same order they appear in the procedure. The following procedure contains a concatenated data set.

//WALK   PROC

//STEP1   EXEC   PGM=PRIMARY

//WORK   DD   DSN=LIBA,DISP=SHR

//   DD   DSN=LIBB,DISP=SHR

To leave a particular DD card unchanged, leave the operand field blank in the overriding DD card.

//   EXEC   WALK

//STEP1.WORK   DD   DSN=LIBRARY

//   DD

//   DD   DSN=LIBC,DISP=SHR

The first DD card is overridden, the second is left unchanged, and a third data set is concatenated. The WORK DD card is interpreted as

```
//WORK    DD    DSN=LIBRARY,DISP=SHR

//  DD    DSN=LIBB,DISP=SHR

//  DD    DSN=LIBC,DISP=SHR
```

A stepname appended to a ddname has no effect if a cataloged procedure is not invoked. The following two steps are treated the same.

```
//  EXEC    PGM=ONE

//IN    DD    DSN=LIB,DISP=SHR
```
            or
```
//  EXEC    PGM=ONE

//GO.IN    DD    DSN=LIB,DISP=SHR
```

CATALOGED PROCEDURES

Cataloged procedures greatly simplify JCL, and all commonly used procedures should be cataloged. A cataloged procedure is a set of JCL statements placed as a member of a partitioned data set on direct-access storage. Cataloged procedures are normally kept in a system library named SYS1.PROCLIB, but MFT and MVT systems permit other libraries to be concatenated to SYS1.PROCLIB by the reader procedures—a great convenience in testing procedures. Since libraries are searched in the order they are concatenated, a first library might contain fully tested procedures, a second library private user procedures, a third library test procedures, etc.

Adding Procedures to the Procedure Library

Each cataloged procedure must be given a unique 1- to 8-character name containing any alphameric (A to Z, 0 to 9) or national (@ $ #) characters. The IBM-supplied utility program IEBUPDTE (rhymes with "up city") adds and replaces procedures as follows:

```
//   EXEC   PGM=IEBUPDTE,REGION=24K
```

The IEBUPDTE program is contained in
SYS1.LINKLIB. The REGION parameter is
needed only for MVT systems.

```
//SYSPRINT   DD   SYSOUT=A
```

SYSPRINT defines a print data set.

```
//SYSUT1   DD   DSN=SYS1.PROCLIB,DISP=OLD
```

SYSUT1 defines the input data set. If procedures
are added to a different library, substitute the
library name for SYS1.PROCLIB.

```
//SYSUT2   DD   DSN=*.SYSUT1,DISP=OLD
```

SYSUT2 describes the output data set—the same
data set used for input.

```
//SYSIN   DD   DATA
```

DATA, described in the next chapter, should
always be used on the SYSIN DD card rather
than * because the card data contains JCL
with // in columns 1 and 2.

```
ADD
REPL
./   - - - -   NAME=name,LIST=ALL
```

[JCL cards forming the procedure]

```
/*
```

Code ADD to add a new procedure, and REPL to replace
an existing procedure. LIST = ALL lists all the cards in the
procedure. The name is the name of the procedure added or
replaced. Any number of ADD or REPL cards, followed by
the JCL making up the procedure, may be included.

A cataloged procedure may consist of many job steps.
Procedures can contain all but the following JCL statements:

1.   EXEC cards requesting cataloged procedures. (A cataloged procedure cannot invoke another cataloged procedure.)
2.   JOB, delimeter (/*), or null (//) cards.
3.   JOBLIB DD cards.
4.   DD * or DD DATA cards.

We can now add a procedure to the library. An obvious procedure to add is one that adds procedures. ADDPROC is an appropriate name for such a procedure.

```
//TEST    JOB    1776,WASHINGTON

//  EXEC    PGM=IEBUPDTE,REGION=24K

//SYSPRINT    DD    SYSOUT=A

//SYSUT1    DD    DSN=SYS1.PROCLIB,DISP=OLD

//SYSUT2    DD    DSN=*.SYSUT1,DISP=OLD

//SYSIN    DD    DATA

./    ADD    NAME=ADDPROC,LIST=ALL

//ADDPROC    PROC

//GO    EXEC    PGM=IEBUPDTE,REGION=24K

//SYSPRINT    DD    SYSOUT=A

//SYSUT1    DD    DSN=SYS1.PROCLIB,DISP=OLD

//SYSUT2    DD    DSN=*.SYSUT1,DISP=OLD

/*
```

Now to add a procedure one need only execute the following step.

```
//  EXEC    ADDPROC

//GO.SYSIN    DD    DATA
```

[ADD and REPL cards followed by JCL cards as
    required]

/*

Often a program must read in card data that seldom
changes from run to run. The following example illustrates
such a program.

//GO   EXEC   PGM=ONE,REGION=88K

//SYSIN   DD   *

[card data]

/*

We might wish to catalog the above step, and since the
card data seldom changes, we would like to catalog it also.
The procedure library contains card images, and any card
data, not just JCL, can be added as a member. The SYSIN
DD card must then point to the member containing the card
data. The following step adds the procedure and the card
data to SYS1.PROCLIB.

// EXEC   ADDPROC

//GO.SYSIN   DD   DATA

./ ADD   NAME=RUN,LIST=ALL

//RUN   PROC

//GO   EXEC   PGM=ONE,REGION=88K

//SYSIN   DD   DSN=SYS1.PROCLIB(CARDS),

// DISP=SHR

./ ADD   NAME=CARDS,LIST=ALL

[card data]

/*

The procedure is named RUN, and the data cards are placed in a member named CARDS. (The cards could have been placed in some other data set if desired.) The program is now executed with a single // EXEC RUN card.

Testing Procedures

One should test each new procedure after adding it to the library. Test cases must not be read in until after the job adding the new procedure completes; otherwise the old procedure will be tested. Since many jobs may depend upon a particular procedure, the procedure should not be replaced until the replacement has been tested. It is perhaps safe to say that any new procedure will not work the first time—it must be tested and debugged before it is ready to replace an existing procedure.

Choose a unique name for testing a procedure and add it to the procedure library. If it works, then add or replace it under its proper name, and delete the testing procedure. The IEHPROGM utility described in Chapter 14 deletes procedures.

Symbolic Parameters

We have seen how cataloged procedures may be modified for execution by overriding parameters on DD cards. This is often inconvenient because the user must know what parameters can be overridden, the stepnames within the procedure, the ddnames of the cards overridden, and the order of the DD cards. Symbolic parameters provide an alternate means of modifying procedures for execution. The following example illustrates symbolic parameters.

```
//RUN    PROC    PROGRAM=ONE,UNIT=2311

//GO    EXEC    PGM=&PROGRAM

//A    DD    UNIT=&UNIT,SPACE=(TRK,20)
```

The ampersands preceding PROGRAM and UNIT mark them as symbolic parameters. The PROC statement allows

default values to be assigned to symbolic parameters. The
RUN procedure can be invoked by a // EXEC RUN card,
and the procedure is interpreted as

        //GO   EXEC   PGM=ONE

        //A   DD   UNIT=2311,SPACE=(TRK,20)

    Values can also be assigned to symbolic parameters on
the EXEC card. Any values coded on the EXEC card override the values on the PROC card for the duration of the run.

        //   EXEC   RUN,UNIT=2314,PROGRAM=TWO

The procedure is now interpreted as

        //GO   EXEC   PGM=TWO

        //A   DD   UNIT=2314,SPACE=(TRK,20)

    Symbolic parameters must always be given values,
either on the PROC card as a part of the procedure or on
the EXEC card invoking the procedure. Otherwise the system considers it a JCL error. The one exception to this is
the DSN parameter. If DSN=&name is coded and no value is
assigned to the name on the PROC or EXEC card, the system interprets &name to mean a temporary data set.

PROC statement

    The PROC statement is coded as *//name* PROC
keyword parameters. The name is optional; it serves only
to help the programmer identify the procedure. The keyword
parameters are separated by commas and may be coded in
any order to assign default values to symbolic parameters.
PROC is needed only if default values are assigned to symbolic parameters. If included, it must be the first card of
the cataloged procedure.

Coding symbolic parameters

A symbolic parameter is preceded by an ampersand and may be 1 to 7 alphameric (A to Z, 0 to 9) characters, the first of which must be alphabetic (A to Z). Symbolic parameters can be coded only in the operand field of JCL cards; they cannot appear in the name or operation field. PGM, DPRTY, PROC, COND, PARM, ACCT, RD, TIME, REGION, and ROLL cannot be used as symbolic parameters because they are EXEC card keyword parameters. A single symbolic parameter can appear on several JCL cards. If more than one value is assigned to a symbolic parameter on a PROC or EXEC card, only the first is used.

```
//RUN    PROC    NAME=LIB1,NAME=LIB2

//STEP1    EXEC    PGM=ONE

//A    DD    DSN=&NAME, . . .

//STEP2    EXEC    PGM=TWO

//B    DD    DSN=&NAME, . . .
```

Each appearance of the symbolic parameter &NAME in the above procedure is assigned a default value of LIB1. One might override this default for a run, and each appearance of &NAME in the procedure is changed. If symbolic parameters had not been used, each DD card would have to be overridden.

The value assigned to a symbolic parameter can be of any length but cannot contain ampersands. If an ampersand appears in the value, no substitution occurs. Values containing special characters other than the ampersand (blank , . / ') (* + - =) must be enclosed in apostrophes. Code a legitimate apostrophe as two consecutive apostrophes.

```
//RUN    PROC    NAME='SYS1.PROCLIB',

//    TAPE='2400-6'
```

A value cannot be continued onto a continuation card. The following card is in error.

//RUN   PROC   NAME='SYS1.,

//   PROCLIB',TAPE='2400-6'

It should be coded as

//RUN   PROC   NAME='SYS1.PROCLIB',

//   TAPE='2400-6'

Symbolic parameters can also be concatenated with regular parameters or portions of regular parameters. The combined text produced by such a concatenation must not exceed 120 characters. (The entire DD card may, of course, contain many more characters.) Two symbolic parameters can also be concatenated.

//RUN   PROC   VOLS=',3,4',NAME=A,IN='NEW,',

//   OUT=KEEP
$$\vdots$$
//A   DD   VOL=SER=(2&VOLS),DSN=SYS1.&NAME,

//   DISP=(&IN&OUT)

The DD card is interpreted as

//A   DD   VOL=SER=(2,3,4),DSN=SYS1.A,

//   DISP=(NEW,KEEP)

If the text follows the symbolic parameter, it must be separated by a period (the period is not considered part of the text). The period is optional if the text begins with a special character other than a period or left parenthesis (, / ') * & + - =).

//RUN   PROC   TAPE=2400,NAME=SYS1
$$\vdots$$
//A   DD   UNIT=&TAPE-2,DSN=&NAME. .P

The DD card is interpreted as

```
//A    DD    UNIT=2400-2,DSN=SYS1.P
```

Nullify symbolic parameters by coding the keyword and equal sign without a value, either on the PROC or EXEC card.

```
//RUN    PROC    VOLS=,NAME=PROCLIB
            .
            .
            .
//A    DD    VOL=SER=(2&VOLS),DSN=SYS1.&NAME
```

The DD card is interpreted as

```
//A    DD    VOL=SER=(2), DSN=SYS1.PROCLIB
```

A delimeter, such as a leading or trailing comma, next to a symbolic parameter is not removed when the parameter is nullified.

```
//RUN    PROC    VOLS=
            .
            .
            .
//A    DD    VOL=SER=(2,&VOLS)
```

The DD card is interpreted as follows, but the system considers this a syntax error and fails the step.

```
//A    DD    VOL=SER=(2,)
```

Symbolic parameters may be coded in any order on PROC or EXEC cards. If NAME and VOLS are symbolic parameters defined in a FORTRAN compile, link edit, and go procedure, the following could be coded.

```
//    EXEC    FORTCLG,NAME='SYS1.FORTERR',

//    REGION.FORT=104K,VOLS=500,COND.GO=EVEN
```

All symbolic parameters given a value on a PROC or EXEC card must appear as symbolic parameters in the procedure. The following procedure is in error because DISK does not appear as a symbolic parameter in the procedure.

```
//RUN    PROC    DISK=2311

//GO    EXEC    PGM=ONE

//A    DD    UNIT=2311,SPACE=(TRK,20)
```

This error can be corrected by recoding the DD card in the procedure.

```
//A    DD    UNIT=&DISK,SPACE=(TRK,20)
```

It can also be corrected by overriding the UNIT parameter with a DD card.

```
//    EXEC    RUN

//GO.A    DD    UNIT=&DISK
```

The preceding example shows that symbolic parameters can be coded on overriding DD cards. DD cards containing symbolic parameters can also be overridden if one is careful not to override a symbolic parameter assigned a value. If the UNIT=&DISK correction is made to the above procedure, the following step is in error because &DISK is given a value on the PROC card but does not now appear in the procedure.

```
//    EXEC    RUN

//GO.A    DD    UNIT=2311
```

Application of symbolic parameters

MFT and MVT systems may have several procedure libraries, but if we use the ADDPROC procedure described earlier in this chapter to add procedures to other than SYS1.PROCLIB, we must override the DSN parameter on the SYSUT1 DD card. Suppose we wish to add a procedure to SYS1.ALTPROC. (Chapter 11 contains an example showing how to create such a library.)

```
//    EXEC    ADDPROC

//GO.SYSUT1    DD    DSN=SYS1.ALTPROC
```

```
//GO.SYSIN    DD    DATA
```

[card data]

```
/*
```

This works fine unless we forget the stepname, ddname, or the parameter to override, or place GO.SYSUT1 after GO.SYSIN. A better method is to make the library name a symbolic parameter and give it a default value of SYS1. PROCLIB.

```
//  EXEC    ADDPROC

//GO.SYSIN    DD    DATA

./  REPL    NAME=ADDPROC,LIST=ALL

//ADDPROC    PROC    NAME='SYS1.PROCLIB'

//GO    EXEC    PGM=IEBUPDTE,REGION=24K

//SYSPRINT    DD    SYSOUT=A

//SYSUT1    DD    DSN=&NAME,DISP=OLD

//SYSUT2    DD    DSN=*.SYSUT1,DISP=OLD

/*
```

ADDPROC is replaced in the library and can now be used to add procedures to any library. Anyone using the old procedure need not change their JCL since the symbolic parameter default value is SYS1.PROCLIB. To add procedures to SYS1.ALTPROC, code the following.

```
//  EXEC    ADDPROC,NAME='SYS1.ALTPROC'

//GO.SYSIN    DD    DATA
```

[card data]

```
/*
```

One final example should serve to show the usefulness of symbolic parameters. The linkage editor step usually contains a DD card named SYSLIB to describe libraries that the linkage editor is to search for subroutines. SYSLIB is often concatenated to describe several subroutine libraries.

```
//LKED    EXEC    PGM=LINKEDIT

//SYSLIB    DD    DSN=SYS1.FORTLIB,DISP=SHR

//    DD    DSN=SYS1.SSPLIB,DISP=SHR
```

The linkage editor searches both SYS1.FORTLIB and SYS1.SSPLIB to find needed subroutines. Now suppose that the above LKED step is part of a FORTRAN compile, link edit, and go procedure named FORTCLG. One might wish to concatenate his own private library to SYSLIB.

```
//    EXEC    FORTCLG
        :
        :
//LKED.SYSLIB    DD

//    DD

//    DD    DSN=PRIVLIB,DISP=SHR
```

PRIVLIB is concatenated to SYS1.FORTLIB and SYS1.SSPLIB. Now consider what happens if the installation changes the FORTCLG procedure by adding a subroutine library. SYSLIB might be changed to

```
//SYSLIB    DD    DSN=SYS1.NEWFORT,DISP=SHR

//    DD    DSN=SYS1.FORTLIB,DISP=SHR

//    DD    DSN=SYS1.SSPLIB,DISP=SHR
```

The PRIVLIB DD card now overrides the SYS1.SSPLIB DD card. If the job uses subroutines in SYS1.SSPLIB, it will fail because SYS1.SSPLIB is no longer searched. The JCL must be changed by adding another // DD card. Symbolic parameters solve this problem very nicely. Suppose the procedure had originally been coded to allow the user to specify a private library as a symbolic parameter.

```
//FORTCLG    PROC    LIB='SYS1.FORTLIB'
                :
                :
//SYSLIB    DD    DSN=SYS1.FORTLIB,DISP=SHR
//  DD    DSN=SYS1.SSPLIB,DISP=SHR
//  DD    DSN=&LIB,DISP=SHR
```

A private library is concatenated by coding the following.

```
//  EXEC    FORTCLG,LIB=PRIVLIB
```

Not only is this method simpler to code with less chance for errors, but, equally important, the installation can freely add libraries to SYSLIB without disturbing anyone's JCL.

SUMMARY

Several data sets may be processed as a single data set by concatenating them together. The data sets must have similar characteristics, but sequential data sets can be concatenated with partitioned data set members.

All DD cards for a step (including STEPLIB DD cards) must immediately follow the EXEC card. DD cards must be ordered in the following circumstances:[†]

1. If DD cards in a step have the same ddname, the first card is used and subsequent DD cards with that name are ignored.
2. Data sets are concatenated in the order of the DD cards.
3. Multiple SYSOUT DD cards to the same output class are printed in the order of the DD cards in MFT and MVT systems. The output in PCP systems is interspersed.

[†]Several of the rules have not been covered yet. They are included here for completeness.

4. DD * or DD DATA cards in PCP systems must be the last DD card in the step.
5. DD cards overriding cataloged procedures must be in the same order as the cards within the procedure. Added DD cards must follow any overriding DD cards. PCP systems require any overriding or added DD * or DD DATA cards to be last.
6. DD cards with referback parameters must follow the DD card to which they refer.
7. The JOBLIB DD card must immediately follow the JOB card.
8. The SYSCHK DD card is placed after the JOB card and any JOBLIB DD card, but before any EXEC card.
9. DD cards defining an indexed-sequential data set must define the index area, prime area, and overflow area, in that order.
10. DD cards obtaining direct-access space with the SPLIT parameter must follow the DD card that allocates the space to be split.
11. PROC card, if included, must be first card in cataloged procedure.

Cataloged procedures greatly simplify JCL. A cataloged procedure may consist of several job steps and contain all but the following JCL cards: JOB, delimeter (/*), null (//), EXEC cards requesting cataloged procedures, JOBLIB DD cards, and DD * or DD DATA cards. The IBM-supplied program IEBUPDTE adds procedures to the procedure library. Symbolic parameters can be coded on cataloged procedure cards to allow parameters to be easily changed.

CHAPTER 10

DD CARDS FOR PERIPHERAL I/O DEVICES

This chapter discusses the DD cards required to read and write data on various peripheral devices. Included are the DD cards for input stream data sets, output stream data sets, unit record devices, and graphic devices. The DDNAME parameter used to postpone the definition of a data set is also described, as are dummy data sets.

INPUT STREAM DATA SETS: *, DATA

Card data is the most common form of input. To include card data in the input stream, code

    //ddname   DD   *

    [card data]

    /*

SYSIN is often used as a ddname for card data. The /* marks the end of the card deck. The card data cannot contain // or /* in columns 1 and 2 if DD * is used. If the card data contains // in columns 1 and 2, as it would if the card data included JCL, code DATA in place of the *.

    //ddname   DD   DATA

    [card data]

    /*

DATA is the same as * except that cards with // in columns 1 and 2 may be included. Both * and DATA are positional parameters and must be coded before any other parameters on the DD card. DD * and DD DATA cards cannot be placed in cataloged procedures because they must immediately precede the card data in the input stream.

144

Special PCP Rules

Programs running on PCP systems can have only one DD * or DD DATA card per step, and it must be the last DD card in the step. Cards are read directly from the card reader, limiting the processing speed to that of the card reader.

Special MFT and MVT Rules

Programs running on MFT or MVT systems may have several DD * or DD DATA cards (with different ddnames) because card input is queued on direct-access storage before the job is executed. If the system encounters card data (any cards not having // or /* in columns 1 and 2) not preceded by a DD * or DD DATA card, it automatically provides a DD * card with a ddname of SYSIN. If a cataloged procedure is invoked, the generated SYSIN card applies to the first step of the procedure. If DD * is specified or assumed and the /* card is omitted, the system assumes a /* for the user when the next card with a // in columns 1 and 2 is encountered.

```
//STEP1    EXEC    PGM=PRIMERO

[card data]

//STEP2    EXEC    PGM=SEGUNDO
```

The above steps are equivalent to

```
//STEP1    EXEC    PGM=PRIMERO

//SYSIN    DD    *

[card data]

/*

//STEP2    EXEC    PGM=SEGUNDO
```

The MFT and MVT readers normally block the cards as they are read in to save storage space and I/O time. Some programs cannot read blocked input, and the DCB subparameter BLKSIZE must be used to unblock the cards. The BUFNO subparameter may also be used to specify the number of buffers. (BUFNO is ignored if the job is submitted via remote job entry.) These two DCB subparameters are the only parameters that can be coded on DD * and DD DATA cards. If BLKSIZE and BUFNO are omitted, default values established in the reader are used.

```
//SYSIN    DD    *,DCB=BLKSIZE=80
```

The block size is set to 80.

```
//SYSIN    DD    DATA,DCB=(BLKSIZE=800,BUFNO=2)
```

The block size is set to 800, and 2 buffers are provided for reading the input.

POSTPONING DEFINITION OF DATA SETS: DDNAME

The DDNAME=ddname parameter, often used with input stream data sets, postpones the definition of the data set until a subsequent DD card is encountered with the specified ddname. DCB subparameters BLKSIZE and BUFNO may be coded with the DDNAME parameter in MVT and MFT systems; no other parameters or subparameters are permitted. The following step requires both BLKSIZE and BUFNO on the DD * card.

```
//GO    EXEC    PGM=INITIAL

//TWO    DD    *,DCB=(BLKSIZE=80,BUFNO=3)
```

[card data]

```
/*
```

One can make this step a cataloged procedure, but DD * and DD DATA cards cannot be placed in cataloged procedures and so the TWO DD card cannot be cataloged. If the procedure is named JOG, the step would consist of

```
//  EXEC    JOG

//GO.TWO    DD    *,DCB=(BLKSIZE=80,BUFNO=3)

[card data]

/*
```

The lengthy DCB parameter makes this procedure in-convenient. The TWO DD card, with BLKSIZE and BUFNO subparameters, can be included in the procedure by using the DDNAME parameter. The procedure is coded as

```
//JOG    PROC

//GO    EXEC    PGM=INITIAL

//TWO    DD    DDNAME=TWO,

//    DCB=(BLKSIZE=80,BUFNO=3)
```

The step is simplified to

```
//  EXEC    JOG

//GO.TWO    DD    *

[card data]

/*
```

BLKSIZE and BUFNO subparameters coded on the DD card pointed to by DDNAME override any subparameters on the DDNAME card. Since DDNAME can refer to any name, SYSIN can be used as well as TWO:

```
//TWO    DD    DDNAME=SYSIN,

//    DCB=(BLKSIZE=80,BUFNO=3)
```

The step is now executed with BLKSIZE set to 800.

```
//  EXEC    JOG
```

    //GO.SYSIN   DD   *,DCB=BLKSIZE=800

[card data]

    /*

    DD cards with a ddname matching a DDNAME parameter
in a cataloged procedure can precede or follow any overriding or added DD cards. The following restrictions apply
to DDNAME: A maximum of five DDNAME parameters, each
referring to unique ddnames, may be included in a single job
step. DDNAME cannot be used on JOBLIB DD cards. A
referback parameter on subsequent DD cards must refer to
the card containing the DDNAME parameter, not to the card
with the matching ddname, and must follow the card with the
matching ddname; otherwise it refers to a dummy data set.
A DDNAME parameter coded in a concatenated data set must
precede both unnamed DD cards and any DD card with the
matching ddname. The following is legal.

    //INPUT   DD   DSN=SYS1.PROCLIB(LIST),

    //   DISP=SHR

    //   DD   DDNAME=SYSIN

    //   DD   DSN=SYS1.PROCLIB(PRINT),DISP=SHR

    The following two data sets are in error. INPUT has a
card with the DDNAME following an unnamed DD card;
SYSIN has a DD card with a matching ddname preceding the
DDNAME card.

    //INPUT   DD   DSN=SYS1.PROCLIB(LIST),

    //   DISP=SHR

    //   DD   DSN=SYS1.PROCLIB(PRINT),DISP=SHR

    //   DD   DDNAME=LATER

    //SYSIN   DD   DSN=SYS1.PROCLIB(LIST),DISP=SHR

    //   DD   DDNAME=SYSIN

DDNAME has one additional use. PCP systems require that any DD * or DD DATA cards overriding cataloged procedures appear last in the input stream. There is also a general restriction that overriding DD cards appear in the order they occur in the procedure. Consider the following procedure.

```
//DOIT    PROC

//GO    EXEC    PGM=INITIAL

//ONE    DD    DSN=SYS1.PROCLIB(LIST),DISP=SHR

//TWO    DD    DSN=LIBRARY,DISP=SHR
```

One might wish to override both DD cards. If ONE is overridden with card data input, the following must be coded.

```
//    EXEC DOIT

//GO.ONE    DD    DDNAME=SYSIN

//GO.TWO    DD    DISP=OLD

//SYSIN    DD    *

[card data]

/*
```

Both the PCP rule that DD * cards be last and the general rule that DD cards be overridden in order are obeyed.

OUTPUT STREAM DATA SETS: SYSOUT

The SYSOUT parameter provides a convenient means of routing output streams to printers, card punches, or other devices. To route an output stream data set to an output device, code

```
//ddname    DD    SYSOUT=class
```

The class can be any alphabetic (A to Z) character.[†] An installation may define separate output classes for special forms, high-volume output, printed or punched output, high-priority output, separated output, etc. SYSOUT=A is traditionally the printer and SYSOUT=B the card punch.

```
//SYSPRINT   DD   SYSOUT=A

//SYSPUNCH   DD   SYSOUT=B
```

The computer operator can direct output classes to a specific output device, or to magnetic tape for later processing — if a printer or punch goes down or for very high-volume output. Output from several jobs can be stacked on a single reel of tape since the tape is not rewound until it reaches the end-of-volume or is dismounted by the operator.

DCB Subparameters

The DCB parameter is generally not required but can be coded if needed. The DCB parameter in PCP systems must be for the specific I/O device, but in MFT and MVT systems it must be for the direct-access device on which the output is queued.

```
//SYSPUNCH   DD   SYSOUT=B,DCB=MODE=C
```

The MODE subparameter produces column binary punched output in PCP but not in MFT or MVT systems. (Column binary is a feature of the card punch but not a feature of a direct-access device.)

```
//SYSPUNCH   DD   SYSOUT=B,DCB=BLKSIZE=800
```

BLKSIZE blocks the card images on direct-access storage in MFT and MVT systems but is ignored in PCP because cards cannot be blocked by a card punch.

[†]Numeric characters (0 to 9) can be used if required, but IBM intends them for future system use.

Special PCP Rules

PCP systems may have a maximum of eight output classes in use at one time, one of which must be SYSOUT=A. Output, written directly onto the device, is interspersed if several data sets are concurrently written to the same output class. If an output class is directed to magnetic tape, only one data set may be open to that output class at a time.

Special MFT and MVT Rules

MFT and MVT systems may have 36 output streams in use at one time. Output is queued onto direct-access storage, and system output writers later write the output onto the appropriate I/O device. The computer operator must start an output writer to a specific device, and each writer may write several classes of output. Be sure to use an output class that will have a writer started to it, or the output will remain queued on direct-access storage. If several data sets are written to the same output class, each data set is printed separately in the order of the DD cards.

UNIT and SPACE parameters

The UNIT parameter in MFT and MVT systems directs the output to a specific intermediate direct-access device; the reader establishes a default intermediate device if UNIT is omitted. Since output for MFT and MVT systems is queued on direct-access storage before it is printed or punched, space must be allocated for each SYSOUT DD card. Default space is allocated by the reader, but the SPACE parameter is required if more (or less) than the default space is wanted. If the step exceeds this space during execution, it is immediately terminated, but all output is printed or punched up to the point at which the data set ran out of space.

The SPACE parameter may also be used to limit the output that a job produces. For example, if one suspects his job will go into an endless loop while printing, he can save computer time (and paper) by limiting the space allocated to the print data set. Chapter 11 describes the SPACE parameter.

Special processing

MFT and MVT systems permit the user to specify a special program to write the output, and to request special output forms. For this, the SYSOUT DD card is coded as

//ddname   DD   SYSOUT=(class,*program,form*)

The program name is the name of a user program contained in SYS1.LINKLIB that writes the output. The form number is a 1- to 4-digit number used to request special output forms (special card stock, paper, etc.). Each installation must establish its own form numbers. The system requests the operator to mount the special form just before the data set is printed or punched, and requests the original form to be remounted when printing is complete.

//PRINT   DD   SYSOUT=(A,MYPRINT)

MYPRINT must be a user program contained in SYS1.LINKLIB. The system loads the program and passes control to it so that it can print or punch the output.

//PRINT   DD   SYSOUT=(A, ,1001)

The operator is requested to mount form 1001 before the output is printed.

//PUNCH   DD   SYSOUT=(B,MYPUNCH,2)

A user program named MYPUNCH punches the output. The operator is requested to mount form 2 prior to punching the output.

UNIT RECORD DEVICES

Unit record devices include printers, card readers and punches, typewriter consoles, and paper tape readers. As the name implies, a single record is processed at a time: one card read or punched, one line typed or printed, etc.

Most unit record devices are preempted for system use in MFT and MVT systems, and one must be careful in requesting them. Card readers are normally allocated to the readers, and card punches and printers are allocated to writers. Since the system can allocate only idle unit record devices to a job, the operator may have to stop the readers or writers to free the device. Programs should normally use the input or output stream DD cards (DD *, DD DATA, or DD SYSOUT) rather than request the card reader, punch, and printers directly.

The card reader, punch, and printers might be used as unit record devices for security so that sensitive data is not queued on direct-access storage, or for processing quantities of data too large to queue on direct-access storage. The DD card for unit record devices is coded as

//ddname   DD   UNIT=address,

//   DCB=(. . .),UCS=(. . .)

The unit may also be requested by type or group, but address is often used because one usually wants a specific device.

DCB Subparameters

The DCB subparameter LRECL can be included for any unit record device. The following DCB subparameters may also be included.

Printer: PRTSP controls printer spacing (0 to 3, PRTSP=1 is assumed). RECFM describes the record format (F, V, U), and printer control characters (A for ASA control characters and M for machine code control characters). Appendix B describes control characters.

Card Reader and Punch: MODE specifies column binary (C) or EBCDIC (E); MODE=E is assumed. If MODE=C is coded, BLKSIZE, LRECL, and BUFL must be specified as

160.[†] RECFM specifies the record format (F, V, U), and control characters (M or A). STACK selects a particular stacker (1 or 2); STACK=1 is default.

Paper Tape: RECFM sets the record format (F or U), and CODE describes special character codes as follows: (CODE=I is assumed.)

I   IBM BCD perforated tape and transmission code (8 tracks).

F   Friden (8 tracks).

B   Burroughs (7 tracks).

C   National Cash Register (8 tracks).

A   USASCII (8 tracks).

T   Teletype (5 tracks).

N   No conversion.

    //DD1   DD   UNIT=00E,DCB=PRTSP=3

        Unit 00E, a printer, is assigned and the spacing is set to 3.

    //DD2   DD   UNIT=2540-2,DCB=(MODE=C,STACK=1,

    //   BLKSIZE=160,LRECL=160,BUFL=160)

        A card punch is requested for punching column binary.

Universal Character Set

The UCS parameter specifies a character set for the 1403 printer with the universal character set feature. UCS

[†]In *column binary* a card column is treated as 12 binary bits, and each column is read into 2 bytes in core. The top 6 rows are read into bits 2 to 7 of the first byte and the bottom 6 rows into bits 2 to 7 of the second byte. Bits 0 and 1 of each byte are set to zero.

allows a print chain or train for a particular character set to be mounted on the printer. A default character set established by an installation when the system is generated is used unless UCS specifies another character set. The character set remains in effect on the printer after the job terminates unless a subsequent DD card requests another character set. To specify a special character set, code

UCS=(code, *FOLD*, *VERIFY*)

The code is a 1- to 4-digit code identifying the character set. Users may add their own character sets to the system and assign codes to them. Character sets for the following codes can be generated into the system.

AN alphameric	QN alphameric (PL/I-scientific)
HN alphameric	RN FORTRAN-COBOL-commercial
PCAN alphameric	SN text printing
PCHN alphameric	TN text printing
PN alphameric (PL/I)	XN high-speed alphameric
QNC alphameric (PL/I-commercial)	YN high-speed alphameric

FOLD causes the folding of the first, second, and third quadrants of the EBCD Interchange Code into the fourth quadrant; that is, hexadecimal characters 01, 21, 81, and C1 all print as uppercase A's, etc. VERIFY causes a printer display of the character set and requests the operator to verify it.

//DD1   DD   UNIT=1403,UCS=QN

The QN character set is requested.

//DD2   DD   UNIT=1403,UCS=(PN,FOLD)

The PN character set is requested. All character codes are folded into the fourth quadrant.

//DD3   DD   UNIT=1403,UCS=(AN, ,VERIFY)

The AN character set is requested and displayed for the operator to verify.

GRAPHIC DEVICES

The DD card for graphic devices is coded as

//ddname   DD   UNIT=address,*DCB=(. . .)*

The unit may also be requested by type or group, but a graphics user usually wants a specific console. UNIT=1130 should be used in the first step and DSN=*.referback in all subsequent steps for graphic devices connected to an IBM 1130 computer. Although two DCB subparameters are allowed (GNCP and GDSORG), they seldom need to be coded.

//GRAPHIC   DD   UNIT=2E0

The graphic device at address 2E0 is requested.

DUMMY DATA SETS: DUMMY, NULLFILE

A sequential data set may be assigned a dummy status in which all I/O operations are bypassed, and device allocation, space allocation, and data set disposition are ignored. An attempt to read a dummy data set results in an immediate end-of-data-set exit; a write request is ignored. Only sequential data sets can be assigned a dummy status.

Dummy data sets are used to test program flow without actually processing data. Unwanted output (listings, punched cards, etc.) may also be suppressed by giving the output data sets a dummy status.

A data set is assigned a dummy status by coding either DUMMY as the first parameter in the DD card or DSN= NULLFILE. Other parameters may also be coded on the DD card as they would be for a real data set, but they are ignored. BLKSIZE and BUFNO may be required for the

OPEN routine to obtain buffers. The following examples illustrate the use of dummy data sets.

> //SYSPRINT   DD   DUMMY

>> Any output produced by SYSPRINT is suppressed.

> //SYSIN   DD   DUMMY

>> Any attempt to read data from SYSIN results in an immediate end-of-data-set exit.

> //OUTPUT   DD   DSN=NULLFILE,

> //   DCB=(BLKSIZE=800,BUFNO=2),DISP=(,CATLG),

> //   VOL=SER=200,UNIT=2314,SPACE=(200,100)

>> The requested volume need not be mounted, no space is allocated, and the data set is not cataloged. OUTPUT must define a sequential data set.

> //OUTPUT   DD   DUMMY,DSN=REAL,

> //   DCB=(BLKSIZE=800,BUFNO=2),DISP=(,CATLG),

> //   VOL=SER=200,UNIT=2314,SPACE=(200,100)

>> This card is equivalent to the preceding card.

A chain of concatenated data sets is broken by an intervening dummy data set. In the following example, only the first data set is read.

> //DD1   DD   DSN=ONE,DISP=SHR

> //   DD   DUMMY

> //   DD   DSN=TWO,DISP=SHR

SUMMARY

The usual forms of the DD card for the various peripheral devices, postponement of data set definition, and dummy data sets are as follows:

1. Input stream data sets—card data must not contain // or /* in columns 1 and 2:

    //ddname   DD   *

    [card data]

    /*

2. Input stream data sets—card data may contain // but not /* in columns 1 and 2:

    //ddname   DD   DATA

    [card data]

    /*

3. Postponing definition of a data set:

    //ddname1   DD   DDNAME=ddname2
    :
    :
    //ddname2   DD   . . .

4. Output stream data sets—SYSOUT=A is normal print output and SYSOUT=B is normal punch output:

    //ddname   DD   SYSOUT=class

    //ddname   DD   SYSOUT=(class,*program,form*)

5. Unit record devices:

    //ddname   DD   UNIT=address,

    //   *DCB=(. . .),UCS=(code,FOLD,VERIFY)*

6. Graphic devices:

    //ddname   DD   UNIT=address

7. Dummy data sets:

    //ddname   DD   DUMMY, . . .

    //ddname   DD   . . .,DSN=NULLFILE, . . .

CHAPTER 11
DIRECT-ACCESS DEVICES

The basic storage unit of a direct-access device is a track, a circumference on the recording surface. Tracks in the same plane parallel to the axis of rotation constitute a cylinder. Access arm movement is required if data resides on different cylinders; thus data can be read or written much faster if it resides all on the same cylinder.

Drums, which contain a single cylinder, are the fastest I/O device, but contain the least amount of data. They are used for small, frequently used data sets—generally portions of the system.

Disks are the most versatile storage device because of their large storage capacity and adequate speed. The IBM 2311 and 2314 disks have removable packs—but an installation generally controls the use of private or mountable packs because it requires about 3 minutes for an operator to change disk packs. Disks are used for storing sequential, partitioned, direct, and indexed-sequential data sets. However, tape or data cells might be more appropriate for large or seldom used sequential data sets.

Data cells, the slowest direct-access device, have the largest storage capacity but can contain only sequential data sets. Data cells are used for storing large or seldom used data sets. Table 2 summarizes the speed and capacity of various direct-access devices.

A volume table of contents (VTOC) is maintained on each direct-access volume as a directory to existing data sets and free space. The installation must initialize each volume before using it. This process is called direct-access storage device initialization (*DASDI*) and is done by the IBM-supplied utility program IEHDASDR. IEHDASDR writes the volume label, allocates space for the table of contents, initializes each track on the volume, and makes alternate tracks available if a track is bad. A volume generally need never be reinitialized.

Table 2. Direct-Access Devices

Device	Capacity (In Million Bytes)	Average Seek Time (In Thousands of a Second)	Average Rotational Delay (In Thousands of a Second)	Data Rate (In Bytes/ Second)
2301 Drum Storage	4.09	0	8.6	1,200,000
2302 Disk Storage	112.79[1]	165	16.7	156,000
2303 Drum Storage	3.91	0	8.6	312,500
2311 Disk Storage Drive	7.25[2]	75	12.5	156,000
2314 Direct-Access Storage Facility	29.17[2,3]	60	12.5	312,000
2321 Data Cell Drive	39.2[4]	100-650	25	55,000

[1] Capacity per module. Model 3 has one module, Model 4 two modules.

[2] Capacity per disk pack. The packs are mountable.

[3] Model A1 may have eight packs on-line, Model A2 five packs.

[4] Capacity per cell. Ten mountable data cells per drive may be on-line.

The table of contents is usually allocated one or two cylinders and is placed in either the first or middle cylinders. A table of contents in the first cylinders maximizes the largest contiguous amount of space that can be allocated. Placing the table of contents in the middle minimizes seek time since the access arm generally has half as far to travel between the table of contents and any data set. The first track on the volume contains the volume label and points to the table of contents.

SPACE ALLOCATION

All new direct-access data sets must be allocated
space, either by requesting the amount of space, by asking
for specific tracks on a volume, by requesting cylinders and
splitting them between data sets, or by suballocating space
obtained from an earlier data set. Direct-access storage is
always allocated in units of tracks, regardless of how it is
requested, and so the minimum space that can be allocated
is one track.

When space is requested, the system looks in the table
of contents to see if it is available, and allocates the space
by updating the table of contents. The system attempts to
allocate space in contiguous tracks (tracks on the same
cylinder) and adjacent cylinders. If contiguous space is
unavailable, the system tries to satisfy the request with up
to five noncontiguous blocks of storage.

If space is still unavailable and the user has not requested a specific volume, the system looks for space on
other appropriate volumes. If space cannot be found, PCP
systems terminate the job, whereas MFT and MVT systems
issue a message to the operator asking him whether the job
should be canceled or held. Unless the operator is able to
mount another pack or wait for some other job to terminate
and release its space, he must cancel the job.

Direct-access space allocated in noncontiguous blocks
is read and written as if it were one large block; the system
automatically compensates for the noncontiguous space.
However, data sets can be read or written faster if they
reside on the same cylinder because a relatively slow mechanical movement is required to position the access arm
between noncontiguous blocks. High-activity data sets should
be allocated contiguous space on the same cylinder.

Requesting A Quantity of Space: SPACE

The usual method of requesting space is to ask for a
quantity of space and let the system select the appropriate
tracks. In multiprogramming environments in which several
jobs may request space concurrently, the system is in a

much better position to know what space is available. Space may be requested in units of block size, tracks, or cylinders as follows:

<pre>
          CYL
          TRK   index
          blocksize   directory
    SPACE=(---------,(quantity,increment,---------))
</pre>

The blocksize, TRK, or CYL requests that space be allocated in units of number of bytes per block, tracks, or cylinders. (The average record length cannot exceed 65,535 bytes.)

The quantity is the number of units (blocks, tracks, or cylinders) to allocate. This space is called the *primary allocation* and is always allocated on a single volume. For example, SPACE=(80,2000) requests 2000 blocks of 80 bytes each, and SPACE=(CYL,20) requests 20 cylinders.

The increment is the number of units to allocate if the primary allocation is exceeded. This space is called a *secondary allocation*, and 15 secondary allocations can be given to a data set. Both the quantity and increment must be large enough to contain the largest block written, or space is allocated and erased as the system tries to find a space large enough for the record.

The directory reserves space for the names of members of partitioned data sets, and the index reserves index space for indexed-sequential data sets.

Requesting blocks of space: blocksize

The blocksize is usually the most convenient means of requesting space since a block corresponds to the user's data. The blocksize is also device-independent so that the same amount of space is allocated whether the device is a disk, drum, or data cell.

The system computes the actual number of tracks to allocate based upon the number of blocks that completely fit on a track. (Tables 3 and 4 describe the capacity of various

Table 3. Direct-Access Storage Device Capacities

Device Type	Volume Type	Track Capacity[a]	Tracks per Cylinder	No. of Cylinders	Total Capacity[a]
2311	Disk	3625	10	200	7,250,000
2314	Disk	7294	20	200	29,176,000
2302	Disk	4984	46	246	56,398,944
2303	Drum	4892	10	80[b]	3,913,600
2301	Drum	20483	8	25[c]	4,096,600
2321	Cell	2000	20[d]	980[d]	39,200,000

[a]Capacity indicated by bytes.

[b]Number of cylinders served by a single access arm. Each module has two access arms.

[c]There are 25 logical cylinders in a 2301 drum.

[d]A volume is equal to one bin in a 2321 data cell.

Table 4. Direct–Access Device Overhead Formulas

| Device | Bytes Required by Each Data Block | | | |
| | Blocks with Keys | | Blocks without Keys | |
	Bi	Bn	Bi	Bn
2311	81+1.049(KL+DL)	20+KL+DL	61+1.049(DL)	DL
2314	146+1.043(KL+DL)	45+KL+DL	101+1.043(DL)	DL
2302	81+1.049(KL+DL)	20+KL+DL	61+1.049(DL)	DL
2303	146+KL+DL	38+KL+DL	108+DL	DL
2301	186+KL+DL	53+KL+DL	133+DL	DL
2321	100+1.049(KL+DL)	16+KL+DL	84+1.049(DL)	DL

Bi is any block but the last on the track.

Bn is the last block on the track.

DL is data length.

KL is key length.

$$\text{blocks/track} = 1 + \frac{\text{track capacity} - Bn}{Bi}$$

(Truncated to nearest integer.)

direct-access devices.) For example, SPACE=(1000,8) allocates three 2311 tracks because each 2311 track contains 3625 bytes and three 1000-byte blocks fit on a track. Although SPACE=(4000,2) requests the same total storage, four 2311 tracks are allocated because two tracks are required to contain each block. Space is always rounded up to a whole number of tracks.

The blocksize should equal the BLKSIZE subparameter in the DCB. If secondary allocation takes place, the system computes the amount of secondary space to allocate by multiplying the increment times the BLKSIZE subparameter rather than the blocksize in the SPACE parameter.

If the blocks have keys, KEYLEN=keysize should be coded as a DCB subparameter so that the system can include space for the keys. The blocksize should be an average for variable or undefined format records. The system does not account for the space saved when track overflow (described in Chapter 14) is requested. The CONTIG and ROUND subparameters explained later are used to allocate contiguous space.

Requesting tracks or cylinders: TRK, CYL

Since space is always allocated in units of track, TRK allows the user to request an exact amount of space. TRK is device-dependent: SPACE=(TRK,1) results in 3625 bytes on a 2311 disk and 7294 bytes on a 2314 disk. TRK might be used for data sets with track overflow since the system does not compensate for it if blocksize is used.

CYL requests complete cylinders, resulting in faster access by eliminating the need for access arm movement. CYL is also device-dependent; SPACE=(CYL,1) obtains 36,250 bytes on a 2311 disk, 145,880 bytes on a 2314 disk, and the entire space on a drum since a drum is composed of a single cylinder. CYL must be used for indexed-sequential data sets.

One must compute the amount of space required if TRK or CYL is used, taking into consideration device type, track capacity, tracks per cylinder, cylinders per volume, block size, key length, and device overhead. Table 3 lists the characteristics of direct-access devices.

Device overhead refers to the space required on each track for hardware data, for example, address markers and gaps between blocks. Device overhead varies with each device and also depends on whether the blocks are written with keys. To compute the actual space needed for each block, use the formulas in Table 4.

For example, if a data set without keys containing 100 blocks is blocked at 800 bytes, we can use Tables 3 and 4 to compute the number of blocks per track. The formula is

$$1 + \frac{3625 - 800}{61 + 1.049(800)} = 4 \text{ blocks, per track}$$

Since 100 blocks must be stored, 25 tracks are required. At this point the reader might well consider requesting space in blocks and letting the computer do these calculations for him; SPACE=(800,100) and SPACE=(TRK,25) are equivalent for a 2311 disk.

The UNIT parameter must not request a group name defining more than one type of device. For example, if SYSDA defines both 2311 and 2314 disks, UNIT=SYSDA, SPACE=(TRK,1) yields 3625 bytes if a 2311 is selected, and 7294 bytes if a 2314 is selected; one would not know which.

Secondary allocation: increment

If an increment is coded and the primary space allocation is exceeded, a secondary allocation called an *extent* is allocated based upon the increment times the units. The system will allocate a maximum of 15 extents; if more are needed, the step is terminated.

As an example, SPACE=(800,(10,20)) results in a primary allocation of 10 blocks of 800 bytes each, and each extent is allocated 20 blocks of 800 bytes. The maximum space that could be allocated is then 10 + 20(15) = 310 blocks of 800 bytes.

Since it is often hard to estimate how much storage is needed, secondary allocations permit one to make a reasonable guess but still obtain more space if the guess is low. Secondary allocations also conserve space by permitting data sets to grow without tying up the maximum space they will ever need, when they are created.

Extents are usually not contiguous, and so the access time increases as extents are allocated. High–usage data sets should usually not have extents. The MXIG and ALX subparameters described later provide an alternative to extents.

The primary space allocation is made in up to 5 non-contiguous blocks if contiguous storage is unavailable, and each noncontiguous block subtracts one from the number of extents permitted. Thus from 2 to 5 fewer extents are permitted if the primary space is not a single contiguous block.

The system does not reserve space for extents before they are needed so that if a volume reaches capacity and an extent is required, the step must be terminated because space is unavailable. This problem is common in multiprogramming systems where several jobs may concurrently request space on a public volume and space cannot be guaranteed to be available. One solution is to allow the data set to extend onto other volumes by making it a multivolume data set with the VOL parameter.

    //DD1   DD   UNIT=2311,SPACE=(800,(100,50)),

    //   VOL=(, ,2)

    If secondary allocation is required and the volume containing the primary allocation is full, space is obtained from a second 2311 volume.

Primary space allocation is always made on a single volume. Multivolume direct-access data sets must be given increments so that space can be allocated on additional volumes. Increments cannot be given to indexed-sequential data sets and are ignored for checkpoint data sets.

If the data set was created without an increment specified, the SPACE parameter may later specify an increment.
If the data set was created with an increment, the SPACE
parameter can also override it with a different increment.
In both cases the new increment is effective only for the
duration of the step and does not change the original increment or the 15-extent limit. For example, a data set might
be created by

    `//A    DD    DSN=HOLDIT,DISP=(,CATLG),`

    `//  UNIT=DISK,SPACE=(100,(10,20))`

Later one might add to it and wish to increase the size
of the extents.

    `//ADD    DD    DSN=HOLDIT,DISP=(MOD,KEEP),`

    `//  SPACE=(100,(0,200))`

> Each extent allocated during the step is given 200
> blocks of 100 bytes. Later runs will revert back
> to an extent size of 20 blocks of 100 bytes.

Be careful when you override a DD card in a cataloged
procedure containing a SPACE parameter. If the overriding
card describes an existing data set, one would usually not
code a SPACE parameter. However, if a secondary allocation is required, the SPACE parameter on the overridden
card specifies the increment, rather than the increment
specified when the data set was created. Code SPACE= on
the overriding DD card to nullify the SPACE parameter and
avoid this problem.

Directory or index space: directory, index

Partitioned data sets must have space allocated for a
directory containing the names, aliases, and locations of
each member. The directory is allocated in units of 256-
byte blocks and each block can contain about 5 entries:
member names or aliases. (Each member can have up to
16 aliases.) To estimate the number of directory blocks,

sum the member names and aliases, divide by 5, and round up to the nearest integer. For example, if a partitioned data set has 30 members and 4 members have a single alias, allocate 34/5 or 7 directory blocks: SPACE=(800,(20,100,7)).

Allow a liberal margin for adding new members and aliases when creating the data set because the directory cannot be extended later. If it fills up, the data set must be re-created. (Chapter 13 describes how to re-create a partitioned data set.) Space for the directory is also allocated in full track units, and any unused space on the track is wasted unless there is enough room to contain a block of the first member. The directory space is obtained from the primary allocation and must be considered in estimating the total space required.

Indexed-sequential data sets may be allocated space for the index in the SPACE parameter. Chapter 14 describes indexed-sequential data sets in detail.

Special space options: RLSE, CONTIG, MXIG, ALX, ROUND

Several positional subparameters may be coded with the SPACE parameter to release unused space and allocate space for faster access. (Only CONTIG is permitted for indexed-sequential data sets.)

```
        CYL
        TRK                         index
        blocksize                   directory
SPACE=(---------,(quantity,increment,---------),

        ALX
        MXIG
        CONTIG
    RLSE,- - - - - -,ROUND)
```

Releasing space: RLSE

RLSE releases all unused space when the data set is closed. It permits one to allocate more space than perhaps

is needed without wasting space. For example, if SPACE=
(800,20 RLSE) is coded and only 4 blocks are written, the
space for the remaining 16 blocks is released. If an extent
is allocated and is only partially used, the remainder of the
extent is also released. If space is requested in cylinders,
only excess cylinders are released; otherwise excess tracks
are released. (RLSE is ignored if TYPE=T is coded in the
CLOSE macro in assembly language.)

Space is released only if the data set is not empty and if
the data set is closed after being opened for output. RLSE
can also be used to release space in an existing data set.
Code SPACE=(0,0,RLSE) on a DD card referring to the data
set to release any excess space when the data set is closed.
(Code SPACE=(units,(,increment),RLSE) if the existing data
set may require secondary allocation.)

At first glance it appears that RLSE should always be
used, but there are some drawbacks. RLSE is slow because
it requires considerable I/O time to release the space. Then
any added data in a subsequent step must be placed in an extent, with the resultant slower processing time.

If you override a DD card in a cataloged procedure with
a DD card defining an existing data set, be sure to code
SPACE= to nullify any SPACE parameter on the overridden
DD card. If you do not, and the SPACE parameter on the
overridden card contains the RLSE subparameter, excess
space in the data set is released when it is closed.

Minimizing access time: CONTIG, MXIG, ALX

CONTIG, MXIG, and ALX are mutually exclusive positional parameters used to allocate contiguous space. Since
contiguous space minimizes access arm movement, the
access time is decreased. CONTIG requests that space be
allocated only on contiguous tracks and cylinders; that is, all
tracks on a cylinder are contiguous, and if more than one
cylinder is needed, the cylinders are also contiguous. Always
code CONTIG if track overflow is used.

MXIG allocates the largest contiguous free area on a
volume, but only if that area is as large or larger than the

amount requested. This may result in considerably more space being allocated than was requested (anywhere from the amount requested to the entire volume), and it should be used only for large data sets as an alternative to requesting secondary allocation. RLSE can release excess space.

ALX builds up a list of the five largest contiguous free areas on the volume and allocates all of these areas that are as large or larger than the space requested. One might obtain a single area as large as the entire volume, five areas all much larger than requested, etc. Since ALX can also allocate much more space than was requested, it should be used only for very large data sets as an alternative to requesting secondary allocation. RLSE can release excess space.

SPACE=(100,(20,10), ,CONTIG)

Space is allocated only if it is contiguous.

SPACE=(100,(1000, ,5),RLSE,ALX)

Somewhere between 100,000 bytes and the entire volume are allocated in up to 5 areas whose minimum size is 100,000 bytes. Excess space is released.

SPACE=(100,(1000,10), ,MXIG)

Anywhere between 100,000 bytes and the entire volume could be allocated with all space being contiguous.

Rounding up to cylinders: ROUND

Space requested by blocksize can be allocated on cylinder boundaries by coding ROUND. The system computes the space needed, rounds up to the nearest cylinder, and allocates complete cylinders so that the space begins on the first track of a cylinder and ends on the last track of a cylinder. CONTIG must be coded if contiguous cylinders are wanted. ROUND ensures that the data is placed on the

minimum number of cylinders possible by starting on a
cylinder boundary. This decreases access time because the
access arm movement is minimized.

SPACE=(1000,195, , ,ROUND)

Six 2311 cylinders or two 2314 cylinders would be
allocated. The cylinders might not be contiguous.

SPACE=(1000,(195,10),RLSE,CONTIG,ROUND)

Six 2311 cylinders or two 2314 cylinders would be
allocated. The cylinders are contiguous, secondary
allocation is permitted, and excess cylinders are
released.

Requesting Specific Tracks: ABSTR

Space can be allocated by giving the starting track
address and the number of tracks to allocate. This always
gives contiguous space but should be used only for location-
dependent data sets. It is sometimes used for very high
usage data sets to place them near the volume table of contents. Space is allocated only if all the tracks are available.
To request absolute tracks, code

$$\textit{index}$$
$$\textit{directory}$$
SPACE=(ABSTR,(quantity,address,---------))

The quantity is the number of tracks desired and the
address is the relative track address of the first track
wanted. (The address of the first track on a volume is 0,
but it cannot be allocated because it contains a pointer to
the table of contents.) The directory requests directory
space for partitioned data sets, and index requests index
space for indexed-sequential data sets.

SPACE=(ABSTR,(200,2400))

Two hundred tracks are requested, starting at
relative track address 2400.

Splitting Cylinders between Data Sets: SPLIT

SPLIT splits the tracks on a cylinder between several
data sets to reduce the processing time of data sets that
have corresponding records. For example, a personnel file
might be divided into several data sets, one containing names,
another salary, and another work experience. For each name
there is a record in corresponding data sets containing salary
and work experience. If cylinders are split among the data
sets, the corresponding records in each data set can be read
without access arm movement.

To split cylinders, place the associated DD cards in
sequence, and specify the space required for the first data
set and the total space required for all data sets on the first
DD card. Each subsequent DD card then requests its portion
of the total space. To request space in units of cylinders,
code the following on the first DD card.

SPLIT=(number,CYL,(quantity,*increment*))

The quantity is the total cylinders to allocate for all
data sets, the number is the number of tracks on each cylinder to allocate to the first data set, and the increment
specifies the number of cylinders of secondary allocation.
The secondary allocation is given only to the data set ex-
hausting its allotted space—it is not split with other data
sets. Each succeeding DD card must contain SPLIT=number,
giving the number of tracks per cylinder to allocate to its
data set.

//DD1   DD   SPLIT=(5,CYL,1),DSN=ONE,

//   DISP=(,CATLG),UNIT=2314

One cylinder is allocated for all data sets. Data
set ONE is allotted 5 tracks on the cylinder.

//DD2   DD   SPLIT=15,DSN=TWO,DISP=(,CATLG)

Data set TWO is allocated 15 tracks on the
cylinder. The unit parameter is not required.

To request space in units of blocks, code the following on the first DD card.

SPLIT=(percent, blocksize,(quantity,*increment*))

The blocksize is the average block size, the quantity is the total number of blocks for all data sets, and the percent is an integer between 1 and 100 specifying the percentage of tracks per cylinder to allot to the first data set. The increment is the number of blocks of secondary allocation. The system rounds up to an integral number of cylinders for both primary and secondary allocation. Each succeeding DD card must contain SPLIT=percent, giving the percentage of tracks on each cylinder to allot to it. (KEYLEN=length must be coded if the blocks have keys.)

//DD1   DD   SPLIT=(20,800,(30,10)),DSN=ONE,

//   DISP=(,CATLG),UNIT=2314

> Thirty 800-byte blocks are allocated to all data sets, and ten 800-byte blocks of secondary allocation are permitted. Data set ONE is allocated 20 percent of the tracks on each cylinder.

//DD2   DD   SPLIT=80,DSN=TWO,DISP=(,CATLG)

> Data set TWO is allotted the remaining 80 percent of the tracks on each cylinder.

The average block length for split data sets cannot exceed 65,535 bytes. SPLIT cannot be used for indexed-sequential, partitioned, or direct organization, or for data sets residing on drums. The space allocated to split data sets is not released until all data sets sharing the cylinders are deleted.

Suballocating Space among Data Sets: SUBALLOC

SUBALLOC allows space to be reserved and suballocated in contiguous order to several data sets. For example,

an installation may control direct-access space by allotting
a fixed amount of space to each user who then suballocates
this space for his data sets.

A data set must first be created to reserve the space
for suballocation. Space can be reserved by any of the three
previous methods: requesting an amount of space, requesting specific tracks, or splitting data sets between cylinders.
This data set can be used only for suballocation because
space is removed from the front of it. It is effectively deleted when all its space is suballocated. To suballocate
space, code the following on a subsequent DD card.

```
            CYL
            TRK
            blocksize
     SUBALLOC=(---------,(quantity,increment,directory),

        referback)
```

The blocksize, TRK, CYL, quantity, increment, and
directory have already been discussed. The increment
applies only to the suballocated data set, not to the original
data set. The referback points to a previous DD card describing the data set from which to suballocate. The system
suballocates space only if it is contiguous, and space obtained by suballocation cannot be further suballocated. Suballocated space can be released individually for each data
set, without all suballocated space being released.

```
    //STEP1   EXEC   PGM=ONE

    //DD1   DD   SPACE=(800,100, ,CONTIG),DSN=ALL,

    //   DISP=(,KEEP),UNIT=2314
```

Space is reserved for suballocation.

```
    //DD2   DD   SUBALLOC=(800,20,DD1),

    //   DSN=DATA1,DISP=(,CATLG)
```

Twenty 800-byte blocks are suballocated from ALL
for DATA1. The UNIT parameter is not required.

```
//STEP2    EXEC    PGM=TWO

//DD3   DD    SUBALLOC=(800,(30,20),STEP1.DD1),

//    DSN=DATA2,DISP=(,CATLG)
```

Thirty 800-byte blocks are suballocated from
ALL for DATA2, and a secondary allocation
of twenty 800-byte blocks is permitted.

DATA SET LABELS: LABEL

The LABEL parameter must be coded if the direct-
access data set has user labels in addition to the standard
labels. To specify user labels, code LABEL=(,SUL). The
LABEL parameter is more commonly used for data set protection (Chapter 14) and for magnetic tape labels (Chapter
12). Since user labels are seldom used, a full description of
LABEL is deferred until these later chapters.

USING DIRECT-ACCESS DATA SETS

To create a data set on direct-access storage, allocate
space with either the SPACE, SPLIT, or SUBALLOC parameter. Always code the UNIT, DSN, and DISP parameters,
except in the rare circumstances when it is apparent they
are not needed; for example, UNIT is not needed if VOL=REF
is coded. The VOL parameter is needed if the data set is to
be placed on a specific volume or on several nonspecific volumes or if a private pack is mounted. DCB subparameters
are coded as required: LRECL, BLKSIZE, BUFNO, and
RECFM are perhaps the most common.

To retrieve an existing data set, code UNIT, VOL, DSN,
and DISP. The LRECL, BLKSIZE, and RECFM DCB subparameters can be obtained from the data set label, but
BUFNO must be coded if it is wanted. Omit UNIT and VOL
if the data set is cataloged or passed.

The following example shows the creation and retrieval
of temporary and nontemporary data sets.

```
//STEP1    EXEC    PGM=WON

//DD1    DD    UNIT=2311,DSN=&&PASSIT,

//  DISP=(,PASS),SPACE=(800,(10,5)))
```

A temporary data set is created and passed to a subsequent step.

```
//DD2    DD    UNIT=2314,DSN=SAVIT,DISP=(,CATLG),

//  SPACE=(800,(20,10),RLSE)
```

A nontemporary data set is created and cataloged for later use.

```
//DD3    DD    UNIT=2314,DSN=KEEPIT,DISP=(,KEEP),

//  VOL=SER=PACK01,SPACE=(TRK,10)
```

A nontemporary data set is created but not cataloged.

```
//STEP2    EXEC    PGM=DOS

//DD4    DD    DSN=&&PASSIT,DISP=(OLD,DELETE)
```

The passed data set is retrieved.

```
//DD5    DD    DSN=SAVIT,DISP=SHR
```

The cataloged data set is retrieved.

```
//DD6    DD    DSN=KEEPIT,UNIT=2314,DISP=OLD,

//  VOL=SER=PACK01
```

The kept data set is retrieved.

In the next example, suppose space must be reserved for a data set containing 100,000 cards with a blocking factor of 10. The DCB subparameters are thus LRECL=80, BLKSIZE=800, and RECFM=FB. We expect the data set will be used often, and so we should try to minimize access time by making the space contiguous.

Next we must select a device. Assume that we can place the data set on any of several permanently mounted 2314 disk packs grouped under the name DISK but that no pack can be expected to have more than 30 contiguous cylinders free. How many cards can be contained in 30 cylinders, and how many volumes will be required?

We can use Table 4 to compute the number of blocks per track:

$$1 + \frac{7294 - 800}{101 + 1.043(800)} = 7.94 \, ,$$

which truncates to 7. Since there are 20 tracks per cylinder, each 2314 cylinder contains 140 blocks, and 30 cylinders contain 4200 blocks or 42,000 cards. Thus 3 volumes are required to contain 100,000 cards, allocating a maximum of 30 cylinders per volume. The DD card is coded as

    //DD1   DD   VOL=(, , , 3),UNIT=DISK,

    //   SPACE=(800,(4200,4200),RLSE,CONTIG,ROUND),

    //   DISP=(,CATLG),DSN=BIG,DCB=(LRECL=80,

    //   RECFM=FB,BLKSIZE=800)

One final example, this time a partitioned data set. In Chapter 9 we added cataloged procedures to a procedure library. How would we reserve space for such a library? Since the library contains card images, the record length is 80, and for simplicity we assume that the records are unblocked.

Now we must estimate the space required. Suppose we estimate the average procedure will contain 10 cards, that we will likely have 50 procedures, but that we want to allow space for an additional 150 more. Our primary space allocation must be for 50(10), and the secondary for 150(10) blocks of 80 bytes. Since secondary allocation can occur 15

times, each extent should be for 150(10)/15 or 100 blocks of
80 bytes. Directory space must be reserved for (50+150)/5
or 40 blocks. The following step reserves space for the
library.

//STEP1   EXEC   PGM=IEFBR14

    The null program is used because no actual
    program needs to be executed.

//DD1   DD   DSN=IT,DISP=(,CATLG),UNIT=2311,

//   SPACE=(80,(500,100,40))

DEDICATED WORK FILES

MVT systems may have dedicated work files for temporary data sets. The data set is allocated to an initiator/
terminator when it is started, and is scratched when the
initiator/terminator is stopped. Since an initiator/terminator
is dedicated to a single job at a time, that job may use what-
ever work files have been dedicated to the initiator/terminator.
This can save a significant amount of time since data sets
used by several jobs, such as compiler and linkage editor
scratch files, need be allocated space only once. Several
initiator/terminators may have dedicated work files with the
same name.

To use a dedicated work file, one must code the data set
name, preceded by one or two ampersands, of the dedicated
work file, and all other parameters required by new data
sets, e.g., UNIT, SPACE, DISP, DCB, etc. If conflicting
parameters are given, the dedicated work file is ignored and
a temporary data set is created.

For example, suppose SYSUT1 is a dedicated work file
specified in the cataloged initiator/terminator procedure as
follows:

//SYSUT1   DD   SPACE=(CYL,2),UNIT=2314

Several steps could reuse the same dedicated work file
if they contained the following DD card.

```
//A    DD    DSN=&&SYSUT1,UNIT=2314,
//  SPACE=(CYL,2)
```

PCP systems may also be given dedicated work files by allocating permanent data sets. Since only a single job is run at a time, each job may reuse the permanent data set.

SUMMARY

Direct-access space is allocated by one of the following methods:

1.   Request an amount of space.

```
        CYL
        TRK                          index
        blocksize                    directory
SPACE=(---------,(quantity,increment,---------,
```

```
        ALX
        MXIG
        CONTIG
    RLSE,------,ROUND)
```

2.   Request specific tracks.

```
                              index
                              directory
SPACE=(ABSTR,(quantity,address,---------))
```

3.   Split cylinders.

```
SPLIT=(number,CYL,(quantity,increment))
```

```
SPLIT=number
    or
SPLIT=(percent,blocksize,(quantity,increment))
```

```
SPLIT=percent
```

4.   Suballocate.

```
        CYL
        TRK
        blocksize
SUBALLOC=(---------,(quantity,increment,directory),
    referback)
```

CHAPTER 12
MAGNETIC TAPES

Magnetic tape consists of a reel of 1/2-inch-wide magnetic tape. A full reel contains about 2400 feet of tape and is equivalent in storage to 480,000 cards punched in all 80 columns, when blocked at 4800 bytes per block. A byte of data is recorded in a column across the width of the tape with the position of each bit along the width called a track.

There are two methods of recording the binary digits on the tape. The older method, still in use, records binary ones with a positive charge and binary zeros by the absence of a charge. An additional parity bit is also recorded to make the number of 1-bits in a column either even or odd (unfortunately neither is standard). When the tape is read, the hardware checks for an even or odd number of 1-bits to see if the data is intact and notes any parity error. Newer System/360 tape units record binary ones with a positive charge and binary zeros with a negative charge. Not only is this method more reliable, but it also eliminates the confusing even or odd parity—odd parity is standard.

Second-generation IBM computers had 6-bit bytes, and so the data was recorded on seven tracks. Since System/360 computers have 8-bit bytes, the newer tape units record data on nine tracks. Different tape drives are required to process 7- or 9-track tapes, but the same reel of tape can be used for either 7- or 9-track recording—as long as it is consistent.

Data is recorded along the length of each track in densities of 200, 556, 800, and 1600 bits per inch (bpi). Seven-track drives can process 200-, 556-, and 800-bpi tapes, whereas 9-track drives must be either 800 or 1600 bpi. (A dual-density feature must be installed on 9-track drives to process both 800- and 1600-bpi tapes.) More data can be stored on a tape at higher densities, and the transmission rate is also increased.

The usable portion of a tape reel is marked by two small aluminum strips; one pasted about 10 feet from the start of the tape to mark the load point and allow a leader for threading; and the other about 14 feet from the end of the reel to mark the end-of-volume and allow unfinished blocks to be completely transmitted. The VOL=SER parameter can specify that other tape reels be mounted when the end-of-volume is reached.

All old data on a tape is erased as the tape is written. The computer operator must insert a small plastic *file-protect ring* into the circular groove provided for it on the tape reel before the tape can be written upon. If the ring is removed, the tape can be read, but is fully protected against being accidently written upon. The operator must be told whether to file protect a tape or not; it cannot be specified by JCL.

Blocks written on a tape are separated by an interblock gap—a length of blank tape 0.75 inch long for 7-track tapes and 0.6 for 9-track. The end of a data set or file is marked by a 3.5-inch gap followed by a special block written by the hardware called a *file* or *tape mark*. Several data sets can be contained on a single reel of tape.

Tapes are read by moving the tape past the read head to transmit the data into contiguous ascending core locations. If an error is detected, the system attempts to reread the block several times before pronouncing an I/O error. The user's program can be notified if the file mark or end-of-tape marker is read. Tapes can also be read backwards by moving the tape in the opposite direction, placing the data in descending order of addresses in core storage.

A tape is written by transmitting data in core in increasing order of addresses onto the tape as it passes the write head. The data is immediately read back as it passes the read head to ensure that it is recorded correctly. Tapes can also be backspaced and forward spaced over blocks or files, rewound to the load point, and unloaded, but only assembly programs can perform all these operations.

MAGNETIC TAPE LABELS: LABEL

The LABEL parameter tells the type of label, the relative file number on the tape, and whether the data set is to be processed for input or output. The complete LABEL parameter is coded as

$$IN \quad RETPD=nnnn$$
$$OUT \quad EXPDT=yyddd$$

LABEL=(*file,type,PASSWORD*,- - -, - - - - - - - - - -)

PASSWORD, EXPDT, and RETPD specify data set protection and are explained in Chapter 14. The usual form of the LABEL parameter for tape is

$$IN$$
$$OUT$$

LABEL=(*file,type*, ,- - -)

Relative File Number: file

If the data set is not the first file on the tape, file must give the relative file number to position the tape properly. The file is a 1- to 4-digit sequence number describing the data set's position relative to other data sets on the volume. If the file is omitted or zero is coded, 1 is assumed. (The tape is spaced to the end-of-volume if the file is higher than the number of data sets on the volume.) The file can be the relative sequence number over several labeled tape volumes, but it must be the relative sequence number for each unlabeled volume.

The file is recorded in the catalog if the data set is cataloged. However, it is not passed with the data set, so that if a DD card refers back to a passed data set, the file number must be supplied.

```
//STEP1   EXEC    PGM=WON

//DD1    DD     DSN=ALL,UNIT=TAPE,VOL=SER=421,

//   DISP=(OLD,PASS),LABEL=2
```

```
//STEP2    EXEC    PGM=TOO
```

```
//DD2    DD    DSN=*.STEP1.DD1,DISP=(OLD,KEEP)
```

DD2 refers to the first file of the tape rather than the second file described by DD1. DD2 should be coded as

```
//DD2    DD    DSN=*.STEP1.DD1,DISP=(OLD,KEEP),
```

```
//    LABEL=2
```

Label Type: type

Magnetic tapes may contain both volume and data set labels, either standard as provided by IBM, nonstandard as devised by the installation, or a combination of both. A tape volume label is a block written on the tape by the installation using the IBM-supplied utility program IEHINITT, before the tape is used. (The 1- to 6-character label is usually pasted on the tape reel to help the operator locate the tape.) The volume label is not separated from the first data set on the tape by a file mark.

Data sets on labeled tape consist of a header block, a tape mark, the data set itself, a tape mark, a trailer block, and then two tape marks. The header block contains the description of the data set: record format, record size, block size, and data set name. The trailer block contains the same information as the header block so that the tape can be read backwards.

Data set labels are automatically created by the system when the data set is created if standard labels are requested. If one specifies that there be no label, neither volume or data set labels are created. The tape would then contain the first data set, a tape mark, the next data set, a tape mark, etc. The last data set on the tape is followed by two tape marks.

One may specify the following types of labels.

SL   Standard Labels (assumed if type is omitted)

NSL   NonStandard Labels

SUL   Both Standard and User Labels

BLP   Bypass Label Processing

NL   No labels

Standard labels: SL

If SL is coded or the type is omitted, the system assumes standard labels and reads in the first file to see whether it contains a valid label. It then checks the volume serial number in the label with that supplied in the VOL=SER parameter. If they do not check, the operator is instructed to mount the proper volume.

If the tape does not have a standard label and a specific volume is not requested with VOL=SER, the operator is requested to supply label information, and a volume label is then written on the tape. If the label being read is of a different density than that specified or assumed on the DD card and if the tape is mounted on a multiple-density drive, the density is changed and the system attempts to read the label again. If a tape is mounted that is written with a different number of tracks than that expected, the job is abnormally terminated.

When the serial numbers check, the system positions the tape to the proper file. If the tape is being written, the data set name given by DSN is written into a data set label. If the tape is being read, the DSN parameter is checked against the name in the data set label, and the program is terminated if the names do not check. One must supply the volume serial number, file number, and data set name for each nontemporary tape data set created.

A trailer label is written on the current volume if an end-of-volume condition is encountered while writing a tape, and processing continues on the next volume. Standard labels are created by the IBM-supplied IEHINITT utility program before the tape is used and are not changed thereafter.

Nonstandard Labels: NSL

NSL gives control to installation-written routines for label processing.

Standard and user labels: SUL

SUL is identical to SL except that user data set labels are additionally processed by installation-provided routines.

Bypass label processing: BLP

BLP positions the tape to the proper file without checking for volume or data set labels. Data set labels are not created when a data set is written. As a consequence, no DCB parameters can be obtained from the label when the data set is read; they must be coded in the program or in the DCB parameter on the DD card. BLP must be used to write on blank tapes or on tapes containing previous data of a different parity, or tracks.

If a tape containing standard labels is written on with BLP, the volume label is overwritten. If a tape with standard labels is read with BLP, the first file contains the volume label and the header block for the first data set, the second file contains the data set, and the third file contains the trailer block.

Unlabeled tapes should be dismounted at the end of the step by using DISP=(. . ,DELETE) so that the system will not use them for scratch. BLP is an option that must be generated into a PCP system, or specified in a MFT or MVT cataloged reader procedure. If the BLP option is not specified and BLP is coded, it is treated as NL.

No labels: NL

NL is exactly like BLP except that NL reads in the first file on the tape to ensure that it does not contain a volume label. NL can produce some unexpected results. Blank tapes, because they do not contain a tape mark, are read to the end-of-volume. If the tape contains previous data of a different parity, or track, an I/O error results and the program is terminated. One must know what is on a tape to use NL—if he does not know, he should use BLP. If the tape does not have the proper label and a specific volume is not requested with VOL=SER, the operator is requested to supply label information, and a volume label is then written on the tape. If the tape originally contains a standard label, a new label is only written if any retention date has expired and if the tape does not contain password protected data sets.

```
//A   DD   LABEL=(,BLP),UNIT=TAPE
```

The tape is positioned to file 1 without label checking.

```
//B   DD   LABEL=2,DSN=MYDATA,DISP=OLD,
//   VOL=SER=300,UNIT=2400
```

The tape is positioned to file 2, and standard labels are assumed.

```
//C   DD   LABEL=(3,NL),UNIT=2400
```

The tape is positioned to file 3. The tape must not have a label.

```
//D   DD   LABEL=(1,SL),UNIT=TAPE,DSN=IT
//E   DD   UNIT=TAPE,DSN=IT
```

D and E are equivalent since the LABEL parameters in D are assumed if LABEL is omitted.

Processing for Input or Output: IN/OUT

If the basic sequential access method is used, the OPEN macro coded in assembly language can specify INOUT, allowing the data set to be opened for input and later be used for output without reopening it. (OUTIN can be coded for the reverse.) Coding LABEL=(, , ,IN) or LABEL=(, , ,OUT) overrides INOUT or OUTIN, respectively, so that the data set can be used for input or output only.

The IN and OUT LABEL subparameters are primarily for FORTRAN programs. FORTRAN opens data sets for INOUT or OUTIN, depending upon whether the first use of the data set is a READ or WRITE. Since this opens data sets for both output and input, the file-protection ring must always be inserted even if the tape is only read, negating the protection afforded by file protecting a tape. Likewise, operator intervention is required for reading data sets that have retention checks. Coding LABEL=(, , ,IN) opens the data set for input only, allowing the file-protection ring to be removed and retention protected data sets to be read without operator intervention.

    //A   DD   LABEL=(2,SL, ,IN), . . .

The data set can only be read.

DCB SUBPARAMETERS

The usual DCB subparameters DSORG, LRECL, BLK-SIZE, BUFNO, and RECFM can also be specified as needed for tapes. Fixed, variable, and undefined record formats are all permitted, but variable formats cannot be written on 7-track drives unless they have the data conversion feature. The block size should be at least 18 bytes long to eliminate mistaking blocks for noise. A DEN subparameter may be required to specify density, and TRTCH is needed for 7-track tapes.

Tape Density: DEN

The following list gives the various values of DEN.

DEN	7-track density	9-track density
0	200 bpi (default)	-
1	556 bpi	-
2	800 bpi	800 bpi (default for 800 bpi drives)

DEN	7-track density	9-track density
3	–	1600 bpi (default for 1600 and dual-density drives)

DEN is required for 7-track drives unless the tapes are 200 bpi density (and few are). DEN is required for 9-track drives only if an 800-bpi tape is used on a dual-density drive.

Tape Recording Technique: TRTCH

TRTCH is used for 7-track drives to specify parity, data conversion, and translation. Parity can be even or odd, data conversion permits binary data to be recorded by 7-track drives, and translation is used to read or write BCD tapes. The following options are possible.

TRTCH omitted	Odd parity, translation off, conversion off. (This mode of processing tapes is used to process data from second-generation computers.)
Write	Only the rightmost 6 bits are written onto tape; the 2 high-order bits are ignored.
Read	Each character on tape is read into the 6 rightmost bits of each byte; the 2 high-order bits are set to zero.
TRTCH=E	Same as omitting TRTCH except parity is even.
TRTCH=T	Odd parity, translation on, conversion off. (BCD/EBCDIC translation.)
Write	Each 8-bit EBCDIC character is converted to a 6-bit BCD tape character.
Read	Each 6-bit tape character is converted to an 8-bit EBCDIC character.
TRTCH=ET	Same as TRTCH=T except parity is even.
TRTCH=C	Odd parity, translation off, conversion on. (This mode is used to record

	binary data on 7-track tapes.) Read backwards forces conversion off.
Write	Three 8-bit bytes (24 bits) are written as four 6-bit tape characters (24 bits). If storage data is not a multiple of 3 bytes, 2 or 3 tape characters are written as needed, and unused bit positions of the last character are set to zero.
Read	Four 6-bit tape characters are read as three 8-bit bytes. If the data is not a multiple of 4 characters, the last 1, 2, or 3 characters are read into core, and the remaining bits of the unfilled byte are set to zero.

USING TAPES

Tapes can contain only sequential data sets. To create a data set on tape, always code the UNIT, DSN, DISP, and VOL parameters, except in those rare circumstances when it is apparent they are not required; for example, DSN is not required for temporary data sets. Code DCB subparameters as needed; LRECL, BLKSIZE, BUFNO, RECFM, DEN, and TRTCH are the most common. LABEL is needed unless the data set is on the first file of a standard-labeled tape.

To access an old data set on tape, code UNIT, VOL, DSN, and DISP. LABEL and DCB subparameters are coded as needed. DCB subparameters can be obtained from the data set label only if the tape has standard labels. (DEN and TRTCH are not stored in the data set label.) Omit UNIT and VOL if the data set is cataloged or passed. If the data set is not cataloged or is not on the first file, LABEL must give the file number. The following example shows several uses of tapes.

```
//STEP1    EXEC    PGM=ENA

//A    DD    UNIT=TAPE9
```

A scratch data set is placed on file 1 of a standard-labeled 9-track tape.

```
//B    DD    UNIT=TAPE7,VOL=SER=250,
//     DSN=SALARY,LABEL=(2,BLP),
//     DCB=(DEN=2,TRTCH=C),DISP=(,PASS)
```

A data set created on file 2 of an unlabeled 7-track tape is passed.

```
//C    DD    UNIT=TAPE9,DSN=TENURE,LABEL=2,
//     VOL=(PRIVATE,RETAIN,SER=451),
//     DISP=(,CATLG)
```

A data set created on file 2 of a 9-track tape is cataloged. The tape is kept mounted at the end of the step.

```
//STEP2    EXEC    PGM=DIA
//D    DD    DSN=*.STEP1.B,LABEL=(2,BLP),
//     DISP=(MOD,KEEP),DCB=(DEN=2,TRTCH=C)
```

The data set on the 7-track tape is retrieved.

```
//E    DD    DSN=TENURE,DISP=OLD
```

The data set on the 9-track tape is retrieved.

SUMMARY

The usual form of the LABEL parameter for magnetic tapes is

$$
\text{LABEL}=(file,---, ,---)
$$

with the choices

$$
\frac{SL}{NL}
$$

NSL

SUL   IN

BLP   OUT

The complete form of the LABEL parameter is

$$
\begin{array}{lll}
\underline{SL} \\
\overline{NL} \\
NSL \\
SUL & IN & RETPD{=}days \\
BLP & OUT & EXPDT{=}yyddd \\
\end{array}
$$

LABEL=(*file*,- - - ,*PASSWORD*, - - -,- - - - - - - - -)

The special DCB subparameters for tape are

DEN=0   200-bpi tapes, default for 7-track drives.

DEN=1   556-bpi tapes.

DEN-2   800-bpi tapes, default for 800-bpi 9-track drives.

DEN=3   1600-bpi tapes, default for dual-density and 1600-bpi 9-track drives.

TRTCH is for 7-track drives only.

TRTCH omitted	Odd parity, translate off, conversion on.
TRTCH=E	Same as omitting TRTCH except parity is even.
TRTCH=T	Odd parity, translate on, conversion off. (Translates EBCDIC to BCD on write and BCD to EBCDIC on read.)
TRTCH=ET	Same as TRTCH=T except parity is even.
TRTCH=C	Odd parity, translate off, conversion on. (For writing binary data on 7-track drives.)

CHAPTER 13

THE LINKAGE EDITOR

The linkage editor, although not a part of JCL proper, is used for many JCL applications, and an understanding of its function is necessary to use many System/360 facilities. This chapter also illustrates the use of partitioned data sets, shows how programs can be retained as members of partitioned data sets, and describes how to create a subroutine library. The chapter further shows how to compress or re-create a partitioned data set that has reached its storage capacity.

THE LINKAGE EDITOR

The linkage editor program processes object modules, linkage editor control cards, and other load modules to produce load modules that can be executed. A single linkage editor step can process several object and load modules to produce either single or multiple load modules.

An object module is a sequential data set containing relocatable machine instructions and data; it is produced by a language compiler. Object modules are usually placed in a temporary data set to be passed to a subsequent linkage editor step; they can also be punched onto cards as an object deck for later linkage editing.

The linkage editor processes the object modules to form a load module suitable for execution. A load module must be made a member of a partitioned data set on a direct-access device; it cannot be punched onto cards or used from tape. The load module is placed into a temporary data set if it is not to be used again. One may elect to place it in a nontemporary data set so that the program can be loaded into core later and executed without the compilation or linkage editor steps. Replacement subroutines can be link edited with an old load module to produce a new load module.

193

The basic unit processed by the linkage editor is a *control section*, a unit of program (instructions and data) that is itself an entity. A control section, the smallest separately relocatable unit of a program, is usually a subroutine, procedure, or block of COMMON storage.

Several sources of input can be made available to the linkage editor with DD cards. A primary input, defined by a DD card whose ddname is SYSLIN, is always required. It is often a temporary data set passed from a compile step, concatenated with the input stream; allowing both newly compiled subroutines and previously punched object decks to be included.

Several additional sources of input can, if needed, be included with linkage editor control cards. For example, when replacement subroutines are compiled and link edited, the old object module is made an additional input source so that those subroutines not recompiled can be included.

Finally, subroutine libraries can be searched for required subroutines. For example, functions used by a FORTRAN program can be automatically looked up in a library. Subroutine libraries are described by a DD card whose ddname is SYSLIB, and several libraries can be concatenated together.

The linkage editor processes the primary input first, and any additional input next, and it searches the subroutine libraries last if any unresolved references remain. If two modules are encountered with the same name, only the first is used.

JCL for the Linkage Editor

The linkage editor, a program named LINKEDIT, is contained in SYS1.LINKLIB. (An installation can create several linkage editor programs of various sizes and assign them other names.)

```
//LKED    EXEC    PGM=LINKEDIT,REGION=96K,
                  MAP
                  XREF
//   PARM=(LIST,- - - -,NCAL,LET,HIAR,OVLY)
```

The linkage editor step is traditionally named LKED. The REGION parameter is required only in MVT systems, and the actual region size needed may vary at particular installations.

The PARM subparameters, which can be coded in any order, request various options. LIST lists the linkage editor control cards and is usually specified. MAP produces a storage map showing the relative locations of control sections and helps the user estimate the region size needed for his program. XREF includes MAP plus a cross-reference table of the load module.

NCAL cancels the automatic library call mechanism and is often used for creating subroutine libraries so that the load module contains a single subroutine. LET marks load modules as executable even if minor errors are found; for example, external references left unresolved by NCAL. HIAR allows control sections to be directed into hierarchy storage in MVT systems, and OVLY permits an overlay structure. (Several other parameters beyond the scope of this manual have been omitted.)

The LINKEDIT program also requires a SYSPRINT DD card to describe a print data set, a SYSUT1 DD card to allocate a scratch data set, and a SYSLIN DD card to describe the primary input. A SYSLMOD DD card is required to describe the data set that is to contain the load module, a SYSLIB DD card is needed for automatic call lookup, and other DD cards may be included to describe additional sources of input. The following example illustrates the use of the linkage editor in a FORTRAN compile, link edit, and go cataloged procedure.

```
//FORTCLG    PROC

//FORT    EXEC    PGM=IEYFORT,REGION=100K
```

The FORTRAN G compiler is named IEYFORT and is contained in SYS1.LINKLIB. REGION is needed only for MVT systems, and the actual amount of core needed may vary at particular installations.

//SYSPRINT   DD   SYSOUT=A

SYSPRINT describes a print data set.

//SYSPUNCH   DD   SYSOUT=B

SYSPUNCH describes a punch data set and is
needed only if an object deck is punched.

//SYSLIN   DD   DSN=&&LOADSET,

//   DISP=(MOD,PASS),UNIT=SYSDA,

//   SPACE=(80,(200,100)),DCB=BLKSIZE=80

SYSLIN describes the data set that is to contain
the object module produced by the compiler. A
disposition of MOD is used so that if there are
several compile steps, the object modules are
all placed in one sequential data set.

//LKED   EXEC   PGM=LINKEDIT,PARM=LIST,

//   COND=(4,LT,FORT),REGION=96K

COND bypasses the link edit step unless the
compile step returns a completion code less
than 4.

//SYSLIB   DD   DSN=SYS1.FORTLIB,DISP=SHR

SYSLIB points to the library used for the automatic call lookup.

//SYSPRINT   DD   SYSOUT=A

SYSPRINT defines a print data set.

//SYSLIN   DD   DSN=&&LOADSET,

//   DISP=(OLD,DELETE)

//   DD   DDNAME=SYSIN

SYSLIN describes the primary input; the output from the compiler concatenated with the input stream.

```
//SYSLMOD    DD    DSN=&&GOSET(GO),

//    UNIT=SYSDA,SPACE=(1024,(50,20,1)),

//    DISP=(,PASS),DCB=BLKSIZE=1024
```

SYSLMOD defines the data set to contain the load module produced.

```
//SYSUT1    DD    UNIT=(SYSDA,SEP=(SYSLIN,

//    SYSLMOD)),DCB=BLKSIZE=1024,

//    SPACE=(1024,(50,20))
```

SYSUT1 defines a scratch data set used by the linkage editor.

```
//GO    EXEC    PGM=*.LKED.SYSLMOD,

//    COND=((4,LT,FORT),(4,LT,LKED))
```

GO executes the program created by the linkage editor. COND bypasses the step unless both the compiler and linkage editor return completion codes less than 4.

```
//FT05F001    DD    DDNAME=SYSIN

//FT06F001    DD    SYSOUT=A

//FT07F001    DD    SYSOUT=B
```

Data sets are required for the FORTRAN input and output.

The entire procedure is now executed as follows.

```
//    EXEC    FORTCLG
```

```
//FORT.SYSIN    DD    *

[FORTRAN source cards]

/*

//LKED.SYSIN    DD    *

[object decks]

/*

//GO.SYSIN    DD    *

[card data]

/*
```

Linkage Editor Control Cards

Several linkage editor control cards may be included for special processing. (Some cards beyond the scope of this manual have been omitted from the following discussion.) The linkage editor control cards can be placed before or after any object modules or other control cards.

1. ENTRY specifies the first instruction to be executed in a load module. It can be a control section name or entry name within a control section. Each load module must have an entry point. If the ENTRY card is omitted, the system assumes the first byte of the first control section is the entry point—unless an assembly- or compiler-produced END statement specifies an entry point. (The entry point given by an END statement is not retained if the load module is link edited again.) An ENTRY card is coded as

   bENTRY   name[†]

      The name must be the name of an instruction, not data.

[†]The b represents a blank and indicates that the card cannot begin in column 1.

bENTRY   SUB1

Execution begins at SUB1.

2.   ALIAS allows a load module to be referred to by up to
      16 aliases. For example, two subroutines might be com-
      bined into a single load module in a subroutine library
      because the use of one subroutine always requires the
      other. If the load module is given the name of one sub-
      routine, and the other subroutine happens to be called,
      it will not be found. The second subroutine name should
      be made an alias of the load module so that both can be
      found regardless of which subroutine is called.

      A module referred to by an alias will begin execution at
      the external name specified by the alias. If the alias is
      not an external name, execution begins at the main entry
      point. The ALIAS card is coded as

         bALIAS   name, . . .,name[†]

            Sixteen aliases can be assigned on one or several
            ALIAS cards.

         bALIAS   GO,PROCEED,ARRIBA

            The load module can now be referred to by its
            aliases GO, PROCEED, and ARRIBA.

3.   INCLUDE specifies additional sources of linkage editor
      input to be included. The included data set can also
      contain an INCLUDE card, but no data following the
      INCLUDE card in the inserted data set is processed.

      INCLUDE is most often used to include an old load
      module when subroutines within it must be recompiled
      and link edited. The linkage editor first processes the
      new subroutines and then includes all the old load

[†]To continue a linkage editor control card, interrupt the
card after a comma anywhere before column 72, code a
nonblank character in column 72, and continue in column
16 of the next card.

module except the replaced subroutines. The INCLUDE card can be coded in two ways.

    bINCLUDE   ddname, . . . ,ddname

       or

    bINCLUDE   ddname(member, . . . ,member), . . . ,

       ddname(member, . . . ,member)

The ddname is the name of a DD card describing the data to include. It can be either a library or sequential data set containing both object modules and control cards, or a library containing just load modules. Several INCLUDE cards are permitted. A member name must be coded for all members to be included from a library. Code just the ddname for sequential data sets.

    bINCLUDE   INPUT1,DD1

    bINCLUDE   INPUT2,DD2(ONE,TWO),DD3(SQRT)

> Three sequential data sets described by the INPUT1, DD1, and INPUT2 DD cards are included. Members ONE and TWO are also included from the library described by the DD2 card, and member SQRT is included from the library described by DD3.

4.   LIBRARY names control sections to be looked up in libraries other than the libraries described by the SYSLIB DD card. LIBRARY also allows external references to go unresolved for a particular run or for the life of the load module. (The NCAL option on the EXEC card cancels all automatic call lookups.) The LIBRARY card can be coded in the following ways.

    bLIBRARY   ddname(member, . . . ,member), . . . ,

       ddname(member, . . . ,member)

A DD card with the given ddname must be included to describe the library. The member names of each control section to look up in the library must be given.

bLIBRARY   (name, . . . ,name)

The control sections named are left unresolved for the run—no automatic call lookup takes place for the named control sections. For example, a subroutine in a library might be referred to in a program but might not be called during a particular run. Since the subroutine will not be called, the reference can be left unresolved to save core storage by not loading the subroutine. (LET should also be coded on the EXEC card.)

bLIBRARY   *(name, . . . ,name)

The asterisk appended to the names causes the external references to go unresolved for the entire life of the load module.

The above parameters can all be coded on one or several LIBRARY cards.

bLIBRARY   DD1(SUB1,SUB2),(HALT),*(ALTO)

SUB1 and SUB2 are looked up in the library described by the DD1 DD card. No automatic subroutine lookup is made for HALT or ALTO. Furthermore, ALTO is left unresolved for the life of the load module.

5.   HIARCHY directs control sections into hierarchy storage in MVT systems. A REGION parameter must request the storage, and HIAR must be coded on the EXEC card. The HIARCHY card is coded as

bHIARCHY   1,name, . . . ,name

The named control sections are loaded into hierarchy 1 storage. Several control sections can be named on one or several HIARCHY cards. Control sections are loaded into main core if they are not listed on a HIARCHY card.

bHIARCHY   1,SUB1,SUB6

SUB1 and SUB6 are loaded into bulk core.

Creating Program Libraries

Suppose now that a FORTRAN program is to be compiled and retained in a data set named PROGRAM. A member name must be selected, 1 to 8 alphameric (A to Z, 0 to 9) or national (@ $ #) characters, beginning with an alphabetic (A to Z) or national character. Perhaps EIGEN is an appropriate name. The FORTCLG cataloged procedure can be used, but we must override the SYSLMOD DD card to create the nontemporary data set.

```
//   EXEC    FORTCLG

//FORT.SYSIN    DD    *

[MAIN source deck]

[SUB1 source deck]

/*

//LKED.SYSLMOD    DD    DSN=PROGRAM(EIGEN),

//    DISP=(,CATLG),SPACE=(1024,(10,5,10))
```

> The PROGRAM data set is created and the load module is added as a member named EIGEN. The SPACE parameter is also overridden to allocate a more precise amount of space and to enlarge the directory space.

```
//LKED.SYSIN    DD    *

[SUB2 object deck]

/*

//GO.SYSIN    DD    *

[card data]

/*
```

Three routines, MAIN, SUB1, and SUB2, are combined into a load module named EIGEN in the PROGRAM data set. Several other programs could be placed in PROGRAM as long as they are given different member names. The program can now be executed in a single step.

```
//GO    EXEC    PGM=EIGEN,REGION=60K
```

REGION is needed only in MVT systems to request the amount of core required by the program.

```
//STEPLIB    DD    DSN=PROGRAM,DISP=SHR
```

The STEPLIB DD card describes the data set containing the program to execute.

```
//FT06F001    DD    SYSOUT=A
```

```
//FT07F001    DD    SYSOUT=B
```

```
//FT05F001    DD    *
```

[card data]

```
/*
```

Now suppose that SUB1 contains an error and must be replaced.

```
//  EXEC    FORTCLG
```

```
//FORT.SYSIN    DD    *
```

[SUB1 source deck]

```
/*
```

```
//LKED.SYSLMOD    DD    DSN=PROGRAM(EIGEN),
```

```
//    DISP=SHR,SPACE=
```

SYSLMOD is again overridden to describe the data set which is to contain the new load module. Since EIGEN is already a member of PROGRAM, it is replaced by the new load module. The SPACE= parameter is coded to nullify the SPACE parameter on the overridden SYSLMOD card so that it does not change the secondary allocation specified when PROGRAM was created.

//LKED.SYSIN   DD   *

bENTRY   MAIN

The MAIN routine is no longer loaded first, and so we must tell the system that it is the entry point.

bINCLUDE SYSLMOD

The old load module is included as additional input.

/*

//GO.SYSIN   DD   *

[card data]

/*

Creating Subroutine Libraries

The linkage editor can also create private subroutine libraries. The NAME card delimits a load module, names it, and permits several load modules to be produced by a single link edit step. Place the NAME card after the last object module that is to be included in the load module. Any ALIAS cards must precede the NAME card. The NAME card is coded as

bNAME   name

    or

bNAME   name(R)

Any name can be selected for the load module, but since that name is the one matched in a library lookup, the subroutine name should be used. The (R) is coded if the subroutine replaces an existing subroutine in the library. (If (R) is omitted for a replacement module, the new module is added and renamed TEMPNAME.)

bNAME   SUB1

SUB1 is added.

bNAME   SUB2(R)

SUB2 is replaced.

Suppose we wish to create a private subroutine library named MYLIB and place SUB1 and SUB2 in it. We should use a link edit only procedure, but since we do not have one, we can modify the FORTCLG procedure.

//JOBNAME   JOB   (2211,60),JONES,

//   MSGLEVEL=1,RESTART=STEP1.LKED

The RESTART parameter can be used to start at other than the first job step.

//STEP1   EXEC   FORTCLG,PARM.LKED=(LIST,

//   NCAL,LET),COND.GO=ONLY

NCAL and LET are made options so that each load module contains only a single subroutine. The GO step is bypassed by making its execution depend upon previous steps failing—an unlikely occurrence.

//LKED.SYSLMOD   DD   SPACE=(1024,(10,5,10)),

//   DISP=(,CATLG),DSN=MYLIB

SYSLMOD is overridden to describe the MYLIB data set.

//LKED.SYSLIN   DD   *

The first DD card in SYSLIN must be overridden because the data set is not passed from the previous step.

bINCLUDE   DD1(SUB1)

SUB1 is included here. SUB1 is a member of the data set described by the DD1 DD card below.

bNAME   SUB1

The load module containing SUB1 is named SUB1.

bINCLUDE   DD1(SUB2)

SUB2 is included here.

bNAME   SUB2

The load module containing SUB2 is named SUB2.

/*

//LKED.DD1   DD   DSN=PROGRAM,DISP=SHR

The DD1 DD card describes PROGRAM, which contains SUB1 and SUB2.

MYLIB now contains the two subroutines. The library can be used by concatenating it with the SYSLIB DD card.

// EXEC   FORTCLG

//FORT.SYSIN   DD   *

[FORTRAN source decks]

/*

//LKED.SYSLIB   DD

A DD card with a blank operand field is used to space over DD cards in the cataloged procedure.

```
//    DD    DSN=MYLIB,DISP=SHR
```

MYLIB is concatenated to SYS1.FORTLIB.

```
//GO.SYSIN    DD    *
```

[card data]

```
/*
```

It now remains to be shown how to replace a subroutine in the library. The following job replaces SUB1.

```
//STEP1    EXEC    FORTCLG,PARM.LKED=(LIST,
//    NCAL,LET),COND.GO=ONLY
```

We need only the compile and link edit steps so the GO step is bypassed.

```
//FORT.SYSIN    DD    *
```

[SUB1 source deck]

```
/*
//LKED.SYSLMOD    DD    DSN=MYLIB,DISP=SHR,
//    SPACE=
//LKED.SYSIN    DD    *
bNAME    SUB1(R)
```

The NAME card follows the primary input—the SUB1 object deck.

```
/*
```

Only one compiled subroutine can be replaced at a time in the above job because there is no way to insert NAME cards between object modules produced by the compiler. If several subroutines are replaced, first compile them to obtain object decks, then place the appropriate NAME card behind each object deck and submit a second run to link edit the object module.

Overlay Structures

If a program is too large to fit into core, the linkage editor can separate the program into several segments, each small enough to fit. Each segment is then loaded into core as needed, overlaying the previous segment.

Segmenting the program

A *segment* is the smallest unit of a program (one or more control sections) that can be loaded as one logical entity during program execution. The *root segment* (first segment) is that portion of the program which must remain in core throughout execution. If your entire program must be in core during execution, it cannot be segmented or overlaid.

A program is segmented by following the flow of control within the program to determine the dependencies among the subroutines. For example, suppose a program reads an entire input deck, performs some processing, and finally prints the results. We can break this program into the following four segments:

1. A root segment containing the program's main routine.

2. A segment containing subroutines that read the input deck.

3. A segment containing subroutines that perform the processing.

4. A segment containing subroutines that print the results.

The following diagram, called an *overlay tree structure*,[†] illustrates the program's structure. The main routine calls the read routines, causing the first segment to be loaded. When the main routine calls the processing subroutines, they overlay the read routines. The output subroutines will in turn overlay the processing subroutines.

```
                          │ Main
                          │ Routine (Root Segment)
          ────────────────┼──────────────────────────┐
          │               │                          │
       Read            Processing                  Output
       Routines         Routines                   Routines
          │               │                          │
          │               │                          │
```

Each vertical line in the diagram represents a segment. The following diagram illustrates a more complex program with nine segments:

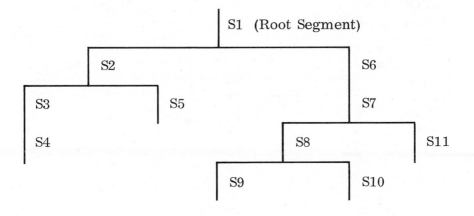

[†] Multiple structures are possible but are beyond the scope of this manual.

S1 through S11 represent subroutines (S1 would be the main routine), and the tree structure shows the segmentation. If we follow down the tree structure, say from S1 to S2 to S5, without backtracking, we establish a *path*. Segments in a path can all be in core at the same time, and a subroutine can call only other subroutines in its path; that is, S3 can call S4, but not S5; whereas S2 can call S3, S4, or S5.

OVERLAY control card

The linkage editor OVERLAY control card describes the overlay structure to the linkage editor. Begin by naming the origin of each segment (the horizontal lines on the tree structure). The names are arbitrary, 1 to 8 alphameric (A to Z, 0 to 9) characters, the first of which must be alphabetic (A to Z). The names FIRST, SECOND, THIRD, and FOURTH are chosen for the example as shown:

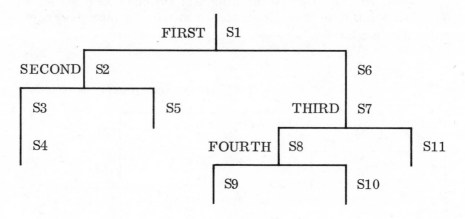

The OVERLAY card is coded as

bOVERLAY   name

The name is the name of the segment origin, that is, FIRST, SECOND, etc. The normal JCL for an OVERLAY run consists of the following.

// EXEC   procedure,PARM.LKED=OVLY

The procedure is any cataloged procedure with a link edit step.

$\vdots$

//LKED.SYSIN   DD   *

[object decks and OVERLAY cards]

/*

$\vdots$

The PARM.LKED=OVLY parameter tells the linkage editor that OVERLAY cards follow. To arrange the object decks and OVERLAY cards, follow down the paths of the tree structure, and describe each segment by an OVERLAY card followed by the appropriate object decks. Work from top to bottom and left to right. An example of the above tree structure can clarify this simple process.

//LKED.SYSIN   DD   *

[S1 object deck]

bOVERLAY FIRST

[S2 object deck]

bOVERLAY SECOND

[S3, S4 object decks]

bOVERLAY SECOND

[S5 object deck]

bOVERLAY FIRST

[S6, S7 object decks]

bOVERLAY THIRD

[S8 object deck]

bOVERLAY FOURTH

[S9 object deck]

bOVERLAY FOURTH

[S10 object deck]

bOVERLAY THIRD

[S11 object deck]

/*

If the object modules are contained in a data set on direct-access storage rather than in card form, they can easily be included in an OVERLAY structure by use of the linkage editor INCLUDE card. Place the INCLUDE card where the object modules are to go.

INSERT control card

It is often inconvenient to insert control sections physically after the appropriate OVERLAY cards. Rather than rearranging the control sections themselves, one can put the control sections anywhere in the primary input and then use the INSERT card to tell the linkage editor how to arrange them.

Place an INSERT card naming the control sections after the OVERLAY card defining the segment in which they are to appear. Place the INSERT card before any OVERLAY cards if the control section belongs in the root segment. INSERT is coded as follows.

bINSERT   name, . . . ,name

The control sections named are inserted wherever the INSERT card is placed. The control sections can be object modules passed from a previous compilation step, object decks, or object and load modules brought in by an INCLUDE card. The control sections themselves can appear anywhere in the primary input—before or after the INSERT card. If the control sections named on the INSERT card are not found in the primary input, the automatic library search mechanism is used.

The following example illustrates the use of INSERT and INCLUDE cards in segmenting the program in the preceding example. Assume S6 is contained in a sequential data set SUBS, S3 and S8 are passed from a compilation step, and S10 and S11 are contained in a partitioned data set MORSUBS.

>   // EXEC   FORTCLG,PARM.LKED=OVLY

> The FORTRAN compile, link edit, go procedure is invoked.

>   //FORT.SYSIN   DD   *

> [S3 source deck]

> [S8 source deck]

>   /*

>   //LKED.A   DD   DSN=SUBS,DISP=SHR

> A DD card must define SUBS.

>   //LKED.B   DD   DSN=MORSUBS,DISP=SHR

> MORSUBS must also be defined.

>   //LKED.SYSIN   DD   *

> [S1,S2,S4,S5,S7,S9 object decks]

>   -- Place all object decks somewhere.

>   bINCLUDE   B(S10,S11)   -- Include other primary input.

```
bINSERT    S1              -- Insert S1 here.

bOVERLAY FIRST

bINSERT    S2              -- Insert S2 here.

bOVERLAY SECOND

bINSERT    S3,S4           -- Insert S3, S4 here.

bOVERLAY SECOND

bINSERT    S5              -- Insert S5 here.

bOVERLAY FIRST

bINCLUDE   A               -- Include SUBS here.

bINSERT    S7              -- Insert S7 here.

bOVERLAY THIRD

bINSERT    S8              -- Insert S8 here.

bOVERLAY FOURTH

bINSERT    S9              -- Insert S9 here.

bOVERLAY FOURTH

bINSERT    S10             -- Insert S10 here.

bOVERLAY THIRD

bINSERT    S11             -- Insert S11 here.

/*
```

COMPRESSING DATA SETS

Partitioned data sets tend to grow as new members are
added and old members are replaced. Both new and replacement members are added to the end of the data set, and the

name is entered into the directory with the location where the member was stored. It is important to remember that a replacement member does not occupy the same space as the old member—the space occupied by the old member is unavailable for allocation until the data set is re-created or compressed.

As members are added and replaced, the data set may become full. The IBM-supplied utility program IEBCOPY compresses data sets to reclaim space occupied by replaced members. (Data sets with the track overflow feature cannot be compressed.) The following cataloged procedure shows how to compress data sets.[†]

//COMPRESS   PROC

//GO   EXEC   PGM=IEBCOPY,PARM=COMPRESS,

//   REGION=20K

IEBCOPY is contained in SYS1.LINKLIB. PARM=COMPRESS requests a compress operation. REGION is needed only for MVT systems.

//SYSPRINT   DD   SYSOUT=A

SYSPRINT defines a print data set.

//SYSUT1   DD   DSN=&NAME,DISP=OLD

SYSUT1 describes the data set to compress. The data set name is made a symbolic parameter for the user to code on the EXEC card. If the data set is not cataloged, the user must override SYSUT1 to include UNIT and VOL parameters.

[†] Several examples in this and the next chapter are given in the context of cataloged procedures to help the reader in writing his own procedures.

```
//SYSUT2    DD    DSN=*.SYSUT1,DISP=OLD,

//   VOL=REF=*.SYSUT1
```

> SYSUT2 describes the output data set—the same data set described by SYSUT1. (The VOL parameter is added in case SYSUT1 does not describe a cataloged data set.)

```
//SYSIN    DD    DUMMY
```

> No SYSIN is required so it is made a dummy.

Suppose now that a data set named MAPS must be compressed. If the data set is cataloged, the step consists only of

```
//   EXEC    COMPRESS,NAME=MAPS
```

If maps is not cataloged, SYSUT1 must be overridden to include the unit and volume information.

```
//   EXEC    COMPRESS,NAME=MAPS

//GO.SYSUT1    DD    UNIT=2311,VOL=SER=300
```

If a data set has exhausted its primary and secondary allocations or its directory space, compressing it will do no good; it must be re-created. IEBCOPY also re-creates data sets.

```
//RECREATE    PROC

//GO    EXEC    PGM=IEBCOPY,REGION=20K

//SYSPRINT    DD    SYSOUT=A

//SYSUT1    DD    DSN=&NAME,DISP=(OLD,DELETE)
```

> SYSUT1 describes the old data set; it is deleted because a new data set is created.

```
//SYSUT2   DD    DSN=*.SYSUT1,DISP=(,CATLG),
//   UNIT=(SYSDA,SEP=SYSUT1),
//   SPACE=&SPACE,DCB=*.SYSUT1
```

The new data set must be created on a different volume. For convenience, the value for the SPACE parameter has been made a symbolic parameter.

```
//SYSIN   DD   DUMMY
```

The MAPS data set can now be re-created and allocated more space.

```
//   EXEC   RECREATE,NAME=MAPS,
//   SPACE='(1024,(30,20,50))'
```

SUMMARY

The linkage editor is used to prepare programs for execution, retain them as members of partitioned data sets, and create subroutine libraries. This is all accomplished by a combination of JCL and linkage editor control cards. Programs too large to fit into core storage can be segmented so that the various segments overlay each other.

The IEBCOPY utility program compresses partitioned data sets to reclaim storage occupied by old members. If more space is required, IEBCOPY can allocate more space and re-create the data set.

The most often used linkage editor parameters specified by PARM on the EXEC card are:

LIST   Lists linkage editor control cards.

MAP or XREF   Produces a storage map showing relative locations of control sections; in addition XREF produces a cross-reference table.

NCAL   Cancels the automatic library call
                    mechanism.

LET   Marks load modules as executable
                    even if minor errors are found.

HIAR   Permits control sections to be directed
                    into hierarchy storage.

OVLY   Allows control sections to be segmented
                    for overlay.

The common linkage editor control cards are:

bENTRY   name

          Name the entry point.

bALIAS   name, . . .

          Assign aliases to load modules.

bINCLUDE ddname, . . .

          Include sequential data sets as linkage
          editor input.

bINCLUDE ddname(member, . . .), . . .

          Include members of partitioned data
          sets as linkage editor input.

bLIBRARY ddname(member, . . .), . . .

          List member names to look up in a
          library.

bLIBRARY (name, . . .)

          Permit external references to go
          unresolved for a run.

bLIBRARY *(name, . . .)

          Permit external references to go
          unresolved for the life of the load
          module.

bHIARCHY   1,name,. . .

> Direct control sections into hierarchy storage.

bNAME   name

> Name a load module to be added.

bNAME   name(R)

> Name a replacement load module.

bOVERLAY   name

> Name an overlay segment.

bINSERT   name, . . . ,name

> Insert control sections in an overlay structure.

CHAPTER 14

MISCELLANEOUS JCL FEATURES

This chapter wraps up some of the loose ends remaining: the command, null, and comments cards, data set maintenance, generation data groups, and multivolume data sets. Data set protection is described, as are several items effecting I/O performance. Finally, in the time-honored tradition of saving the hardest for the last, direct and indexed-sequential data sets are described.

COMMAND CARD SPECIFICATION

Operator commands are normally entered from the console, but frequently used commands can be coded on command cards to be read in through the input stream. Command cards should be limited to operator use because they affect machine operation.

The commands must be synchronized with the execution of jobs because the commands are executed as they are read in (except for SET and START in PCP systems). The command card is placed before a JOB, EXEC, null, or another command card. They cannot be continued onto a continuation card. Command cards are codes as

// command operands

The command is the operator command, and the operands depend upon the type of command. The following commands can be entered on command cards in the various systems.

PCP:	DISPLAY	SET	STOP	VARY
	MOUNT	START	UNLOAD	
MFT:	CANCEL	LOG	REPLY	STOP
	DISPLAY	MODIFY	RESET	UNLOAD
	HALT	MOUNT	SET	VARY
	HOLD	RELEASE	START	WRITELOG

MVT:	CANCEL	LOG	REPLY	STOP
	DISPLAY	MODIFY	RESET	UNLOAD
	HALT	MOUNT	SET	VARY
	HOLD	RELEASE	START	WRITELOG

Examples

    //   VARY   293,OFFLINE

    //   DISPLAY   Q

NULL CARD SPECIFICATION

The null card contains // in columns 1 and 2 with the remaining columns blank and causes the system to look for the next JOB card; any intervening cards are ignored. A null coded on distinctive colored cards is often used to help operators separate jobs. It is also used by operators to avoid having to end-of-file the card reader. The reader must be closed in order to read in the last card, and an operator command is required to reopen it. The operator can place four null cards behind the last job in the reader so that the job can be completely read in without closing the reader.

COMMENTS CARD SPECIFICATION

The comments card contains //* in columns 1 to 3, with the remaining columns containing any desired comments. They can be placed before or after any JCL card following the JOB card to help document the JCL. Comments cards are listed in the system output with *** in columns 1 through 3. Comments cards cannot be continued, but the user can code //* on the following card and resume the comments. Comments can also be coded on any JCL card by leaving a blank field after the last operand.

    //A   DD   UNIT=2311,   A 2311 DISK IS USED.

    //*THE FOLLOWING CARD REQUESTS THE

//*SPECIFIC VOLUME TO USE.

// VOL=SER=200   VOLUME 200 IS USED.

The system lists the above comments but ignores them when interpreting the JCL. The JCL is interpreted as

//A   DD   UNIT=2311,VOL=SER=200

DATA SET MAINTENANCE

Cataloged Data Sets

When a data set is cataloged, the name, unit, and the volume or volumes on which it resides are entered into a system data set named SYSCTLG. The file number is also recorded for tape data sets. Thereafter one can refer to the data set by name, without giving the unit, volume, or file number.

The catalog is usually contained entirely on the system residence volume, but it can be extended onto other volumes to save space, or if part of the catalog and its related data sets are to be moved from one computer to another. Any volume containing a portion of the catalog is called a *control volume*. Control volumes are created by the IBM-supplied IEHPROGM utility program which builds an index in an existing catalog to point to another volume. Since IEHPROGM has other important uses, the reader should be familiar with it.

The IEHPROGM Utility

The IBM-supplied utility IEHPROGM scratches data sets or members of data sets, catalogs and uncatalogs data sets, and renames data sets or members of data sets. It also builds and deletes indexes, index aliases, and indexes for generation data groups. (IEHPROGM has several other uses for system maintenance not described here.) IEHPROGM is executes as follows.

//PROC   MAINT

//GO   EXEC   PGM=IEHPROGM,REGION=48K

IEHPROGM is contained in SYS1.LINKLIB. The
REGION parameter is needed only for MVT
systems.

//SYSPRINT   DD   SYSOUT=A

A print data set is required.

//SYSTEM   DD   DSN=SYS1.SVCLIB,DISP=OLD

A DD card must define the system residence
volume. Any unique ddname can be used.

//DDn   DD   UNIT=device,VOL=SER=volume,

//   DISP=OLD

A DD card with a unique ddname must be included for each volume named by the VOL or CVOL
parameters on the data cards described below.
If DD cards are not included in the procedure,
one must include them when the procedure is
invoked. The device type (2311, SYSDA, etc.)
and the volume serial number must be coded.

The procedure is invoked as follows.

//   EXEC   MAINT

//GO.SYSIN   DD   *

[card data]

/*

Any number of data cards can be included in a run. Data
cards consist of an operations field starting in column 2 or
beyond, one or more blank fields, and an operand field. If
the data extends beyond column 71, interrupt it either in

column 71 or after any comma, code a nonblank character
in column 72 (optional if card is interrupted after a comma),
and continue it anywhere in columns 14 through 16 of the
following card. The following data cards can be included.

1. SCRATCH scratches a data set or member of a data set
    residing on direct-access storage. SCRATCH is similar
    to a disposition of DISP=(. . ,DELETE), except that
    DELETE also uncatalogs data sets, whereas SCRATCH
    does not. SCRATCH can also delete a member of a
    partitioned data set. It has one other advantage over
    DELETE: a job containing a DD card with a disposition
    of DELETE is terminated if the data set cannot be found,
    whereas IEHPROGM continues on to the next data card.

    bSCRATCH   DSNAME=name,VOL=device=volume,

    MEMBER=name,PURGE[†]

    DSNAME names the data set; it cannot be abbreviated as
    DSN. VOL names the device type and volume serial num-
    ber on which the data set resides. If the data set resides
    on several volumes, code VOL=device=(volume, . . . ,
    volume). MEMBER names a data set member to scratch.
    Omit MEMBER to scratch an entire data set. PURGE is
    needed for data sets with retention protection.

    bSCRATCH   DSNAME=MYDATA,VOL=2314=300,

    PURGE

    The MYDATA data set which resides on volume
    300 of a 2314 disk and has a retention check is
    scratched.

    bSCRATCH   DSNAME=TEST,VOL=2311=400,

    MEMBER=ONE

    Member ONE of the TEST data set residing on
    volume 400 of a 2311 disk is scratched.

[†]A b represents a blank and serves as a reminder that the
card cannot begin in column 1.

2.   RENAME changes the name or alias of data sets or
     members of data sets residing on direct-access storage,
     but does not change the catalog. UNCATLG and CATLG
     can be used to uncatalog and recatalog the new name.

     bRENAME   DSNAME=name,VOL=device=volume,

     NEWNAME=name, *MEMBER=name*

     DSNAME gives the current name of the data set, VOL
     names the device type and volume serial number on
     which the data set resides, and NEWNAME gives the
     new data set or member name. MEMBER names the
     member to rename. Omit it to rename the entire data
     set.

     bRENAME   DSNAME=MYDATA,VOL=2311=400,

     NEWNAME=TMPRY

     The MYDATA data set is renamed TMPRY.

     bRENAME   DSNAME=LIB,VOL=2311=400,

     NEWNAME=SQRT,MEMBER=SQQT

     Member SQQT of the LIB data set is renamed
     SQRT.

3.   CATLG catalogs a data set, building any higher-level
     indexes needed. For example, if A.B.C is cataloged,
     indexes are built for A and A.B. This differs from a
     disposition of DISP=(. . ,CATLG) which cannot build
     higher-level indexes.

     bCATLG   DSNAME=name,VOL=device=volume,

     CVOL=device=volume

     DSNAME names the data set. VOL names the device
     type and volume serial number containing the data set
     to catalog. If the data set resides on several volumes,
     code VOL=device=(volume, . . . ,volume). The volumes

must be listed in the order in which the data set was created on them.

If the data set resides on tape, include the file number by coding VOL=device=(volume,file, . . . ,volume,file). CVOL is seldom required; it specifies the device type and volume serial number on which the catalog search for the index is to begin. The search begins on the system residence volume if CVOL is omitted. CVOL is used to catalog data sets on other than the system residence volume.

    bCATLG   DSNAME=MYDATA,VOL=2400=(200,1)

        A data set named MYDATA residing on file 1 of tape volume 200 is cataloged.

    bCATLG   DSNAME=SHIP,VOL=2314=300

        Data set SHIP residing on volume 300 of a 2314 disk is cataloged.

4. UNCATLG uncatalogs a data set but does not remove higher-level indexes from the index structure. For example, if A.B.C is uncataloged, A and A.B remain as indexes. UNCATLG is identical to a disposition of DISP=(. . ,UNCATLG).

    bUNCATLG   DSNAME=name,*CVOL=device=volume*

    bUNCATLG   DSNAME=TAX.STATE

        The data set TAX.STATE is uncataloged. The index TAX remains.

5. BLDX builds an index for data set names. Either BLDX or CATLG must be used before data sets can be cataloged with levels of names. For example, a DD card containing DSN=TAX.STATE,DISP=(,CATLG) must have an index built for TAX. BLDX builds all higher-level indexes needed. Thus, if an index is built for A.B.C, indexes are also created for A and A.B if they do not exist. The user could then name data sets as A.name, A.B.name, and A.B.C.name.

bBLDX   INDEX=index,*CVOL=device=volume*

bBLDX   INDEX=SMITH.DATA

The user can now catalog data sets of the form SMITH.DATA.name.

6. DLTX deletes the lowest level of index. Thus, deleting A.B.C does not disturb the index for A or A.B. The index is not deleted if it has other entries; for example, deleteing A.B.C does not disturb the C index if a data set named A.B.C.D is cataloged.

bDLTX   INDEX=index,*CVOL=device=volume*

bDLTX   INDEX=SMITH.DATA

The index for SMITH.DATA is removed, leaving only the index for SMITH.

7. BLDA assigns an alias to the highest-level index. For example, if X is made an alias of Z, a data set could be referred to as either Z.B or X.B.

bBLDA   INDEX=index,ALIAS=alias,

CVOL=device=volume

bBLDX   INDEX=CITY,ALIAS=TOWN

TOWN is made an alias of the index named CITY.

8. DLTA deletes aliases created by BLDA.

bDLTA   ALIAS=alias,*CVOL=device=volume*

bDLTA   ALIAS=TOWN

The alias TOWN is deleted.

9. CONNECT connects volumes by placing a highest-level index pointing to the second control volume into the catalog. The user must create a SYSCTLG data set on the second volume and build an index in it.

bCONNECT   INDEX=index,VOL=device=volume,

CVOL=device=volume

INDEX gives the name of the index to create, and VOL
names the device type and volume serial number to
record in the index. CVOL names the volume to connect
to if the new volume is to be connected to other than the
system residence volume. Several volumes can be
connected.

bCONNECT   INDEX=JONES,VOL=2311=300

Volume 300 is made a control volume. A
SYSCTLG data set must be created on it, and
an index for JONES must be built. If the user
refers to a data set named JONES.name, the
system residence volume points to the catalog
in volume 300, and the search continues from
there.

10. RELEASE releases connected volumes by deleting the
high-level index created by CONNECT. The index is not
deleted on the second volume.

bRELEASE   INDEX=index,*CVOL=device=volume*

bRELEASE   INDEX=JONES

The index for JONES is deleted in the system
residence volume, disconnecting volume 300.

11. BLDG builds indexes for generation data groups. An
index must be built for each generation data group before it can be created. (DLTX can be used to delete
indexes.)

bBLDG   INDEX=name,ENTRIES=number,

DELETE,EMPTY,CVOL=device=volume

INDEX specifies the fully qualified name of the generation data group, and ENTRIES specifies the number of
generations to retain (maximum of 255). DELETE

scratches old generations as they are removed from the index. EMPTY removes all generations from the index when a generation overflows the number of ENTRIES specified. Only the oldest generation is removed if EMPTY is omitted.

    bBLDG   INDEX=APOLLO.EIGHT,ENTRIES=2,

        DELETE

        An index is built for APOLLO.EIGHT, and 2 generations are retained. Old generations are scratched as they are removed from the index.

Examples

    In the following example a data set named IT, cataloged on volume 200, is renamed THAT. Since the data set is cataloged, it must be uncataloged and recataloged under the new name.

    // EXEC   MAINT

    //GO.A   DD   UNIT=2314,VOL=SER=200,

    // DISP=OLD

        A DD card must define volume 200.

    //GO.SYSIN   DD   *

    bRENAME   DSNAME=IT,VOL=2314=200,

        NEWNAME=THAT

    bUNCATLG   DSNAME=IT

    bCATLG   DSNAME=THAT,VOL=2314=200

    /*

    The next example creates an index named STATE, connecting volume 500 to the system residence volume.

A data set named STATE.UNION is then cataloged on the new control volume.

```
//   EXEC   MAINT

//GO.A   DD   DSN=SYSCTLG,UNIT=2314,

//   DISP=(,KEEP),SPACE=(TRK,(10,1)),

//   VOL=SER=500,DCB=DSORG=PS
```

DD card A refers to volume 500 and creates the catalog. Ten tracks are allocated for the catalog, and an extent of 1 track is allowed.

```
//GO.SYSIN   DD   *

bCONNECT   INDEX=STATE,VOL=2314=500

bCATLG   DSNAME=STATE.UNION,VOL=2314=500,

   CVOL=2314=500

/*
```

GENERATION DATA GROUPS

A generation data group is a group of data sets that are chronologically or functionally related. They are processed periodically, often by adding a new generation, retaining previous generations, and perhaps discarding the oldest generation. For example, an income tax report is a generation data group with a new generation added each year, chronologically and functionally related to previous years. When a new generation is added, the four previous reports must be retained for legal purposes, but the fifth may be discarded.

Cataloged generation data groups are referred to by a name and a relative generation number. For example, DSN=TAX.STATE(0) would refer to the current tax report, DSN=TAX.STATE(-1) to last year's tax report, etc. A new generation is added by calling it DSN=TAX.STATE(+1).

The advantages of generation data groups are that all data sets have the same name and the system keeps track of adding and deleting successive generations. Generation data groups can be sequential, direct, or partitioned organization and can reside on any device appropriate to their organization. Generation data groups are used like any other data set except for the relative generation number in the DSN parameter.

Two steps are required to create a generation data group: a generation data group index must be created in the system catalog (SYSCTLG) with the IBM-supplied IEHPROGM utility program, and a dummy or real data set must be created on the volume containing SYSCTLG, whose data set label contains DCB subparameters for the generation data group.

As an example, a generation data group named TAX. STATE is created. The following two steps build the generation data group index and create a dummy data set.

//STEP1   EXEC   MAINT

The MAINT cataloged procedure, discussed earlier in this chapter, is used.

//GO.SYSIN   DD   *

bBLDG   INDEX=TAX.STATE,ENTRIES=5,DELETE

INDEX names the generation data group, ENTRIES specifies the number of generations to retain, and DELETE scratches old generations as they are removed from the index.

/*

//STEP2   EXEC   PGM=IEFBR14

//BUILDIT   DD   DSN=TAX.STATE,DISP=(,KEEP),

//   SPACE=(TRK,1),VOL=REF=*.STEP1.GO.SYSTEM,

//   DCB=(LRECL=80,RECFM=FB,BLKSIZE=800)

BUILDIT creates a dummy data set with appropriate DCB subparameters for the generation data group. The dummy data set must be on the volume containing the generation data group index, but cannot be cataloged. DSORG, OPTCD, KEYLEN, and RKP could also have been coded as DCB subparameters.

A generation data group can now be created.

```
//STEP1    EXEC    PGM=CREATE
```

Assume CREATE is a program which creates a data set.

```
//GEN    DD    DSN=TAX.STATE(+1),UNIT=2314,
//    DISP=(,CATLG),SPACE=(80,200)
```

The system automatically searches for a data set named TAX.STATE which contains the required DCB subparameters. It then creates a generation data set and catalogs it. A disposition of CATLG must be used for all new generation data sets. DCB subparameters can be coded on the DD card to override or add parameters from the dummy data set.

Generation (0) is always the current generation, (-1) is the preceding generation, (-2) the second generation, etc. Generation (+1) indicates a new generation and causes all generations to be pushed down one level at the end of the job. Generations are referred to by the same number throughout an entire job and the generation numbers are not updated until the job terminates.

```
//STEP1    EXEC    PGM=ONE
//INPUT    DD    DSN=TAX.STATE(0),DISP=OLD
```

This is the current generation.

```
//OUTPUT    DD    DSN=TAX.STATE(+1),

//   DISP=(,CATLG),SPACE=(80,200)
```

This creates a new generation.

```
//STEP2    EXEC    PGM=TWO

//NEXT    DD    DSN=TAX.STATE(+2),DISP=(,CATLG),

//   SPACE=(80,200)
```

This creates another new generation. It cannot
be referred to as (+1) because the indexes are
not updated until the end of the job. At that time,
(+2) becomes (0), (+1) becomes (-1), and (0)
becomes (-2).

The dummy data set can be cataloged by giving it a
different name, but it must still be placed on the volume
containing SYSCTLG.

```
//STEP2    EXEC    PGM=IEFBR14

//BUILDIT    DD    DSN=DUMMYDS,DISP=(,CATLG),

//   SPACE=(TRK,1),UNIT=2314,VOL=SER=100,

//   DCB=(LRECL=80,RECFM=FB,BLKSIZE=800)
```

Any generation data group can use DUMMYDS to supply
DCB subparameters.

```
//STEP1    EXEC    PGM=CREATE

//GEN    DD    DSN=TAX.STATE(+1),UNIT=2314,

//   DISP=(,CATLG),SPACE=(80,200),

//   DCB=(DUMMYDS,BLKSIZE=400)
```

The DCB parameter points to the data set containing the DCB subparameters. Subparameters
can also be added or overridden as shown.

MULTIVOLUME DATA SETS

Sequential data sets too large to be contained on a single tape or direct-access volume can be extended onto several volumes. The VOL parameter may request specific volumes or a maximum number of nonspecific volumes, and can specify a starting volume sequence number. The UNIT parameter may mount volumes in parallel or defer mounting until the volumes are needed. Use parallel mounting only if there are few volumes and if the volumes are processed quickly. One should defer mounting in multiprogramming systems so as not to monopolize the I/O units, especially if volume processing is slow. If there are more volumes than I/O units, mounting must be deferred.

A disposition of DISP=(MOD,CATLG) should be used when extending multivolume cataloged data sets, even if the data set is already cataloged. CATLG records new volume serial numbers in the catalog as the data set is extended.

The SPACE parameter must request extents for a new direct-access data set if it is to extend onto multiple volumes, and the track overflow feature cannot be used. A disposition of MOD is used to extend direct-access data sets onto multiple volumes.

Volume switching during writing occurs when space is exceeded on a direct-access volume, or when the end-of-volume marker is reached on tape volumes. During reading, volume switching occurs when a direct-access extent is read that resides on another volume or when an end-of-file mark or end-of-volume is encountered on tape. The following example shows the creation, extension, and retrieval of multivolume tape and direct-access data sets.

```
//STEP1   EXEC   PGM=CREATE

//A   DD   DSN=MULTI,DISP=(,CATLG),UNIT=TAPE,

//   VOL=(PRIVATE, , ,4,SER=(100,200))
```

A tape data set is created on volumes 100 and 200. The operator must assign and mount up

to 2 more volumes if they are required. All
volumes used are recorded in the catalog.

```
//B    DD    DSN=MEGA,DISP=(,CATLG),UNIT=DISK,

//    SPACE=(1600,(200,100))
```

A direct-access data set is created on nonspecific volumes.

```
//STEP2   EXEC   PGM=EXTEND

//C    DD    DSN=MULTI,DISP=(MOD,CATLG),

//    UNIT=(,P,DEFER),VOL=PRIVATE
```

All volumes of MULTI are mounted in parallel,
and if more volumes are required, the operator
must assign and mount them. Any new volume
serial numbers are entered into the catalog.

```
//D    DD    DSN=MEGA,DISP=(MOD,CATLG),

//    UNIT=(, ,DEFER)
```

The MEGA data set is extended onto volumes as
needed.

```
//STEP3   EXEC   PGM=RETRIEVE

//E    DD    DSN=MULTI,DISP=OLD,UNIT=(, ,DEFER),

//    VOL=(, ,2)
```

The volumes are mounted one at a time as
required. Processing begins on the second
volume.

```
//F    DD    DSN=MEGA,DISP=OLD,UNIT=(, ,DEFER)
```

The volumes are mounted one at a time as
required.

DATA SET PROTECTION: RETPD, EXPDT, PASSWORD

Data sets can be protected by retention checks or passwords. Operator response is required before data sets with retention protection can be modified; they cannot be scratched except by using the IEHPROGM utility discussed earlier in this chapter. The operator must respond with the password before a password-protected data set can be opened.

Retention Check: RETPD, EXPDT

The LABEL parameter coded on the DD card can assign a retention period to tape or direct-access data sets, and the operator must give his assent before a data set with an unexpired retention date can be modified. When the retention period expires, the data set becomes like any other data set without a retention check—it can be modified or scratched without the operator's approval.

System data sets should always have a retention check to prevent their being inadvertently modified or scratched. Retention checks should be used with discretion on other data sets because the operator must reply to all retention checks, and this may keep him quite busy.

To request a retention period, code LABEL=RETPD= days, specifying the number of days (9999 maximum) in the retention period. Alternatively, code LABEL=EXPDT= yyddd to request an expiration date. The yy is the two-digit year, and ddd is the three-digit day number. A retention period of zero days is assumed if retention is not specified.

Password Protection: PASSWORD

A measure of security can be given to data sets by protecting them with a password. The PASSWORD subparameter, coded when the data set is created, indicates that a password is needed to open the data set. One must record the data set name and a chosen 8-character password in a system data set named PASSWORD. The

installation will usually give the PASSWORD data set itself
password protection. The operator must respond with the
password before a data set can be opened for reading or
writing. If he fails after two tries, the job is terminated.

Password protection does not yield a high measure of
security. A clever programmer can circumvent the protection, and a second party—the operator—must know the
password. Password protection is adequate for noncritical
data sets but may not be appropriate for highly sensitive
data sets such as payroll. It is inadequate for government
classified information. To request that a data set be protected by password, code LABEL=(, ,PASSWORD).

Retention periods and password protection are usually
assigned when the data set is created, but retention periods
can be changed or removed later in any job step that opens
the data set.

PASSWORD is a positional subparameter and RETPD
and EXPDT are keyword subparameters. They may all be
coded in any combination with other LABEL subparameters.

```
//A   DD   LABEL=(2,SL,PASSWORD,IN,RETPD=30),...

//A   DD   LABEL=(, ,PASSWORD,EXPDT=99360),...
```

I/O PERFORMANCE FEATURES

Several DCB subparameters can be used to affect I/O
performance. Generally they involve a tradeoff between
storage capacity and speed of processing. The SEP and AFF
parameters are used to direct data sets onto different
channels.

Write Validity Check

The DCB subparameter OPTCD=W requests a write validity check for any direct-access data set. As data is written onto the device, it is immediately read back in to ensure it was transferred correctly from core. This verification requires an extra revolution of the device and is quite slow. Validity checking is always performed on the 2321 data cell whether requested or not, but it is not usually required for other devices.

Track Overflow

Track overflow is used to conserve direct-access storage space. The system normally writes complete blocks on each track by checking to see whether the next block will fit on the remainder of the track. If not, it writes the block on the next track. If the block size is greater than the track capacity, each block begins on a new track and continues onto as many tracks as required.

If the record overflow feature is available on the device (standard on 2314 and 2301, optional on 2302, 2303, 2311, and 2321), the DCB subparameter RECFM=FT, RECFM=FBT, etc., can request that blocks which do not fit completely on a track be partially written on that track and continued onto the next contiguous track. This saves storage space; particularly if the records are long.

For example, a 2311 disk track contains 3625 bytes. If the block size is 2000 bytes, only one block fits on a track, wasting 1625 bytes. Coding DCB=RECFM=FBT to request track overflow would allow this wasted space to be reclaimed.

The CONTIG subparameter in the SPACE parameter should be used to allocate contiguous space. Since all tracks must be contiguous, the data set cannot extend onto another volume. Track overflow cannot be used for indexed-sequential data sets, FORTRAN data sets which use backspace, and REGIONAL(3) data sets in PL/I with U or V record formats. Nor can it be used if the DCB subparameter BFTEK=E (exchange buffering) or OPTCD=C (chained scheduling) is coded.

Spanned Records

Variable-length records on direct-access devices can be spanned over blocks so that if a record does not fit within a block, it is written in segments. For example, if BLKSIZE= 800 and two 300-byte records are written, a third 600-byte record is split into a 200-byte segment to fill the block, and the remaining 400 bytes are placed in the next block. If a 1300-byte record is written next, 400 bytes fill the last block, 800 bytes are placed in the next block, and the remaining 100 bytes are placed in another block.

Spanned records are requested by coding the DCB subparameter RECFM=VS or RECFM=VBS. Spanned records allow efficient blocking to be set independent of the record size.

Standard Blocks

A data set on direct-access storage is considered to have standard blocks if all blocks (except possibly the last) have the same length, and each is completely contained on a track. Track overflow must not be requested, nor may the block size exceed track capacity.

The DCB subparameter RECFM=FS or RECFM=FBS tells the system that standard blocks are used. Since all blocks are the same length and each is completely contained on a track, all tracks contain the same number of blocks in the same relative locations. The system can then compute the exact track address of each block. This saves one rotation in reading or writing and may speed up I/O considerably.

Chained Scheduling

Several I/O operations can be initiated by a single I/O request by chaining them together. For example, a single I/O request might cause three blocks to be read into three separate buffers. The blocks are read sequentially, but no delay occurs when one block finishes and another begins.

Code the DCB subparameter OPTCD=C to request chained scheduling. Chained scheduling requires about 2000 bytes more core storage, and at least three buffers should be provided by coding the DCB subparameter BUFNO.

Chained scheduling decreases CPU time, channel start/stop time, and rotational delays on direct-access devices, but should be used only for very heavy I/O jobs. Since it tends to monopolize a channel, other data sets should be placed on other channels. Chained scheduling cannot be used if track overflow is requested, if other than simple buffering is used, or if indexed-sequential data sets, direct data sets, or paper tape readers are used.

Channel Separation: SEP, AFF

A *channel* is the path by which data is transmitted between an I/O device and core storage. If a job step is reading or writing several data sets all on the same channel, the congestion may lengthen the running time of the job. The SEP and AFF parameters can be used to direct data sets onto different channels. One should first find out what the channel configuration is on his computer before using SEP or AFF.

To separate a data set from a channel used by other data sets in the same step, code SEP=ddname or SEP=(ddname, . . . ,ddname). The ddname is the name of 1 to 8 previous DD cards in the same step.

```
//STEP1   EXEC   PGM=ALPHA

//A   DD   UNIT=2314, . . .

//B   DD   UNIT=2314,SEP=A, . . .
```

The data set described by the B DD card is separated from the channel used by the A DD card.

```
//C   DD   UNIT=2314,SEP=(A,

//   B), . . .
```

C is separated from the channels used by A and
B. The ddnames can be interrupted for continuation after a complete ddname, including the
comma following it.

//D   DD   UNIT=2314,SEP=(A,B), . . .

D has the same channel separation as C.

The AFF parameter is used to copy a SEP parameter
from a previous DD card by coding AFF=ddname. The DD
card named D in the above step could also be coded as

//D   UNIT=2314,AFF=C, . . .

D is not necessarily placed on the same channel
as C; it merely uses the same SEP parameter.

Channel separation requests are ignored if the possibil-
ity for separation does not exist (e.g., not enough channels),
if a unit is requested by hardware address, if a volume is
premounted and recognized by the automatic volume recognition feature, or if an old data set resides on a permanently
mounted volume.

Channel separation should be used with discretion. In a
multiprogramming environment where several jobs are
running concurrently, the impact of a single job upon channel
usage may not be significant. Channel separation restricts
unit assignment and may result in unnecessary dismounting
of volumes. Channel separation should be used only for new
data sets, or old data sets on mountable volumes, where a
significant savings is expected.

DIRECT DATA SETS

Direct data organization permits each record to be
accessed directly, without regard to its position relative to
other records. Each record contains a key that describes
the record's location in the data set. The addressing can be
direct or indirect.

For *direct addressing*, the key contains an absolute or
relative track address. A *relative track address* is relative
to the first track in the data set. The key can also contain
the *relative record number* so that one can compute the
track address, knowing the address of the first track and the
number of records per track.

The second method of direct data organization, *indirect
addressing*, is more complex. One must perform some
mathematical manipulation on the key to compute the track
address. The method of organizing the data and performing
the conversion of the key into a record address is left to the
user.

Direct data sets can be created in COBOL (ORGANIZA-
TION RELATIVE or DIRECT, ACCESS RANDOM), FORTRAN
(DEFINE FILE), PL/I (REGIONAL DIRECT), and assembly
language.

Direct data set DD cards differ from sequential data
sets only in that the SPLIT parameter cannot be used for
space allocation and that different DCB subparameters may
be needed—DSORG=DA or DSORG=DAU must be coded to tell
the system it is a direct data set. If the records are written
with keys, KEYLEN must be coded to specify the key length
in bytes. Keys must be of a fixed length and be in every
record.

Direct data sets are usually processed randomly.
Records are read deleted, added, or replaced, and the next
record processed does not depend upon the position of the
record being processed. Direct data sets can, of course,
be processed sequentially if one knows the key of each
record and then orders the keys sequentially. Individual
records can be located faster with direct organization than
with indexed-sequential organization because no index
search is required. However direct organization is slower
if it is processed sequentially because the queued-access
technique cannot be used—each record is located when it is
needed, and the transmission of records cannot be overlapped with the processing of the records.

INDEXED-SEQUENTIAL DATA SETS

Indexed-sequential data sets can be created by assembly language, COBOL, PL/I, and RPG. An indexed-sequential data set can be accessed sequentially or directly. Each record must contain an identifying key, and the records are arranged in collating sequence on the keys.

For example, suppose a public library maintains a data set containing a record for each book and there are 150,000 books. Each record might contain the title, author, publisher, and other information about the book. The title could be used as the key to arrange the books in alphabetic order.

Sequential processing works well when all the records must be processed, as they would for an inventory, but suppose a book titled "Zelda's Zilch" requires a change. When a single record must be changed, direct accessing is much faster. Likewise books are added and deleted from the data set directly without having to process the entire data set.

Records

Indexed-sequential data sets can be created only on direct-access devices; they are composed of records, blocks, tracks, and cylinders. A record has the following format.

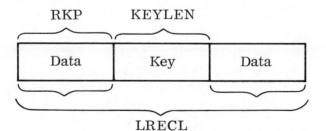

RKP (the relative location of the key within the record), KEYLEN (the key length; KEYLEN=255 is maximum), and LRECL (the record length) are all DCB subparameters whose values are given in bytes. Each record can be flagged as active (to be processed) or inactive (to reserve space or indicate a deleted record). In our library example, a record might consist first of 40 characters for the title, then 20 characters for the author, 20 more characters for the publisher, and finally 20 characters for other information. (RKP=0, KEYLEN=40, and LRECL=100; RKP=0 is assumed if omitted.) The records are placed on the tracks in the order of the key—the book title.

Blocks

Several records can be placed in a block to conserve direct-access storage space and to very significantly increase processing speeds. The key of the last record in the block is appended to the front of the block to aid in locating a particular key. A block has the following format.

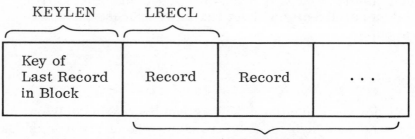

Tracks

As many integral blocks are placed on a track as space permits. The total number of tracks containing records is called the *prime area*. The tracks must be arranged on cylinders, but the cylinders need not be contiguous.

A track index is automatically created for each cylinder on the first tracks of the cylinder. Two entries are required for each track; a normal entry pointing to the track, and an overflow entry pointing to an overflow area in case the records overflow the track.

As records are added to a data set, all the records
following it on the track are moved down to make room.
Any records forced off the track are placed in an overflow
area, and an appropriate entry is made in the track index.
Several records forced off a track are linked together.
Records in overflow areas are unblocked and require an
extra 10 bytes for the link field. A deleted record is simply
flagged as inactive to save a time-consuming moveup operation, but it is discarded if forced off a track. Tracks can
also be flagged as inactive in the track index to reserve
space. The track index entry has the following format.

KEYLEN   10 Bytes

Key of Last Record in Track	Location of Track

Overflow Areas

Two overflow areas, a cylinder overflow area and an
independent overflow area, can be reserved either singu-
larly or in combination. A *cylinder overflow area* is reserved by allocating a specified number of tracks on each
cylinder for overflow. Any records overflowing tracks on
that cylinder are placed in this area. This has the advantage of minimizing access time by ensuring that overflow
records are placed on the same cylinder. However, cylinder overflow areas are not shared so that if an area for one
cylinder becomes full, unused space on other cylinders
cannot be used.

An *independent overflow area* can be shared by all
cylinders, conserving storage space. The independent overflow area is given a separate space allocation called the
overflow area. The price is increased access time because
an independent overflow area must be placed on a different
cylinder from the original data.

The best method of reserving space for overflow
records is to set the cylinder overflow area at a reasonable
value and to provide an independent overflow area to contain
records when cylinder overflow areas become full.

Cylinder Index

A *cylinder index* is automatically created if the data set
resides on more than a single cylinder. An entry is added
for each cylinder and has the same format as the track index
entries.

Master Index

One can request that an entry be created in a *master
index* for each specified number of tracks of cylinder index.
A master index obviates having to search the entire cylinder
index to locate a record, allowing one to focus quickly on the
relevant cylinder indexes, and is particularly useful for
large data sets. A second- and third-level master index are
also created for every specified number of tracks of lower-
level index. Assembly language programs can request that
the master index be held in core storage to decrease the
search time. The area reserved for the master index and
cylinder index is called the *index area*. The format of each
master index entry is the same as for track index entries.

Accessing Indexed-Sequential Data Sets

The following steps show how the system locates a
record 'directly' with a key.

1.   If a master index does not exist, the search begins
      at step 2. Otherwise the master index is searched
      for the first entry containing a key greater than the
      key desired. If the master index points to a lower
      index, it is searched in a similar manner. Even-
      tually a master index entry is found that points to
      a cylinder index known to contain the desired key.

2. If there is no cylinder index, the data set must be contained on a single cylinder and the search continues at step 3. Otherwise the cylinder index is searched for the first entry with a key greater than the key desired. When found, that entry will point to a cylinder containing a record with the desired key.
3. The track index occupying the first tracks of the cylinder is searched for the first entry with a key greater than the key wanted. The track index points to a track containing the record.
4. The track is then searched for the record with the desired key.

To speed up the search, the master and cylinder indexes should both be placed on the same cylinder. Search time is also decreased by locating the cylinders containing the master and cylinder indexes on a separate volume from the prime area. If it must be on the same volume, it should be placed on a cylinder contiguous to the prime area or, better yet, on cylinders in the middle of the prime area. (The prime area would then not be contiguous.)

An indexed-sequential data set is processed sequentially by locating each cylinder in the cylinder index and processing all the tracks sequentially. Overflow tracks greatly increase sequential processing times, particularly if they are on independent overflow areas.

Creating Indexed-Sequential Data Sets

An indexed-sequential data set may require space allocation for three separate areas: the prime area, the index area, and the independent overflow area. A prime area must always be provided, but the index and independent overflow areas are optional. The DD cards for an indexed-sequential data set must be coded in the following order.

```
//ddname   DD   DSN=name(INDEX), . . .

//  DD   DSN=name(PRIME), . . .

//  DD   DSN=name(OVFLOW), . . .
```

The ddname is coded on the first DD card only. INDEX, PRIME, and OVFLOW must always be coded in that order, maintaining the order if INDEX or OVFLOW is omitted. A temporary data set is indicated by coding DSN=&&name(. .) on each DD card. If the data set consists of only a prime area, PRIME need not be coded; that is, DSN=name and DSN=name(PRIME) are identical if the data set is created with one DD card.

The DCB subparameter DSORG=IS or DSORG=ISU must be coded on each DD card. Any other DCB subparameters coded on one card must be consistent with DCB subparameters coded on the other cards. Volume mounting cannot be deferred so that UNIT=(. . , . . ,DEFER) is not permitted.

The SPACE parameter

The SPACE parameter must be coded in one of two ways for indexed-sequential data sets, but the same method must be used on all DD cards describing the data set. To request an amount of space, code

SPACE=(CYL,(quantity, ,*index*), ,*CONTIG*)

Space is allocated on cylinders. The index specifies the number of cylinders to reserve for the index area if it is to be imbedded in the prime area. CONTIG causes contiguous cylinders to be allocated and must be coded on all DD cards if it is coded on one. If more than one unit is requested, the specified space is allocated on each volume. Specific tracks can be requested by coding

SPACE=(ABSTR,(quantity,address,*index*))

Space is allocated on the absolute tracks requested. The quantity must be equivalent to an integral number of cylinders, and the address must be the first track on a cylinder other than the first cylinder of the volume. If more than one unit is requested, space is allocated beginning at the address specified and continuing through the volume onto the next volume until the request has been satisfied. The volume table of contents on the second and succeeding volumes must

be contained on the first of each volume. The index specifies the number of tracks to reserve for the index area. The
specific track method of requesting space is often used for
indexed-sequential data sets because the relative placement
of the prime, index, and overflow areas affects access time.

Indexed-sequential data sets can be cataloged with
DISP=(,CATLG) only if the data set is created with a single
DD card. The IEHPROGM utility described earlier in this
chapter can catalog indexed-sequential data sets defined by
more than one DD card, provided that all DD cards request
the same type of unit.

Example of space allocation

Since space allocation for indexed-sequential data sets
is quite complicated, the library example suggested earlier
is used to show each step involved. Tables 3 and 4 in Chapter 11 provide the formulas for space allocation:

$$\text{Blocks/track} = 1 + \frac{\text{track capacity} - Bn}{Bi}$$

where Bi is any block but the last and Bn is the last block on
the track. Track capacity, Bi, and Bn depend upon the type
of device. Our example will use a 2314 disk and so the
equation is

$$\text{Blocks/track} = 1 + \frac{7294 - (45 + \text{KEYLEN} + \text{BLKSIZE})}{146 + 1.043(\text{KEYLEN} + \text{BLKSIZE})}$$

The library data set contains 150,000 records, each
100 bytes long. The title is used as the key and contains 40
bytes. Assume there are 20 records per block so the data
set has DCB subparameters of KEYLEN=40, LRECL=100,
and BLKSIZE=2000.

Prime area

The prime area may reside on more than one volume of
the same device type. Any unused space in the last cylinders

of the prime area is used as an independent overflow area. The prime area is allocated in cylinders and the first tracks in each cylinder are used for track indexes. (The first volume allocated to the prime area cannot be the volume from which the system is loaded.)

1. Compute the number of records per track in the prime area.

$$\text{Blocks/track} = 1 + \frac{7294 - (45 + \text{KEYLEN} + \text{BLKSIZE})}{146 + 1.043\,(\text{KEYLEN} + \text{BLKSIZE})}$$

$$= 1 + \frac{7294 - (45 + 40 + 2000)}{146 + 1.043\,(40 + 2000)} = 3.29$$

which truncates to 3 blocks per track.

Records/track = (blocks/track)(records/block) =

3(20) = 60

2. Compute the tracks per cylinder needed to contain the track indexes. Records are unblocked and consist of a key plus 10 bytes of data.

Track index entries/track =

$$1 + \frac{7294 - (45 + \text{KEYLEN} + 10)}{146 + 1.043\,(\text{KEYLEN} + 10)}$$

$$= 1 + \frac{7294 - (45 + 40 + 10)}{146 + 1.043\,(40 + 10)} = 37.33$$

which truncates to 37 entries per track.

Tracks/cylinder for track index =

$$\frac{2\,(\text{tracks/cylinder}) + 1}{\text{index entries/track} + 2}$$

Table 3 in Chapter 11 tells us that a 2314 disk has 20 tracks per cylinder.

Tracks/cylinder for track index =

$$\frac{2(20) + 1}{37 + 2} = \frac{41}{39}$$

The first 1-2/39 tracks of each cylinder are used for track indexes. If the unused space (37/39) on the second track can contain blocks of data, it must be considered in determining the number of data records per cylinder.

Blocks/partial track =

$$1 + \frac{(37/39)(7294) - (45 + 40 + 2000)}{146 + 1.043(40 + 2000)} = 3.13$$

which truncates to 3 blocks.

The first two tracks of each cylinder will contain 3(20) or 60 records in addition to the track index.

3. Compute the space (if any) to allocate for a cylinder overflow area. Overflow records are unblocked and require an extra 10-byte link field.

Overflow records/track =

$$1 + \frac{7294 - (45 + KEYLEN + LRECL + 10)}{146 + 1.043(KEYLEN + LRECL + 10)}$$

$$= 1 + \frac{7294 - (45 + 40 + 100 + 10)}{146 + 1.043(40 + 100 + 10)} = 24.47$$

which truncates to 24 overflow records per track.

But for how many overflow records per cylinder should we reserve space? The size depends upon how often we add records and how critical storage space and accessing times are. Faster access times are achieved at a cost in storage space for a larger cylinder overflow area. Suppose we expect to change 5% of the records, and we wish most of these changes to go in the cylinder overflow area to minimize access time. By roughly approximating the number of records per cylinder and taking 5% of this number, we can estimate the number of cylinder overflow records and tracks per cylinder needed.

Overflow records/cylinder =

(data tracks/cylinder)(data records/track) percent

But we cannot compute the number of data records per cylinder until we know the number of overflow records, and the number of overflow records depends upon the number of data records. However we can approximate the number of data records fairly accurately. A 2314 cylinder contains 20 tracks, but about 1 track is used for track indexes, and at least 1 track will be used for the cylinder overflow area (we can recalculate if this estimate is too far off), leaving about 18 tracks for data.

Overflow records/cylinder =

$18(60)0.05 = 54$ records/cylinder

Overflow tracks/cylinder =

$$\frac{\text{overflow records/cylinder}}{\text{overflow records/track}} = \frac{54}{24} = 2.25$$

which we can round to 2 tracks per cylinder (we need not be exact).

The DCB subparameters OPTCD=Y and CYLOFL=tracks are coded on the DD cards defining the data set to request cylinder overflow and reserve tracks on each cylinder. (CYLOFL=99 is maximum.)

4. Compute the total number of cylinders needed for the prime area.

Records/cylinder = (records/track)(tracks of data) +

records of data in track index

Tracks of data = tracks/cylinder - tracks for index -

tracks for overflow

Records/cylinder = 60(20 - 2 - 2) + 60 = 1020

$$\text{Total cylinders} = \frac{\text{total records}}{\text{records/cylinder}} = \frac{150{,}000}{1020} = 147.06$$

which rounds up to 148 cylinders.

Index area

A cylinder index area is required if the prime area occupies more than 1 cylinder. A master index area can also be requested to decrease search time. The index area, comprising the cylinder and master indexes, can be imbedded in the prime area, placed in any unused space at the end of the prime area, or allocated space with a separate DD card. If space is allocated separately, the index area need not be on the same device type as the prime area, but it must be contained on a single volume. Any unused space left in the last cylinders of the index area is used for an independent overflow area, provided that it is the same device type as the prime area.

5. Compute space required for cylinder index (if the prime area occupies more than 1 cylinder). The same formula used to compute track entries is used for cylinder entries, and since we are using the same type of device, there are 37 cylinder index entries per track.

Tracks for cylinder index =

$$\frac{\text{number of cylinders} + 1}{\text{entries/track}} = \frac{148 + 1}{37} = 4.03$$

6. Compute space required for master index (if desired). To request a master index, code the DCB subparameters OPTCD=M and NTM=tracks. NTM specifies the number of tracks of cylinder index per master index entry (NTM=99 is maximum). Now we must decide how many

tracks of cylinder index per master index entry are needed. This involves a trade between storage space and access time. Smaller NTM values decrease access time and increase storage requirements. Perhaps 2 tracks of cylinder index per master index entry is a happy compromise. The master index entries are the same size as cylinder index entries so that 37 entries will fit on a track.

Tracks for first-level master index =

$$\frac{\text{cylinder index tracks/NTM} + 1}{\text{index entries/track}}$$

(If cylinder index tracks is greater than NTM.)

Tracks for second-level master index =

$$\frac{\text{tracks for first level/NTM} + 1}{\text{index entries/track}}$$

(If tracks for first level is greater than NTM.)

Tracks for third-level master index =

$$\frac{\text{tracks for second level/NTM} + 1}{\text{index entries/track}}$$

(If tracks for second level is greater than NTM.)

Tracks for first-level master index =

$$\frac{4.03/2 + 1}{37} = 0.08$$

Second- and third-level master indexes are not required and so the total index space is (4.03 + 0.08) or 4.11, which rounds up to 5 tracks.

Independent overflow area

The independent overflow area contains records overflowing from the cylinder overflow area. The independent overflow area can be allocated with a separate DD card, but must be the same device type as the prime area and must be contained on a single volume.

7. Compute the size of the independent overflow area (if desired). The size of the independent overflow area depends upon how often records are added or changed and how much space was reserved for the cylinder overflow area. We allowed 5% for cylinder overflow; perhaps 5% is appropriate for the independent overflow area also.

Independent overflow area cylinders =

prime area cylinders (percent) = 148(0.05) = 7.4

which rounds to 7 cylinders (again we need not be exact).

To summarize the space requirements, 148 cylinders are needed for the prime area, 5 tracks for the index area, and 7 cylinders for the independent overflow area. Since a 2314 volume has only 200 cylinders, perhaps the prime area should be allocated on more than one volume.

Using Indexed-Sequential Data Sets

To retrieve an indexed-sequential data set, code DSN, UNIT, VOL, and DISP. The DCB subparameter DSORG=IS or DSORG=ISU must be coded unless the data set was passed. UNIT and VOL can be omitted if the data set is contained on a single volume and was passed or cataloged. The DSN parameter is coded without the terms INDEX, PRIME, or OVFLOW. A separate DD card must be coded if the index area resides on a different unit. The following examples show various ways space can be allocated for the library data set, and the means of coding DD cards to retrieve the data set.

1. Separate areas for index, prime, and independent over-
    flow.

```
//STEP1    EXEC    PGM=CREATE

//A    DD    DSN=LIB(INDEX),DISP=(,KEEP),

//    SPACE=(CYL,1, ,CONTIG),UNIT=2314,

//    VOL=SER=200,DCB=(DSORG=IS,OPTCD=YM,

//    CYLOFL=2,NTM=2)
```

The data set is named LIB. Only 5 tracks are
needed for the index area, but all space must be
allocated in integral cylinders. CONTIG must be
coded on all DD cards if it is coded on any one
of them.

```
//    DD    DSN=LIB(PRIME),DISP=(,KEEP),

//    SPACE =(CYL,74, ,CONTIG),UNIT=(2314,2),

//    VOL=SER=(300,400),DCB=*.A
```

Seventy-four cylinders (148 total) are allocated
on each of the 2 volumes for the prime area.

```
//    DD    DSN=LIB(OVFLOW),DISP=(,KEEP),

//    SPACE=(CYL,7, ,CONTIG),UNIT=2314,

//    VOL=SER=500,DCB=*.A
```

DCB subparameters must be consistent on all
the DD cards.

```
//STEP2    EXEC    PGM=READ

//B    DD    DSN=LIB,DCB=DSORG=IS,DISP=OLD,

//    UNIT=(2314,4),VOL=SER=(200,300,400,500)
```

The volume serial numbers must be listed in the
same order when the data set is retrieved as
they were when the data set was created.

2. Separate index area, independent overflow area at end
of the prime area.

```
//STEP1   EXEC   PGM=CREATE

//A   DD   DSN=LIB(INDEX), . . .

//  DD   DSN=LIB(PRIME),DISP=(,KEEP),

//  SPACE =(CYL,78, ,CONTIG),UNIT=(2314,2),

//  VOL=SER=(300,400),DCB=*.A
```

The prime area space is increased to provide
room for the independent overflow area.

```
//STEP2   EXEC   PGM=READ

//B   DD   DSN=LIB,DCB=DSORG=IS,DISP=OLD,

//  UNIT=(2314,3),VOL=SER=(200,300,400)
```

3. Index area placed at end of prime area, separate
independent overflow area.

```
//STEP1   EXEC   PGM=CREATE

//A   DD   DSN=LIB(PRIME),DISP=(,KEEP),

//  SPACE=(CYL,74, ,CONTIG),UNIT=(2314,2),

//  VOL=SER=(300,400),DCB=(DSORG=IS,OPTCD=YM,

//  CYLOFL=2,NTM=2)

//  DD   DSN=LIB(OVFLOW), . . .

//STEP2   EXEC   PGM=READ
```

```
//B   DD   DSN=LIB,DISP=OLD,DCB=DSORG=IS,
//   UNIT=(2314,3),VOL=SER=(300,400,500)
```

4. Imbedded index area, separate independent overflow
    area.

```
//STEP1   EXEC   PGM=CREATE
//A   DD   DSN=LIB(PRIME),DISP=(,KEEP),
//   SPACE=(CYL,(149, ,1), ,CONTIG),UNIT=2314,
//   VOL=SER=400,DCB=(DSORG=IS,OPTCD=YM,
//   CYLOFL=2,NTM=2)
```

> A 1-cylinder index area is imbedded in the prime
> area. Since the index area must be contained on
> a single volume, the prime area must be allocated
> on one volume.

```
//   DD   DSN=LIB(OVFLOW), . . .
//STEP2   EXEC   PGM=READ
//B   DD   DSN=LIB,DCB=DSORG=IS,DISP=OLD,
//   UNIT=(2314,2),VOL=SER=(400,500)
```

5. Index area placed at end of prime area, independent
    overflow area placed at end of index area.

```
//STEP1   EXEC   PGM=CREATE
//A   DD   DSN=LIB,DISP=(,CATLG),
//   SPACE=(CYL,78, ,CONTIG),UNIT=(2314,2),
//   VOL=SER=(300,400),DCB=(DSORG=IS,OPTCD=YM,
//   CYLOFL=2,NTM=2)
```

The prime area is increased to reserve room for the index and independent overflow areas. Since the data set is created with a single DD card, it can be cataloged.

```
//STEP2    EXEC    PGM=READ

//B     DD     DSN=LIB,DCB=DSORG=IS,DISP=OLD
```

6. Imbedded index area, independent overflow area at end of prime area.

```
//STEP1    EXEC    PGM=CREATE

//A     DD     DSN=&&LIB,DISP=(,PASS),

//    SPACE=(CYL,(156, ,1), ,CONTIG),UNIT=2314,

//    VOL=SER=300,DCB=(DSORG=IS,OPTCD=YM,

//    CYLOFL=2,NTM=2)
```

The prime area is increased to reserve room for the imbedded index area and the independent overflow area at the end. The data set must be contained on a single volume. Indexed-sequential data sets can be temporary, and they can be passed if they are created with a single DD card.

```
//STEP2    EXEC    PGM=READ

//B     DD     DSN=*.STEP1.A,DISP=(OLD,DELETE)
```

The DSORG=IS subparameter is not needed if the indexed-sequential data set is passed.

Any one of the six methods may be used to create an indexed-sequential data set. The particular method depends upon the relative sizes of the prime, index, and independent overflow areas, and where these areas are placed.

Index area on a different unit

The index area can be placed on a unit different from the prime area. To take an example, suppose we wished to place the index on a 2311 disk. We must first recompute the space requirement. The formula in Table 4, Chapter 11, for 2311 disk space is

$$\text{Blocks/track} = 1 + \frac{3625 - (20 + \text{KEYLEN} + \text{LRECL})}{81 + 1.049(\text{KEYLEN} + \text{LRECL})}$$

$$\text{Index entries/track} = 1 + \frac{3625 - (20 + 40 + 10)}{81 + 1.049(40 + 10)} = 27.64$$

which truncates to 27 entries per track.

$$\text{Tracks for cylinder index} = \frac{148 + 1}{27} = 5.52$$

$$\text{Tracks for master index} = \frac{5.52/2 + 1}{27} = 0.14$$

Second- and third-level master indexes are not required and so the total index space is (5.52 + 0.14) = 5.66 tracks. A 2311 cylinder contains 10 tracks so that 1 cylinder will be ample. For an example showing creation and retrieval of an indexed-sequential data set residing on two different types of units, let us suppose one already exists, but that the overflow area has become full.

Recreating indexed-sequential data sets

Indexed-sequential data sets must be periodically reorganized because the overflow areas become filled, and overflow records take longer to process. The IBM-supplied utility program IEBISAM copies an indexed-sequential data set, deletes records marked for deletion, and reorganizes the records on the prime area by emptying the overflow areas. IEBISAM is executed as follows:

```
//GO    EXEC    PGM=IEBISAM,PARM=COPY,

//    REGION=12K
```

IEBISAM is contained in SYS1.LINKLIB. PARM=
COPY tells the program to copy the data set.
(IEBISAM has other uses beyond the scope of
this manual.) The REGION parameter is required only in MVT systems.

```
//SYSPRINT    DD    SYSOUT=A
```

A print data set is required.

```
//SYSUT1    DD    DSN=LIB,DCB=DSORG=IS,
//    DISP=(OLD,DELETE),UNIT=2311,VOL=SER=100
//    DD    DSN=LIB,DCB=DSORG=IS,UNIT=(2314,3),
//    DISP=(OLD,DELETE),VOL=SER=(300,400,500)
```

SYSUT1 describes the data set to reorganize.
Two DD cards are needed to describe an indexed-
sequential data set contained on two different
device types. Since the data set is copied, we
can delete the old copy.

```
//SYSUT2    DD    DSN=LIB(INDEX),DISP=(,KEEP),
//    SPACE=(CYL,1),UNIT=(2311,SEP=SYSUT1),
//    DCB=*.SYSUT1
//    DD    DSN=LIB(PRIME),DISP=(,KEEP),
//    SPACE=(CYL,74),UNIT=(2314,2,SEP=SYSUT1),
//    DCB=*.SYSUT1
//    DD    DSN=LIB(OVFLOW),DISP=(,KEEP),
//    SPACE=(CYL,7),UNIT=(2314,SEP=SYSUT1),
//    DCB=*.SYSUT1
```

SYSUT2 describes the re-created data set. It must
be placed on different volumes from the old data
set.

SUMMARY

This chapter completes the discussion of Job Control Language. It is apparent from the size of this manual that JCL can be quite complicated. However it can also be very useful.

Many JCL details are difficult to remember, especially if they are seldom used. Appendix C contains a brief summary of each JCL card for a quick reference. The appendix also refers to the pages in the text where the JCL parameters are discussed in detail.

APPENDIX A
DCB SUBPARAMETERS

BFALN — Fullword (F) or doubleword (D) boundary alignment of each buffer.

BFTEK — Type of buffering (simple or exchange) to be supplied by the control program (S or E). (Queued-sequential access method only.)

BLKSIZE — Maximum block size in bytes (a number.) (Cannot be used with basic indexed-sequential access method.)

BUFL — Length, in bytes, of each buffer to be obtained for a buffer pool (a number).

BUFNO — Number of buffers to be assigned to the data control block. (Cannot be used with indexed-sequential access methods.)

BUFRQ — Number of buffers to be read in advance from the direct-access-device queue. (For use with teleprocessing access methods.)

CODE — Paper tape code in which the data is punched.

    I - IBM BCD perforated tape and transmission code (8 tracks)
    F - Friden (7 tracks)
    B - Burroughs (7 tracks)
    C - National Cash Register (8 tracks)
    A - ASCII (8 tracks)
    T - Teletype (5 tracks)
    N - No conversion

CPRI — Relative priority to be given to sending and receiving operations. (For use with teleprocessing access methods.)

CYLOFL   Number of tracks to be reserved on each cylinder to hold records that overflow from other tracks on that cylinder. (Queued indexed-sequential access method only.)

DEN   Tape recording density.

               0 - 200 bits/inch (7-track only)
               1 - 556 bits/inch (7-track only)
               2 - 800 bits/inch
               3 - 1600 bits/inch (9-track only)

               For 7-track tapes, all information on the reel must be written in the same density (i.e., labels, data, tapemarks). Do not specify DEN for a SYSOUT data set.

DSORG   Organization of the data set.

               PS   - Physical Sequential
               PSU - Physical Sequential Unmovable
               PO   - Partitioned Organization
               POU - Partitioned Organization Unmovable
               IS   - Indexed Sequential
               ISU - Indexed Sequential Unmovable
               DA   - Direct Access
               DAU - Direct Access Unmovable

EROPT   Option to be executed if an error occurs. (Queued-sequential access method only.)

               ACC - Accept
               SKP - Skip
               ABE - Abnormal End of task

GDSORG   Organization of a graphic data set. (For use with the graphics access method.)

GNCP   Maximum number of I/O macro instructions that will be issued before a WAIT macro instruction. (For use with the graphics access method.)

HIARCHY   The number of the storage hierarchy in which
the buffer pool is to be formed (0 or 1).

INTVL   Number of seconds of intentional delay between
passes through a polling list. (For use with
teleprocessing access methods.)

KEYLEN   Length, in bytes, of a key (a number). (Cannot be used with basic indexed-sequential or
queued-sequential access methods.)

LIMCT   Search limits, in tracks or blocks, if the
extended search option (OPTCD=E) is chosen
(a number). (Basic direct access method
only.)

LRECL   Actual or maximum length, in bytes, of a
logical record (a number). For variable-
length spanned records where the logical
record length exceeds 32,756, specify
LRECL=X. (Cannot be used with basic
indexed-sequential or basic direct access
methods.)

MODE   Mode of operation (column binary or EBCDIC)
for a card reader or card punch. (C or E.)

NCP   Maximum number of READ or WRITE macro
instructions issued before a CHECK macro
instruction (number of channel programs).
(Cannot be used with direct or sequential
access methods.)

NTM   Number of tracks to be contained in the master
index of an indexed-sequential data set;
required when a master index (OPTCD=M) is
requested. Through this master index facility,
extensive serial search through a large cylinder index can be avoided.

OPTCD   Optional services to be provided by the control
program.

W - Perform a WRITE validity check.

F - Feedback will be requested in READ or WRITE macro instructions in the program.

E - Use extended search.

R   For the basic direct access method, relative block addresses are used. For the queued indexed-sequential access method, place reorganization criteria information in the RORG1, RORG2, and RORG3 fields of the DCB.

T - Request user totaling facility.

A - Actual addresses are used.

C - Use chained scheduling method.

M - Create master indexes as required.

Y - Use cylinder overflow areas.

I - Use independent overflow area.

L - Delete marked records when new records are added to the data set.

U - Unblock data check (universal character set).

Z - Reduced error recovery procedure occurs for an input data set on magnetic tape when a data check is encountered (sequential access method and EXCP). Should be requested only when it is known that the tape contains errors and not all records need to be processed.

PRTSP   Line spacing on a printer (0, 1, 2, or 3).

RECFM   Characteristics of the records in a data set. These can be used in combination, as required.

U - Undefined-length records.

V - Variable-length records.

F - Fixed-length records.

B - Blocked records.

T - Track overflow used.

S - With fixed-length records, standard blocks, no truncated blocks or unfilled tracks within the data set. With variable-length records, local records spanned over more than one physical block.

A - ASA control character.
M - Machine code control character.

RKP   Relative position of the first byte of the record
key within each logical record (a number).
(Indexed-sequential access method only.)

SOWA   Size, in bytes, of the user-provided work
areas. (For use with teleprocessing access
methods.)

STACK   Stacker bin on a card reader or card punch
(1 or 2).

TRTCH   Tape recording technique for 7-track tape.
These values can be used in combination.

                  C   - Data conversion feature
                  E   - Even parity
                  T   - BCD to EBCDIC translation when
                             reading; and EBCDIC to BCD when
                             writing. Odd parity.
               ET - BCD to EBCDIC translation when
                             reading; and EBCDIC to BDC when
                             writing. Even parity.

APPENDIX B
CONTROL CHARACTERS

Records may contain a control character, to control a printer or punch, as the first byte of data in each record. (The first byte of data for variable-length records is the fifth byte of the record, immediately after the 4-byte record descriptor.) The control character itself is not printed or punched.

The control character may be either a machine code (RECFM= . .M) or an ASA control character (RECFM= . .A). A machine control character is dependent upon the device; refer to the appropriate IBM system Reference Library publication describing the device. ASA control characters are as follows:

EBCDIC Character	Action before Writing Record
b	Space one line before printing (blank code)
0	Space two lines before printing
-	Space three lines before printing
+	Suppress space before printing
1	Skip to channel 1
2	Skip to channel 2
3	Skip to channel 3
4	Skip to channel 4
5	Skip to channel 5
6	Skip to channel 6
7	Skip to channel 7
8	Skip to channel 8
9	Skip to channel 9
A	Skip to channel 10
B	Skip to channel 11
C	Skip to channel 12
V	Select punch pocket 1
W	Select punch pocket 2

These control characters include those defined by USASI FORTRAN. If any other character is specified, it is interpreted as 'b' or V, depending on the device being used, and no error indication is returned.

APPENDIX C
JOB CONTROL LANGUAGE SUMMARY

JOB CARD (PP. 38-47)

A single JOB card must be the first card in a job.

//jobname   JOB

// *(acct number,additional acct information),name,*

// *keyword parameters*

job name (pp. 39-40)—unique 1- to 8-character name (A to Z, 0 to 9, @, $, #).

acct number, additional acct information (pp. 40-41)—supply accounting information to job as specified by installation; may be mandatory.

name (pp. 41-42)—1- to 20-character name for identification; may be mandatory. Enclose name in apostrophes if it contains (blank , / ') (* $ + - =).

MSGLEVEL=(jcl,allocations) (pp. 42-43)—print JCL cards and allocation messages. Code jcl as 0 to print JOB cards only, as 1 to print all JCL cards, and as 2 to print only JCL cards in input stream. Code allocations as 0 to suppress allocation messages, and as 1 to print allocation messages.

PRTY=priority (pp. 43-44)—MFT, MVT only. Numeric job priority. Can range from 0 to 13; 13 is highest. Installation sets default.

MSGCLASS=class (p. 44)—MFT,MVT only. Output class for system messages; MSGCLASS =A is default.

CLASS=class (pp. 44-45)—MFT, MVT only. Job class is single letter (A to O) as set by installation. CLASS=A is default.

270

TYPRUN=HOLD (pp. 45-46)—MFT, MVT only. Hold
job in input queue until released by operator.

COND=((number,comparison), . . . ,(number,compar-
ison)) (pp. 66-69)—specify up to 8 tests for executing subsequent steps if previous steps fail.
Number can range from 0 to 4095. Comparisons
are GT, GE, EQ, LT, LE, and NE. Test is made
at end of each step; if any test is satisfied, all
remaining steps are bypassed. Can be interrupted for continuation after complete test, including comma following it.

ROLL=(be rolled out,cause rollout) (pp. 69-70)—MVT
only. Code YES or NO in appropriate place to
specify rollout/rollin conditions.

REGION=(*mainK,bulkK*) (pp. 71-73)—MVT only. Main
and bulk are the 1- to 5-digit even number of
1024-byte blocks of contiguous core storage to
allocate; system rounds up if number is odd.

RD=restart conditions (pp. 74-76)—specify conditions
for automatic restart and control checkpoints: R
(restart and checkpoints), NC (no restart or
checkpoints), NR (no restart but checkpoints), or
RNC (restart and no checkpoints).

$$*$$
stepname
RESTART=(-------- ,*checkid*) (pp. 76-79)—restart job
later from checkpoint specified by checkid, or
from start of step named. Code * to start from
first step.

TIME=(minutes,seconds) (pp. 64-65)—MVT only. Job
time limit. Minutes can range from 0-1440
(1440 eliminates all time limits), seconds from
0-59. Installation sets default.

EXEC CARD (PP. 48-63)

An EXEC card names a program to execute or invokes a cataloged procedure.

```
                                procedure
                                PROC=procedure
                                PGM=program
                                PGM=*.referback
//stepname    EXEC    ---------------- ,

//   keyword parameters
```

stepname (p. 49)—1- to 8-character name (A to Z, 0 to 9, @, $, #) to identify step.

procedure (p. 55)—1- to 8-character (A to Z, 0 to 9, @, $, #) name of cataloged procedure.

program (pp. 49-54)—1- to 8-character (A to Z, 0 to 9, @, $, #) name of program.

*.referback (pp. 53-54)—backward reference to previous DD card describing program:

  *.ddname

  *.stepname.ddname

  *.stepname of procedure.stepname within procedure.ddname

PARM=value (pp. 56-59)—pass parameters to step. Separate any subvalues by commas. If value contains subvalues or special characters (blank , . / ') (* & + - =), enclose value in apostrophes. Can be interrupted for continuation after complete subvalue, including comma following it, by enclosing value in parentheses and enclosing subvalues containing special characters in apostrophes.

ACCT=(acct information) (p. 59)—supply accounting information to step as specified by installation. Separate subvalues by commas, enclose subvalue in apostrophes if it contains (blank , . / ') (* & + =). Can be interrupted for continuation after complete subvalue, including comma following it.

TIME=*(minutes,seconds)* (pp. 64-65)—MVT only. Step time limit. Minutes can range from 0 to 1440 (1440 eliminates all time limits), seconds from 0 to 59. Installation sets default.

DPRTY=(v1,v2) (pp. 60-61)—MVT only. Dispatching priority is calculated as 16(v1)+v2. The numbers v1 and v2 may range from 0-15.

$$\text{COND}=(\ \overline{\begin{matrix}\text{EVEN}\\\text{ONLY}\\\text{(number,comparison,}stepname)\end{matrix}}\ ,\ \ldots\ )$$

(pp. 66-68)—specify up to 8 tests to determine whether step should be bypassed. EVEN executes step even if previous steps fail, ONLY executes step only if previous steps fail. Number can range from 0 to 4095. Comparisons are GT, GE, EQ, LT, LE, and NE. Stepname causes test to be made against only that step; otherwise tests are made against all previous steps. If any test is satisfied, step is bypassed. Can be interrupted for continuation after a complete test, including comma following it.

ROLL=(be rolled out, cause rollout) (pp. 69-70)—MVT only. Code YES or NO in appropriate place to specify rollout/rollin conditions.

REGION=*(mainK,bulkK)* (pp. 71-73)—MVT only. Main and bulk are the 1- to 5-digit even number of 1024-byte blocks of contiguous core to allocate; system rounds up if number is odd.

RD=restart conditions (pp. 74-76)—specify conditions for automatic restart and control checkpoints: R (restart and checkpoints), NC (no restart or checkpoints), NR (no restart but checkpoints), or RNC (restart and no checkpoints).

Keyword parameters can be coded on cards invoking cataloged procedures by appending the stepname within procedure to keyword. Parameters must be coded on EXEC card in the order steps appear within procedure. If stepname not appended, parameters can be coded in any order and apply to all steps within procedure. See pp. 55-56.

SPECIAL DD CARDS

//JOBLIB   DD   DSN=name,DISP=SHR (pp. 50-52)— a single JOBLIB card (can be concatenated) may be placed immediately after JOB card to describe library containing programs to execute. Cannot be placed in cataloged procedure.

//STEPLIB   DD   DSN=name,DISP=SHR (pp. 52-53)— a single STEPLIB card (can be concatenated) may be placed anywhere after EXEC card to describe library containing program to execute. Can be placed in cataloged procedure.

//SYSUDUMP   DD   SYSOUT=A (pp. 61-62)— a single SYSUDUMP card may be placed anywhere after EXEC card to give a dump of program area if step abnormally terminates.

//SYSABEND   DD   SYSOUT=A (pp. 61-62)—same as SYSUDUMP, but in addition dumps system nucleus.

//SYSCHK   DD   keyword parameters (pp. 78-79)—a single SYSCHK card is placed immediately after JOB and any JOBLIB card to describe checkpoint data set.

DD CARD (PP. 81-122, 144-192)

A DD card must be included after EXEC card for each data set used in step.

<pre>
                          *
                          DATA
                          DUMMY
   //ddname   DD   - - - - - ,keyword parameters
</pre>

ddname (pp. 83-84)—1- to 8-character (A to Z, 0 to 9, @, $, #) name unique to step to identify DD card.

* (pp. 144-146)—indicate that card data follows in input stream. Cards cannot have /* or // in columns 1 and 2.

DATA (pp. 144-146)—indicate that card data follows in input stream. Cards can have // but not /* in columns 1 and 2.

DUMMY (pp. 156-157)—assign dummy status to sequential data set. Can also code DSN=NULLFILE to assign a dummy status.

DDNAME=ddname (pp. 146-149)—postpone definition of data set until DD card with specified ddname is encountered.

SYSOUT=(class,*program,form*) (pp. 149-152)—route data through system output stream. Class can be A to Z; SYSOUT=A is traditionally printer and SYSOUT=B card punch. Program is user-provided program to process output. Form is 1- to 4-digit number to identify special forms.

UCS=(code,*FOLD,VERIFY*) (pp. 154-156)—specify character set for 1403 printer with universal character set feature. Code specifies character set: AN, HN, PCAN, PCHN, PN, QN, QNC, RN, SN, TN, XN, or YN. FOLD folds first, second, and third quadrants of EBCDIC into fourth quadrant. VERIFY displays character set for verification.

DCB=($\overset{\textit{name}}{\underset{\textit{*.referback}}{\rule{0pt}{0pt}}}$,*subparameter*, . . . ,*subparameter*)
(pp. 85-90)—specify parameters to complete defi-
nition of data set. Name is name of cataloged
data set to copy DCB subparameters from. Referback (pp. 84-85) refers back to DD card containing
DCB subparameters to copy. Subparameters can
be coded in any order and are described in Appendix A. Subparameters can be interrupted for
continuation after complete subparameter, including comma following it.

DSN=name (pp. 90-93)—names data set. Name can be
1 to 8 characters (A to Z, 0 to 9, @, $, #, -, or
12-0 multipunch). Precede name by two ampersands to denote temporary data set.

DSN=name	DSN=&&name
DSN=*.referback	
DSN=name(member)	DSN=&&name(member)
DSN=name(generation)	
DSN=name(INDEX)	DSN=&&name(INDEX)
DSN=name(PRIME)	DSN=&&name(PRIME)
DSN=name(OVFLOW)	DSN=&&name(OVFLOW)

UNIT=($\overset{\textit{type}}{\underset{\textit{address}}{\underset{\textit{group}}{\rule{0pt}{0pt}}}}$ ----- , $\overset{\textit{P}}{\underset{\textit{volumes}}{\rule{0pt}{0pt}}}$ ----- ,*DEFER,SEP=(ddname, . . . ,*
ddname)) (pp. 94-101)—specifies I/O unit.

type (pp. 95-97)—type of I/O unit.

group (pp. 97-98)—name assigned by installation
to group of I/O units.

address (p. 95)—hardware address of I/O unit.

P (pp. 99-100)—mount volumes of cataloged
data set in parallel.

volumes (pp. 99-100)—number of volumes to mount in parallel.

DEFER (p. 100)—defer volume mounting until data is opened.

SEP (pp. 100-101)—separate data set from units used by 1 to 8 DD cards named. Can be interrupted for continuation after complete ddname, including comma following it.

UNIT=AFF=ddname (p. 98)   assign data set to I/O unit used by another data set.

DISP=(*current status,normal disposition,abnormal disposition*) (pp. 101-112)—give status of data set at start of step and method of disposing of data set.

```
            KEEP
    NEW  DELETE    KEEP
    MOD  PASS      DELETE
    OLD  CATLG     CATLG
    SHR  UNCATLG   UNCATLG
DISP=( --- , ------- , ------- )
```

NEW (p. 102)—create data set.

MOD (pp. 102-103)—create or extend data set.

OLD (pp. 103-104)—read or extend old data set with exclusive control.

SHR (pp. 104-105)—share data set being read.

KEEP (pp. 107-108)—keep nontemporary data set.

DELETE (p. 108)—delete data set.

PASS (pp. 106-107)—pass data set to following steps.

CATLG (pp. 108-109)—keep and catalog data set.

UNCATLG (pp. 109-110)—keep and uncatalog data set.

VOL=(*PRIVATE,RETAIN,sequence,volumes,*
      REF=name
      REF=*.referback
      SER=(volume, . . . ,volume)
— — — — — — — — — — — — — — — — — — —) (pp. 113-120—specify volume information.

PRIVATE (pp. 116-117)—private mountable volume.

RETAIN (p. 117)—keep private volume mounted between steps.

sequence (pp. 117-118)—sequence number (1 to 4 digits) of cataloged data set with which to begin processing.

volumes (pp. 118-120)—number of volumes (1 to 255) onto which data set may extend.

REF (pp. 114-115)—assign volumes used by another data set.

SER (pp. 114-115)—give 1- to 6-character (A to Z, 0 to 9, @, $, #, -) volume serial numbers. Enclose serial number in apostrophes if it contains (blank , . / ')(* & + =). Can be interrupted for continuation after volume serial number, including comma following it.

              CYL
              TRK   *index*
              blocksize   *directory*
SPACE=(---------,(quantity,*increment*, ---------
              ALX
              MXIG
              CONTIG
RLSE, - - - - - - ,*ROUND*) (pp. 161-172—request a quantity of direct-access space.

blocksize (pp. 162-165)—units requested in blocks.

TRK (pp. 165-166)—units requested in tracks.

CYL (pp. 165-166)—units requested in cylinders.

quantity (pp. 162-166)—number of units of primary storage.

increment (pp. 166-168)—number of units to allocate to each of 15 possible extents.

directory (pp. 168-169)—number of 256-byte blocks to reserve for partitioned data set directory. Assume about 5 members or aliases per block.

index (pp. 168-169)—number of cylinders to allocate to imbedded index for indexed sequential data set.

RLSE (pp. 169-170)—release excess space when set is closed.

CONTIG (p. 170)—allocate contiguous space.

MXIG (pp. 170-171)—allocate largest free space on volume if as large or larger than amount requested.

ALX (p. 171)—allocate 5 largest contiguous free areas on volume that are as large or larger than amount requested.

ROUND (pp. 171-172)—round space requested by size up to integral cylinders.

index
directory
SPACE=(ABSTR,(quantity,address, ---------))
    (p. 172) — allocate tracks specified. Quantity is number of contiguous tracks to allocate, and address is track address of first track.

SPLIT=(number,CYL, (quantity,*increment*))
    (p. 173)   split cylinders between data sets.

Number is number of tracks on each cylinder to allocate to first data set, and quantity is number of cylinders to allocate for all data sets. Code SPLIT=number on subsequent DD cards to allocate tracks to other data sets.

SPLIT=(percent,blocksize,(quantity,*increment*))
(p. 174) —split cylinders between data sets. Percent is percentage of tracks on each cylinder to allocate to first data set, and quantity is number of blocks to allocate to all data sets. Code SPLIT=percent on subsequent DD cards to allocate tracks to other data sets. Percent can be 1 to 100, but must not total more than 100.

CYL
TRK
blocksize

SUBALLOC=(--------- ,(quantity,*increment,directory*), referback) (pp. 174-176)—suballocate space from a previous data set indicated by the referback.

IN   RETPD=nnnn
OUT EXPDT=yyddd

LABEL=(*file,type,PASSWORD*, --- , -----------)
(pp. 183-188, 236-237)—give label information, and specify data set protection.

file (pp. 183-184)—relative file of magnetic tape.

type (pp. 184-187)—type of volume and data set label: SL, NL, NSL, SUL, or BLP.

PASSWORD (pp. 236-237)—give data set password protection.

IN (pp. 187-188)—open sequential data set for input only.

OUT (pp. 187-188)—open sequential data set for output only.

RETPD (p. 236)—give data set retention period (0 to 9999) in days.

EXPDT (p. 236)—give date when retention period expires.

SEP=(ddname, . . . ,ddname) (pp. 240-241)—separate data set from channels used by other data sets described by 1 to 8 ddnames. Can interrupt ddnames for continuation after a complete ddname, including comma following it.

AFF=ddname (pp. 240-241)—copy SEP parameter from previous DD card.

DELIMETER CARD

/* (p. 144)—placed after card decks to mark their end.

PROC CARD

//*procedure*   PROC   *keyword parameters*
(p. 135)—a single PROC card may be placed as the first card of a cataloged procedure to assign default values to symbolic parameters. Symbolic parameter is 1 to 7 characters (A to Z, 0 to 9); first must be A to Z. When coded within procedure, must be preceded by ampersand. Value can be any length and can contain (A to Z, 0 to 9, @, $, #). Can also contain (blank , . / ') (* + - =) if enclosed in apostrophes.

COMMAND CARD

//   command   operands (pp. 220-221)—command cards can be placed before a JOB, EXEC, null, or another command card to enter operator commands from the input stream.

NULL CARD

// (p. 221)—null card can be placed at end of job for identification, to mark end of job, or to allow all cards to be read by card reader.

COMMENTS CARD

//* (pp. 221-222)—comments cards can be placed anywhere
before or after any JCL card following the JOB card.

REFERENCES

Material in this manual has been condensed from the
following IBM Systems Reference Library publications.

1. A22-6810, IBM System/360 System Summary.

2. C20-1649, Student Text Introduction to IBM System/360
   Direct Access Storage Devices and Organization Methods.

3. C20-1684, Student Text Introduction to IBM Data
   Processing Systems.

4. C24-3337, Report Program Generator Language.

5. C26-3756, Assembler(F) Programmer's Guide.

6. C27-6909, Graphic Programming Services for IBM 2250
   Display Unit.

7. C27-6912, Graphic Programming Services for IBM 2260
   Display Station (Local Attachment).

8. C27-6926, Multiprogramming with a Fixed Number of
   Tasks (MFT), Concepts and Considerations.

9. C27-6935, Planning for Rollout/Rollin.

10. C27-6939, Planning for Multiprogramming with a Fixed
    Number of Tasks (MFT).

11. C27-6942, Introduction to Main Storage Hierarchy Sup-
    port for IBM 2361 Models 1 and 2.

12. C28-6380, COBOL(F) Programmer's Guide.

13. C28-6534, IBM System/360 Operating System Introduction.

14. C28-6535, Concepts and Facilities.

15. C28-6538, Linkage Editor.

16. C28-6539, Job Control Language.

17. C28-6540, Operator's Guide.

18. C28-6550, System Programmer's Guide.

19. C28-6554, System Generation.

20. C28-6586, Utilities.

21.   C28-6594, PL/I (F) Programmer's Guide.

22.   C28-6628, System Control Blocks.

23.   C28-6632, Job Control Language Charts.

24.   C28-6646, Supervisor and Data Management Services.

25.   C28-6647, Supervisor and Data Management Macro Instructions.

26.   C28-6656, Checkpoint Restart.

27.   C28-6680, Tape Labels.

28.   C28-6702, Planning Guide for the Loader.

29.   C28-6708, Advanced Checkpoint/Restart Planning Guide.

30.   C28-6817, FORTRAN IV (G and H) Programmer's Guide.

31.   C33-4000, ALGOL Programmer's Guide.

32.   Y28-6607, System/360 Operating System Direct-Access Device Space Management. Program Logic Manual, Program Number 360S-DS-508, Restricted Distribution.

INDEX

NOTES

NOTES